W9-CZL-238

Japanese
DeMYSTiFieD

Second Edition

Eriko Sato, PhD

New York Chicago San Francisco Lisbon London Madrid Mexico City
Milan New Delhi San Juan Seoul Singapore Sydney Toronto

1 2 3 4 5 6 7 8 9 10   QFR   1 9 8 7 6 5 4 3 2

ISBN 978-0-07-179771-9 (book and CD set)
MHID   0-07-179771-8 (book and CD set)

ISBN 978-0-07-179769-6 (book for set)
MHID   0-07-179769-6 (book for set)

e-ISBN 978-0-07-179772-6
e-MHID   0-07-179772-6

Library of Congress Control Number 2012948442

CONTENTS

Contents

AUDIO TRACK LISTING

Track 33 Oral Practice
Track 34 Oral Practice
Track 35 Oral Practice

CHAPTER 9

Track 36 Oral Practice
Track 37 Oral Practice
Track 38 Oral Practice
Track 39 Oral Practice
Track 40 Oral Practice
Track 41 Oral Practice

CHAPTER 10

Track 42 Oral Practice
Track 43 Oral Practice
Track 44 Oral Practice

CHAPTER 11

Track 45 Oral Practice
Track 46 Oral Practice
Track 47 Oral Practice
Track 48 Oral Practice
Track 49 Oral Practice
Track 50 Oral Practice
Track 51 Oral Practice
Track 52 Oral Practice

CHAPTER 12

Track 53 Oral Practice
Track 54 Oral Practice
Track 55 Oral Practice

CHAPTER 13

Track 56 Oral Practice
Track 57 Oral Practice
Track 58 Oral Practice

CHAPTER 20

Track 59 Oral Practice
Track 60 Oral Practice

ACKNOWLEDGMENTS

I am grateful to Karen Young and the other editors and staff at McGraw-Hill for their professional assistance and warm encouragement.

INTRODUCTION

Most people think that it would be wonderful if they could speak one or more foreign languages and communicate directly with people in other countries, travel around the world without an interpreter, explore many different cultures, and learn about many different ways of thinking and living. Our knowledge of foreign languages will definitely widen our horizon and increase our future professional career opportunities. Some people also just enjoy learning foreign languages. There are many differences, but also many similarities among languages. Once you learn one foreign language, the second one will be much easier to learn.

Because you are reading the introduction of *Japanese Demystified*, you must be thinking about studying Japanese, for whatever reason. You may be interested in Japanese traditional, contemporary, or pop culture, for example, karate, cooking, magna, or anime. You may be a high school or college student who is studying Japanese in a classroom or by yourself. You may be thinking of taking a nationwide Japanese proficiency test to boost your opportunities for college admission or employment. You may be a high school teacher of French who is thinking of teaching both French and Japanese for promotion. You may be already fluent in Chinese and thinking of becoming trilingual to get engaged in a trading business. You may be an employee at an American pharmaceutical company that closely collaborates with Japanese counterpart companies. Or, you may have grandparents and a bunch of cousins in Japan!

Japanese Demystified provides you with easy-to-access and easy-to-understand basic grammar explanations ranging from simple sentence structures like *A is B* to complex sentence structures including passive and causative constructions. When you have any grammar questions, you can check the table of contents or scan the bold-face headings in the book and just read the relevant section. However, this book can also be used to develop your knowledge of Japanese grammar step-by-step as you develop your Japanese communication skills using other materials because *Japanese Demystified* is organized based on both linguistic categories and

communicative functions. You can use *Japanese Demystified* as your grammar-building tool, regardless of whether you are studying Japanese in a conversation class, with a tutor, or by yourself.

How to Use This Book

If you are using this book as a grammar reference book, you can scan the table of contents or the bold-face headings to find the grammar topic you are interested in checking. This book discusses most basic grammar points covered during the first one or two years of college Japanese classrooms in the United States.

If you are using this book to build your knowledge of Japanese grammar step by step, you can read each chapter sequentially starting with Chapter 1 and doing all the oral/written practices to reinforce the new material presented in the chapter.

This book has a total of twenty chapters divided into four parts.

Each chapter begins with the statement of its general objectives and then provides a number of relatively short sections featuring specific grammar/function points like "The Question Particle か **ka**" and "Describing People's Appearances." Each section provides an explanation of the given grammar/function point with Japanese examples, as well as some bullets and tables when needed. All the example sentences are written in Japanese orthography, hiragana, katakana, and kanji and are immediately followed by their romanization to help you pronounce them correctly, just in case you are not familiar with some characters.

After one or more sections, you'll find oral and written practice sections that reinforce the new content in the chapter. Oral practices usually ask you to read the phrases and sentences out loud. They are intended to strengthen your understanding of the grammar/function point(s), show how they are actually used in authentic and natural utterances in Japanese, and help you become able to use them for communication. The accompanying audio CD provides you with native speakers' pronunciation of all the sentences in the Oral Practice sections, so you can learn the authentic pronunciations and appropriate rhythms and intonations.

Written practices usually ask you to choose the correct item, fill in the blanks, or write sentences. They are intended to develop and strengthen your ability to form and write Japanese phrases and sentences using the given grammar/function point(s).

Each chapter ends with an open-book quiz with ten multiple-choice questions that review the concepts introduced in the chapter. You should try to achieve a score of 80 percent on the chapter-ending quiz before moving on to the next chapter.

Each part includes five chapters and is followed by a part test with twenty-five multiple-choice questions that review the content of the part. These tests are closed-book tests, and you should try to get 75 percent of the questions correct before moving to the next part.

After the fourth part test, you'll find a final exam with one hundred multiple-choice questions that review the entire contents of the book to see how much you really understood, remembered, and acquired. A good score on this exam is 75 percent. The answers for written practices, chapter quizzes, part tests, and the final exam are provided at the end of the book. You are encouraged to retake part tests and the final exam every few months to measure the level of your retention and to refresh your memory.

がんばってください。

Ganbatte kudasai!

Try your best (and good luck)!

PART ONE

IDENTIFYING PEOPLE AND THINGS

CHAPTER 1

Pronouncing and Writing Japanese Words

In this chapter you'll learn:

Basic Japanese Sounds and Romaji
The Japanese Writing Systems
Familiar Japanese Words

Basic Japanese Sounds and Romaji

In this section, you will learn basic Japanese vowels and consonants, using romaji (**rōmaji**), romanization of Japanese. This book uses the popular Hepburn romaji system with some modifications. Just remember that a vowel with a macron, for example, **ā**, stands for a long vowel, and **n** with an apostrophe, **n'**, shows the separation from the following vowel or **y**. In this section, you will also learn about the pitch accent in Japanese, which is very different from the stress accent in English.

VOWELS

 TRACK 1

Japanese has only five basic vowels, which are **a, i, u, e**, and **o**: **a** is as in the vowel in *Aha*, **i** is as in the initial part of the vowel in *eat*, **u** is as in the initial part of the vowel in *boot*, but without lip rounding; **e** is as in the initial part of the vowel in *eight* and **o** is as in the initial part of the vowel in *oat*.

Romaji	Pronunciation	Example	
a	ah	atama (ah-tah-mah)	*head*
i	ee	ishi (ee-shee)	*stone*
u	oo	unagi (oo-nah-gee)	*eel*
e	eh	eki (eh-kee)	*train station*
o	oh	origami (oh-ree-gah-mee)	*origami*

Long Vowels The five vowels introduced above have long counterparts, which are represented by adding a macron, as in **ā** (or by doubling the vowel, as in **aa**, if there is a morphological boundary). In Japanese, the vowel length can make a difference in meaning. For example, おばさん **obasan** means *aunt*, but おばあさん **obāsan** means *grandmother*. You need to pay attention to the vowel length to understand Japanese correctly.

Oral Practice

 TRACK 2

Practice pronouncing the following Japanese words paying special attention to the vowel length.

obasan	*aunt*
obāsan	*grandmother*

ojisan	*uncle*
ojīsan	*grandfather*
shujin	*one's husband/master*
shūjin	*prisoner*
e	*painting*
ē	*yes*
tori	*bird*
tōri	*street*

Devoiced Vowels The vowels **i** and **u** tend to be whispered or devoiced when they are between two voiceless consonants such as **p, t, k, s, sh, ch, ts,** and **h,** or when they are at the end of the word, preceded by a voiceless consonant. For example, you may not hear the underlined vowels in **k<u>u</u>shi** (*comb*) and **s<u>u</u>kiyaki** (*sukiyaki*) when native speakers of Japanese say them at normal or fast speed. However, you may hear these vowels when they speak extremely slowly and deliberately.

CONSONANTS

Most Japanese consonants written in romaji can be read just as in English, but **r** and **f** are quite different from their English pronunciation. Japanese **r** is made by tapping the tip of the tongue behind the upper teeth, like the brief flap sound **tt** in *lettuce* or *letter* in American English. Japanese **f** is pronounced by bringing the upper and lower lips close to each other, blowing air between them gently.

Some consonants written in romaji are pronounced just slightly differently from English. **W, sh,** and **ch** are pronounced without lip rounding. The sound **g** is often nasalized when it occurs between vowels. When the consonant **n** is followed by a consonant made with the lips (**p, b,** or **m**), it changes to **m.**

Some consonants have a distributional restriction. The consonant **w** occurs only before the vowel **a.** The consonant **y** occurs only before **a, u,** and **o.** The consonant **h** becomes **f** when it is followed by **u.** The consonant **t** becomes **ch** when it is followed by the vowel **i** and **ts** when it is followed by the vowel **u.**

Some consonants, such as **p, t, k,** and **s,** can be doubled, which is actually realized as a single consonant preceded by a brief pause. The latter brief pause is represented by an extra consonant in the romaji system, as in **kitte** (*stamp*) and **gakki** (*musical instrument*).

Oral Practice

 TRACK 3

Practice pronouncing the following Japanese words paying attention to the sound quality of the consonants.

chizu	*map*
fune	*boat*
Honda	*Honda*
kitte	*stamp*
kushi	*comb*
ringo	*apple*
tsunami	*tsunami*
washi	*eagle*
yama	*mountain*

PITCH ACCENT

 TRACK 4

Unlike in English, where an accented syllable is stressed and pronounced louder and longer, an accented syllable in Japanese is not stressed but changes pitch. Each syllable in a Japanese word is either high or low in pitch. For example, the word 雨 **ame** (*rain*) and 飴 **ame** (*candy*) sound exactly the same except for their pitch pattern. 雨 **ame** (*rain*) has an accent on the first syllable, so the pitch falls right after the first syllable. That is, the first syllable **a** in 雨 **ame** (*rain*) is pronounced high, and the second syllable **me** is pronounced low. By contrast, 飴 **ame** (*candy*) has no accent, so there is no pitch fall within this word. The first syllable **a** in 飴 **ame** (*candy*) is low in pitch, and the second syllable **me** is high in pitch. However, the pitch pattern of Japanese words differs greatly depending on the region, and the range of variation in pitch patterns of words is very wide. Therefore, the slight difference in pitch doesn't cause any misunderstanding in general, and you do not have to be too concerned about it when you study Japanese.

The Japanese Writing Systems

Japanese is generally written by combining three writing systems, which are kanji, hiragana, and katakana.

Kanji are Chinese characters that were brought to Japan in around the 5th century AD, and they are used for representing concrete meanings conveyed by nouns, verbs, adjectives, and adverbs. Average Japanese know about 2,000 kanji characters. Hiragana and katakana were created from simplified kanji in Heian Period (794–1192). Each hiragana or katakana represents syllable sound rather than meaning. For example, the hiragana character か and the katakana character カ represent the syllable sound, **ka**. Katakana are mainly composed of straight lines and sharp angles and are used for representing foreign words such as *coffee* and *salad*. (The words borrowed from Chinese are usually written in kanji.) Katakana are also used for representing many instances of onomatopoeia (see Chapter 12) and plant or animal names. Hiragana are composed mainly of curved lines and are used for representing grammatical items, such as verb endings and particles, and words that are not written in kanji or katakana. Accordingly, one Japanese sentence can contain kanji, katakana, and hiragana as shown:

私は中国とアメリカに行きます。
Watashi wa Chūgoku to Amerika ni ikimasu.
I will go to China and America.

In this example, those for 私 I, 中国 *China* and 行 *go* are kanji, those for アメリカ *America* are katakana, and the others (は *as for*, と *and*, に *to*, and きます [*verb inflection*]) are hiragana.

In this book, Japanese words and sentences are written authentically, by combining kanji, hiragana, and katakana, and for your convenience, they are all rewritten in romaji, as in the above example sentence.

HIRAGANA

There are 46 basic hiragana characters. If you learn two diacritics and some conventions, you will be able to write any Japanese word and sentence in hiragana.

 **TRACK 5**

Basic Hiragana The 46 basic hiragana characters are represented in the following table along with romaji letters.

ん n'	わ wa	ら ra	や ya	ま ma	は ha	な na	た ta	さ sa	か ka	あ a
		り ri		み mi	ひ hi	に ni	ち chi	し shi	き ki	い i
		る ru	ゆ yu	む mu	ふ fu	ぬ nu	つ tsu	す su	く ku	う u
		れ re		め me	へ he	ね ne	て te	せ se	け ke	え e
	を o	ろ ro	よ yo	も mo	ほ ho	の no	と to	そ so	こ ko	お o

Japanese children memorize hiragana using a chart like the one above, by reciting hiragana from top to bottom, from right to left, as in **a, i, u, e, o, ka, ki, ku, ke, ko…**

Oral Practice

 TRACK 6

Practice reading the following words written in both hiragana and romaji.

さけ	sake	*rice wine*
すし	sushi	*sushi*
からて	karate	*karate*
さしみ	sashimi	*sliced raw fish*
にほん	Nihon	*Japan*
きもの	kimono	*kimono, traditional Japanese clothing*

 **TRACK 7**

The Diacritics ゛and ゜ There are two diacritics that can be added at the right upper corner of some hiragana. They are the voicing marker, ゛, and the plosive marker ° . The voicing marker is used to convert the initial voiceless consonant of the syllable represented by the given hiragana to its voiced counterpart. For example, placing the **voicing** mark next to か ka gives us が **ga**. The plosive marker can be added to は **ha**, ひ **hi**, ふ **fu**, へ **he**, or ほ **ho**, converting them to syllables with the consonant **p**, as in ぱ **pa**, ぴ **pi**, ぷ **pu**, ぺ **pe**, and ぽ **po**. The hiragana used with these diacritics are all listed in the following table.

ぱ pa	ば ba	だ da	ざ za	が ga
ぴ pi	び bi	ぢ ji	じ ji	ぎ gi
ぷ pu	ぶ bu	づ zu	ず zu	ぐ gu
ぺ pe	べ be	で de	ぜ ze	げ ge
ぽ po	ぼ bo	ど do	ぞ zo	ご go

As you can see, ば, び, ぶ, べ, and ぼ are pronounced **ba**, **bi**, **bu**, **be**, and **bo** with the consonant **b**, both じ and ぢ are pronounced **ji**, and both ず and づ are pronounced **zu**. Note that じ is more commonly used than ぢ to represent the sound **ji**, and ず is more commonly used than づ to represent the sound **zu**.

Oral Practice

 TRACK 8

Practice pronouncing the following words, paying attention to the diacritics.

うなぎ	unagi	*eel*
なごや	Nagoya	*Nagoya (a city in Japan)*
てんぷら	tenpura	*tempura*
ふぐ	fugu	*blow fish*
おりがみ	origami	*origami*
ふじさん	Fujisan	*Mt. Fuji*

Long Vowels Long vowels are represented by two hiragana letters. For example, by placing あ after か ka, we get かあ kā.

Note that the addition of う after a hiragana letter with **o** represents **ō**, and the addition of い after a hiragana **e** usually represents **ē**. That is, when you hear **ō**, you will see either お or う as the second hiragana letter, and when you hear **ē**, you will see either え or い as the second hiragana letter. Check some example words as you go over the following Oral Practice.

Japanese Demystified

Oral Practice

 TRACK 9

Practice reading the following Japanese words out loud.

おかあさん	okāsan	*mother*
おばあさん	obāsan	*grandmother*
おにいさん	onīsan	*older brother*
ちいさい	chīsai	*small*
すうがく	sūgaku	*mathematics*
おねえさん	onēsan	*older sister*
おおさか	Ōsaka	*Osaka*
おとうさん	otōsan	*father*
とおり	tōri	*street*
せんせい	sensei	*teacher* (usually sounds like sensē)
えいご	eigo	*English language* (usually sounds like ēgo)

Double Consonants Double consonants are represented by a small-size つ **tsu**. For example, the word **kitte** (*stamp*) includes a double consonant, and it is written as きって in hiragana. As you can see, the small-size つ is not pronounced, but it represents a brief pause before the next consonant.

Oral Practice

 TRACK 10

Practice reading the following Japanese words, paying attention to double consonants represented by a small つ.

おと	oto	*sound*
おっと	otto	*husband*
みつ	mitsu	*honey*
みっつ	mittsu	*three pieces*
てっぽう	teppō	*gun*
きっさてん	kissaten	*coffee shop*
がっこう	gakkō	*school*

 **TRACK 11**

Palatalized Sounds Japanese syllables are relatively simple. The only complex syllable initial consonants are palatalized consonants, which are pronounced using the palatal area (roof of the mouth), as in **kya**, **myo**, and **ryu**. Such palatalized sounds are represented by a hiragana character that represents the initial consonant plus the vowel **i**, and a small-sized hiragana character, や, ゆ, or よ, depending on the following vowel. The following table lists all the palatalized sounds in Japanese.

りゃ	みゃ	ぴゃ	びゃ	ひゃ	にゃ	ぢゃ	ちゃ	じゃ	しゃ	ぎゃ	きゃ
rya	mya	pya	bya	hya	nya	ja	cha	ja	sha	gya	kya
りゅ	みゅ	ぴゅ	びゅ	ひゅ	にゅ	ぢゅ	ちゅ	じゅ	しゅ	ぎゅ	きゅ
ryu	myu	pyu	byu	hyu	nyu	ju	chu	ju	shu	gyu	kyu
りょ	みょ	ぴょ	びょ	ひょ	にょ	ぢょ	ちょ	じょ	しょ	ぎょ	きょ
ryo	myo	pyo	byo	hyo	nyo	jo	cho	jo	sho	gyo	kyo

Oral Practice

 TRACK 12

Practice reading the following Japanese words, paying attention to the palatalized sounds.

とうきょう	Tōkyō	*Tokyo*
かいしゃ	kaisha	*company*
じゅうどう	jūdō	*judo*
ひゃく	hyaku	*hundred*
びょういん	byōin	*hospital*
りょう	ryō	*dormitory*
りょかん	ryokan	*Japanese-style inn*

Written Practice 1

Write the following words in hiragana.

1. karate (*karate*) _____

2. unagi (*eel*) _____

3. okāsan (*mother*) _____

4. gakkō (*school*) _____

5. Tōkyō (*Tokyo*) _____

KATAKANA

Just like hiragana, katakana has 46 basic characters. They are all listed here.

ン n'	ワ wa	ラ ra	ヤ ya	マ ma	ハ ha	ナ na	タ ta	サ sa	カ ka	ア a
		リ ri		ミ mi	ヒ hi	ニ ni	チ chi	シ shi	キ ki	イ i
		ル ru	ユ yu	ム mu	フ fu	ヌ nu	ツ tsu	ス su	ク ku	ウ u
		レ re		メ me	ヘ he	ネ ne	テ te	セ se	ケ ke	エ e
	ヲ o	ロ ro	ヨ yo	モ mo	ホ ho	ノ no	ト to	ソ so	コ ko	オ o

The diacritics and conventions used in the hiragana system can also be used in the katakana system, except that the long vowels are represented by the elongation mark, which is a horizontal line when written horizontally, but a vertical line when written vertically. Also note that the katakana system allows some combinations of characters that are not available in the hiragana system. For example, it allows combinations like ファ (fa), フィ (fi), フォ (fo), トゥ (tu), ティ (ti), ディ (di), ヴァ (va), ヴォ (vo), ヴェ (ve), ウォ (wo), and ジェ (je), which are helpful for representing the approximate pronunciations of foreign words. The following are some examples of place names written in katakana.

ニューヨーク	Nyūyōku	*New York*
フィリピン	Firipin	*The Philippines*
ロンドン	Rondon	*London*
パリ	Pari	*Paris*
バージニア or ヴァージニア	Bājinia	*Virginia*

The following are some loanwords written in katakana:

ネクタイ	nekutai	*necktie*
ハンドバッグ	handobaggu	*handbag*
コーヒー	kōhī	*coffee*
サッカー	sakkā	*soccer*
テニス	tenisu	*tennis*
レストラン	resutoran	*restaurant*
テレビ	terebi	*TV*
ラジオ	rajio	*radio*
カメラ	kamera	*camera*

Written Practice 2

Write these items in katakana using the basic katakana table provided at the beginning of this subsection as well as the necessary diacritics and conventions.

1. tenisu (*tennis*) _____
2. kamera (*camera*) _____
3. sakkā (*soccer*) _____
4. kōhī (*coffee*) _____
5. Bosuton (*Boston*) _____
6. Nyūyōku (*New York*) _____

KANJI

The average Japanese knows about 2,000 kanji. Unlike hiragana and katakana, each kanji represents meaning rather than sound. For example, the kanji character 人 represents *person*. Most kanji have a Japanese way of pronunciation and a Chinese way of pronunciation, and each of them may also have some variant pronunciations. For example, the Japanese way of pronouncing 人 is **hito**, and the Chinese way of pronouncing it is **nin** or **jin**. Which pronunciation should be used depends on the context.

Many kanji characters were created from pictures. For example, 人 was created from the picture of a standing person viewed side-on. Some kanji were created by

combining two or more kanji. For example, the kanji 明 (*bright*) was created by combining the kanji 日 (*sun*) and 月 (*moon*).

These are some frequently used kanji:

人	hito, jin, nin	*person*
日	hi, nichi, ni	*sun*
川	kawa, gawa, sen	*river*
山	yama, san	*mountain*
口	kuchi, guchi, kou	*mouth*
田	ta, da, den	*rice field*
私	watashi, shi	*I, me*
本	moto, hon	*book, origin, root, true*

The following are examples of kanji used in a compound or a phrase:

日本	Nihon	*Japan*
日本人	Nihon-jin	*Japanese person*
あの人	ano hito	*that person*
山田	Yamada	*Yamada (a family name)*
川口	Kawaguchi	*Kawaguchi (a family name)*
私の本	watashi no hon	*my book*
山と川	yama to kawa	*mountains and rivers*

Written Practice 3

Match the kanji with their meanings.

1. 山 _____   a. mouth
2. 口 _____   b. person
3. 人 _____   c. mountain
4. 川 _____   d. sun
5. 日 _____   e. river

PUNCTUATION AND FORMAT

The Japanese write words and sentences horizontally from left to right, just as in English, or vertically from top to bottom. The Japanese period is 。, and it is placed at the end of each sentence, just as in English. The Japanese comma is 、, and it is placed at the end of a phrase, but unlike in English, there are no strict rules on when and where the comma should be used. No question mark is needed at the end of question sentences in Japanese, although many young people use the English question mark. The quotation marks are 「 」. The following sentences illustrate these punctuation rules:

私は日本人です。
Watashi wa Nihon-jin desu.
I'm Japanese.

あれは山ですか。
Are wa yama desu ka.
Is that a mountain?

はい、そうです。
Hai, sō desu.
Yes, it is.

「はい」と、言いました。
"Hai" to, iimashita.
(I) said, "Yes!"

A surprising fact about written Japanese is that there is no space between words. In addition, a word may be broken between two lines. You can see it in the following e-mail message from Mr. Tanaka to Ms. Yamada. Can you see that the katakana word オフィス **ofisu** (*office*) is broken into two lines?

From: tanaka@abcd.co.jp
To: yamada@efgh.co.jp
Date: 2008年3月9日 9:13
Re: 居酒屋

山田さん

今日、いっしょに居酒屋に行きませんか。私は7時まではオフ
ィスにいます。連絡してください。

田中

Familiar Japanese Words

You already know many Japanese words. Japanese foods and martial arts have been spread all around the world. Japanese traditional culture and contemporary culture have been very popular in many countries. Japanese cities like Tokyo and Kyoto are visited by many tourists from overseas.

JAPANESE FOODS

How many of the following Japanese foods and beverages can you identify?

すし	sushi	*sushi*
刺し身	sashimi	*sliced raw fish*
すき焼き	sukiyaki	*Japanese style beef stew*
うなぎ	unagi	*eel*
てんぷら	tenpura	*tempura*
酒	sake	*Japanese rice wine*

JAPANESE MARTIAL ARTS

How many of the following martial arts do you know?

空手	karate	*karate*
柔道	jūdō	*judo*
剣道	kendō	*kendo*
合気道	aikidō	*aikido*
相撲	sumō	*sumo wrestling*

JAPANESE TRADITIONAL AND POP CULTURE

折り紙 **origami** has been a popular extracurricular activity in many elementary schools and カラオケ **karaoke** has become a popular entertainment among adults all over the world. How many of the following items do you know?

折り紙	origami	*origami*
俳句	haiku	*haiku*

生け花	ikebana	*flower arranging*
着物	kimono	*kimono (traditional Japanese clothing)*
侍	samurai	*samurai*
忍者	ninja	*ninja*
カラオケ	karaoke	*karaoke*

JAPANESE CITIES AND ISLANDS

The largest city in Japan is, of course, 東京 **Tōkyō**. The largest Japanese island is 本州 **Honshū**. How many of the following Japanese cities and islands can you identify?

東京	Tōkyō	*Tokyo*
大阪	Ōsaka	*Osaka*
京都	Kyōto	*Kyoto*
名古屋	Nagoya	*Nagoya*
神戸	Kōbe	*Kobe*
横浜	Yokohama	*Yokohama*
本州	Honshū	*Honshu*
北海道	Hokkaidō	*Hokkaido*
沖縄	Okinawa	*Okinawa*

QUIZ

Circle the letter of the word that corresponds to the given Japanese word.

1. りょう ryō
   - (a) teacher
   - (b) dormitory
   - (c) student
   - (d) school
2. おじいさん ojīsan
   - (a) aunt
   - (b) uncle
   - (c) grandmother
   - (d) grandfather

3. おねえさん onēsan

   (a) grandmother   (c) younger sister

   (b) mother   (d) older sister

4. おとうさん otōsan

   (a) mother   (c) older brother

   (b) father   (d) younger brother

5. ハンドバッグ handobaggu

   (a) hamburger   (c) handkerchief

   (b) hiking   (d) handbag

6. テレビ terebi

   (a) table   (c) telephone

   (b) test   (d) TV

7. 山 yama

   (a) river   (c) person

   (b) sun   (d) mountain

8. 川 kawa

   (a) river   (c) moon

   (b) mountain   (d) sun

9. 日本人 Nihon-jin

   (a) Japan   (c) Japanese language

   (b) Japanese person   (d) Japanese foods

10. うなぎ unagi

   (a) eel   (c) octopus

   (b) shrimp   (d) squid

CHAPTER 2

Identifying People and Things

In this chapter you'll learn:

Referring to People
Naming People and Things
Using Demonstratives
Using Everyday Phrases

Referring to People

In this section, you will learn how to address people appropriately as well as how to name nationalities and occupations.

PEOPLE'S NAMES

Some of the most common Japanese family names are 鈴木 **Suzuki**, 佐藤 **Satō**, and 田中 **Tanaka**. Popular male given names include ひろし **Hiroshi**, たかし **Takashi**, and あきら **Akira**, and popular female given names include けいこ **Keiko**, ようこ **Yōko**, and よしこ **Yoshiko**, which may be written in a variety of different kanji. As in Korean and Chinese, the family name is placed before the given name. The following are examples of Japanese full names:

鈴木広
Suzuki Hiroshi
Hiroshi Suzuki

田中陽子
Tanaka Yōko
Yoko Tanaka

Westerner's names can be represented in katakana following their original word order, but a fat dot is placed between names.

トム・クルーズ
Tomu Kurūzu
Tom Cruise

ヒラリー・ローダム・クリントン
Hirarī Rōdamu Kurinton
Hillary Rodham Clinton

RESPECTFUL TITLES

When addressing or referring to someone, you must use a respectful title after his/her name. The most commonly used gender-neutral and marital-status-neutral respectful title is さん **san**. You can add it at the end of the family name, the given name, or the full-name, as in:

田中さん	Tanaka-san	*Mr./Ms./Mrs. Tanaka*
陽子さん	Yōko-san	*Yoko*
田中陽子さん	Tanaka Yōko-san	*Ms./Mrs. Yoko Tanaka*
マイクさん	Maiku-san	*Mike*
スミスさん	Sumisu-san	*Mr./Ms./Mrs. Smith*

Other respectful titles have more restrictions: くん **kun** is used for boys or for subordinates; ちゃん **chan** is used only for children after their given name to show affection; さま **sama** is used in extremely polite contexts, such as talking to a business customer or client. These respectful titles are used as in the following examples:

広くん	Hiroshi-kun
陽子ちゃん	Yōko-chan
田中様	Tanaka-sama

If the person has a certain position or function, his/her professional title, such as 部長 **buchō** (*division manager*), 社長 **shachō** (*company president*), or 先生 **sensei** (*professor, teacher, medical doctor*, etc.), should be used in professional contexts instead of as a respectful title. For example:

山田社長	Yamada shachō	*President Yamada*
スミス先生	Sumisu sensei	*Professor Smith*

You must be very careful not to place a respectful title or professional title after your own name.

PERSONAL PRONOUNS

The following table lists some of the personal pronouns in Japanese.

	Singular	**Plural**
1st person	私 watashi	私たち watashi-tachi
2nd person	あなた anata	あなたたち anata-tachi
3rd person male	彼 kare	彼ら karera
3rd person female	彼女 kanojo	彼女ら kanojora

NOTE: 私 *is usually read as* **watashi** *but is also read as* **watakushi** *in some cases, and the latter sounds more polite and formal than the former. Males can also use* 僕 **boku** *to refer to themselves, which is slightly more casual than* 私 **watashi**. *Note that personal pronouns are frequently dropped in Japanese conversations. In fact,* あなた **anata** *is actually avoided in a conversation among native speakers, and it is either dropped or substituted by the person's name, as in the following conversation between Tanaka and Yamada:*

Tanaka: 山田さん、これは山田さんのペンですか。

Yamada-san, kore wa Yamada-san no pen desu ka.

Ms. Yamada, is this your pen? (*Literally: Ms. Yamada, is this Ms. Yamada's pen?*)

Yamada: はい、私のペンです。

Hai, watashi no pen desu.

Yes, it is my pen.

EXPRESSING NATIONALITY

One's nationality can be expressed by the name of the country plus 人 **jin**. For example, アメリカ人 **Amerika-jin** means *an American person*. The following are additional examples:

日本人	Nihon-jin	*a Japanese person*
中国人	Chūgoku-jin	*a Chinese person*
イギリス人	Igirisu-jin	*an English person*
フランス人	Furansu-jin	*a French person*
オーストラリア人	Ōsutoraria-jin	*an Australian person*
カナダ人	Kanada-jin	*a Canadian person*

EXPRESSING OCCUPATION

Many terms for occupation have a plain form and a polite form. The plain form is for the speaker and his/her insiders such as family members, and the polite form is for outsiders. The polite forms are also called honorific forms (see Chapter 20). The following table lists some examples:

Plain	Polite	Meaning
教師 kyōshi	先生 sensei	*teacher*
学生 gakusei	学生さん gakusei-san	*student*
会社員 kaishain	会社員さん kaishain-san	*company employee*
弁護士 bengoshi	弁護士さん bengoshi-san	*lawyer*
医者 isha	お医者さん o-isha-san	*medical doctor*
看護師 kangoshi	看護師さん kangoshi-san	*nurse*

Written Practice 1

Match the words on the left with their meanings on the right.

1. 日本人 Nihon-jin   _____   a. doctor
2. 中国人 Chūgoku-jin   _____   b. Japanese
3. 弁護士 bengoshi   _____   c. American
4. アメリカ人 Amerika-jin   _____   d. Chinese
5. 医者 isha   _____   e. lawyer

Naming People and Things

To say *X is Y*, Japanese uses the form XはYです **X wa Y desu**. For example:

私は学生です。
Watashi wa gakusei desu.
I'm a student.

THE TOPIC PARTICLE は WA

In Japanese, most sentences start with a topic. The topic is what the sentence is about. The topic of the sentence presents old shared information, which can serve as an introduction for the coming new piece of information in the sentence. Thus, the topic must be something that is already familiar to the speaker and the listener. In the following sentence, the sentence is about the particular person named *Tom*, whom both the speaker and the listener already know, and the new piece of information about Tom is the fact that he is English.

トムさんはイギリス人です。
Tomu-san wa Igirisu-jin desu.
Tom is English. (Literally: As for Tom, he is English.)

Here, トムさん **Tomu-san** (*Tom*) is the subject of the sentence but also functions as the topic. That's why it is marked by the topic particle は **wa**. (The subject particle is actually が **ga** (see Chapter 5 and 7), but is deleted in this example because が **ga** and は **wa** cannot occur together.) Note that the hiragana は is usually pronounced **ha**, but if it is used as a topic particle, it is pronounced **wa**.

THE COPULAR VERB です DESU

The English copular verb *to be* corresponds to the Japanese copular verb です **desu**. Unlike English verbs, Japanese verbs come at the end of the sentence.

マイクさんはカナダ人です。
Maiku-san wa Kanada-jin desu.
Mike is a Canadian.

陽子さんは学生です。
Yōko-san wa gakusei desu.
Yoko is a student.

Written Practice 2

Reorder the items in each set and form a grammatical sentence with the specified meaning:

1. *Mr. Smith is a student.*
   (学生 gakusei, です desu, は wa, スミスさん Sumisu-san)

   _____

2. *I am Japanese.*
   (日本人 Nihon-jin, 私 watashi, です desu, は wa)

   _____

3. *Mr. Chen is Chinese.*
   (中国人 Chūgoku-jin, チェンさん Chen-san, は wa, です desu)

   _____

Written Practice 3

Using the following passage as an example, write about yourself.

私はトム・ブラウンです。私はアメリカ人です。弁護士です。
Watashi wa Tomu Buraun desu. Watashi wa Amerika-jin desu. Bengoshi desu.
I am Tom Brown. I am an American. (I) am a lawyer.

_____

_____

THE NEGATIVE COPULAR VERB じゃありません JA ARIMASEN

To say X is not Y, say:

XはYじゃありません。
X wa Y ja arimasen.
X is not Y.

It is also possible to say:

XはYではありません。
X wa Y de wa arimasen.

The latter sounds slightly more formal than the former. Some speakers also say:

X はYじゃないです。
X wa Y ja nai desu.

or

X はYではないです。
X wa Y de wa nai desu.

For example:

ブラウンさんはアメリカ人じゃありません。カナダ人です。
Buraun-san wa Amerika-jin ja arimasen. Kanada-jin desu.
Mr. Brown is not an American. (He) is a Canadian.

ホワイトさんは先生じゃありません。学生です。
Howaito-san wa sensei ja arimasen. Gakusei desu.
Ms. White is not a teacher. (She) is a student.

Written Practice 4

Translate the following sentences into Japanese.

1. Mr. Brown is an American. (*Brown*: ブラウン Buraun)

   _____

2. Ms. White is not an American. (*White*: ホワイト Howaito)

   _____

3. Mr. Smith is a student. (*Smith*: スミス Sumisu)

   _____

4. Ms. Yamada is not a student. (*Yamada*: 山田 Yamada)

   _____

INDICATING THE ADDITIONAL ITEM WITH THE PARTICLE も MO

When some state or action that is previously said to apply to one item also applies to another item, the latter additional item is marked by the particle も **mo** in Japanese. For example:

ブラウンさんは学生です。　スミスさんも学生です。
Buraun-san wa gakusei desu. Sumisu-san mo gakusei desu.
Mr. Brown is a student. Mr. Smith is also a student.

Written Practice 5

Fill in the blanks with either は **wa** or も **mo**.

1. 私は学生です。弟 _____ 学生です。

   Watashi wa gakusei desu. Otōto _____ gakusei desu.

2. 私は学生です。兄＿＿＿＿会社員です。

   Watashi wa gakusei desu. Ani _____ kaishain desu.

3. ブラウンさんはカナダ人です。ホワイトさん＿＿＿＿イギリス人です。

   Buraun-san wa Kanada-jin desu. Howaito-san _____ Igirisu-jin desu.

4. チェンさんは中国人です。リーさん＿＿＿＿中国人じゃありません。

   Chen-san wa Chūgoku-jin desu. Rī-san _____ Chūgoku-jin ja arimasen.

5. 田中さんは先生じゃありません。山田さん＿＿＿＿先生じゃありません。

   Tanaka-san wa sensei ja arimasen. Yamada-san _____ sensei ja arimasen.

Using Demonstratives

In this section, you will learn how to refer to people and things using demonstrative adjectives or demonstrative pronouns such as *this* and *that*.

DEMONSTRATIVE ADJECTIVES

A demonstrative adjective can be added right before a common noun like *book*, as in *this book* or *that book*. Different demonstrative adjectives can be used depending on the relative distance among the item, the listener, and the speaker: if the item is within the speaker's domain, この **kono** is used; if the item is within the listener's domain, but outside of the speaker's domain, その **sono** is used; if the item is outside of the speaker's domain as well as the listener's domain, あの **ano** is used. For example,

あの人はマイクさんです。
Ano hito wa Maiku-san desu.
That person over there is Mike.

この車はカローラです。
Kono kuruma wa Karōra desu.
This car is a Corolla.

その犬は秋田犬です。
Sono inu wa Akita-inu desu.
That dog near you is an Akita.

この建物は図書館です。
Kono tatemono wa toshokan desu.
This building is a library.

カフェテリアはあの建物です。
Kafeteria wa ano tatemono desu.
The cafeteria is that building over there.

Written Practice 6

Fill in the blanks with この **kono**, その **sono**, or あの **ano**.

1. You are holding a book, and you are about to say that it is a Japanese book.

   _____ 本は日本語の本です。 _____ hon wa Nihon-go no hon desu.

2. Your friend is reading a book, and you want to ask him whether it is a Japanese book.

   _____ 本は日本語の本ですか。 _____ hon wa Nihon-go no hon desu ka.

3. You are sitting with your friend at a table in a restaurant. Suddenly, you see a woman in the parking lot through the window. You guess that she is Ms. Yamada.

   _____ 人は山田さんですね。 _____ hito wa Yamada-san desu ne.

See Chapter 4 for the confirmation particle ね **ne** at the end of the last sentence.

DEMONSTRATIVE PRONOUNS

For referring to a non-human item, you can just use a demonstrative pronoun such as あれ **are** (*that one over there*), これ **kore** (*this one*), and それ **sore** (*that one near you*) instead of using a demonstrative adjective and a common noun. For example, instead of saying あの車 **ano kuruma** (*that car*), you can just say あれ **are** (*that one*). For example:

あの車はカローラです。あれもカローラです。
Ano kuruma wa Karōra desu. Are mo Karōra desu.
That car is a Corolla. That one is also a Corolla.

あれはカフェテリアです。
Are wa kafeteria desu.
That one is a cafeteria.

体育館はあれです。
Taiikukan wa are desu.
The gym is that one over there.

これは英和辞典です。
Kore wa eiwa-jiten desu.
This one is an English-Japanese dictionary.

それも英和辞典です。
Sore mo eiwa-jiten desu.
That one (near you) is also an English-Japanese dictionary.

Written Practice 7

Choose the appropriate item in the parentheses.

1. (これ, この) 車はカローラです。(Kore, Kono) kuruma wa Karōra desu.
2. (あれ, あの) は図書館です。(Are, Ano) wa toshokan desu.
3. (それ, その) 建物は体育館です。(Sore, Sono) tatemono wa taiikukan desu.
4. 郵便局は (あれ, あの) 建物です。Yūbinkyoku wa (are, ano) tatemono desu.
5. (あれ, あの) 人は山田さんです。(Are, Ano) hito wa Yamada-san desu.
6. (あれ, あの) 学生は川口さんです。(Are, Ano) gakusei wa Kawaguchi-san desu.

Using Everyday Phrases

This section introduces useful everyday phrases for introducing yourself, greeting, parting, thanking, and apologizing.

INTRODUCING YOURSELF

Before introducing yourself to someone you met for the first time, say はじめまして **Hajimemashite**. Its literal translation is *beginning*, but its function is to signal your intention to introduce yourself to the person. Then, tell your name, and say よろしく **Yoroshiku**. よろしく **Yoroshiku** literally means *favorably*, but it just shows your good intentions for your future relationship with the person. When the other person says よろしく **Yoroshiku** to you before you say it to him/her, you should say こちらこそよろしく **Kochirakoso yoroshiku**, which means *It is me (who should say) yoroshiku.*

Oral Practice

🔘 **TRACK 13**

Practice saying the following out loud.

> はじめまして。鈴木です。よろしく。
> Hajimemashite. Suzuki desu. Yoroshiku.
> *Hi! I'm Mr. Suzuki. Pleased to meet you!*

> はじめまして。高橋です。こちらこそよろしく。
> Hajimemashite. Takahashi desu. Kochirakoso yoroshiku.
> *Hi! I'm Ms. Takahashi. Pleased to meet you, too!*

GREETING AND PARTING

As in English, phrases for greeting differ depending on the time of the day. In the morning, say おはようございます **Ohayō gozaimasu** (*Good morning*), in the afternoon, say こんにちは **Konnichiwa** (*Good afternoon*), and in the evening, say こんばんは **Konbanwa** (*Good evening*). Instead of おはようございます **Ohayō gozaimasu**, you may say just おはよう **Ohayō** if you are greeting your family, friends, or subordinates. Note that the hiragana は in こんにちは **Konnichiwa** and こんばんは **Konbanwa** is read as **wa**.

When you have to part with a person you may see again later during the same day, say じゃあ、また **Jā, mata** (*See you later*). If the person is your superior such as your teacher, say じゃあ、しつれいします **Jā, shitsurei shimasu** instead. It is a modest and sophisticated expression to signal your intention to part from your superior. If you are sure that you will not see the person again during the same day, also say さようなら **Sayōnara** (*Good-bye*). Note that one does not say さようなら **Sayōnara** to one's own family members.

Oral Practice

 TRACK 14

Practice saying *Hi* and *Bye*.

先生、おはようございます。
Sensei, ohayō gozaimasu.
Professor, good morning!

ああ、鈴木さん。おはよう。
Ah, Suzuki-san. Ohayō.
Oh, Ms. Suzuki. Good morning.

じゃあ、しつれいします。
Jā, shitsurei shimasu.
Okay, see you later.

ええ。じゃあ、また。
Ē. Jā, mata.
Yes. See you later.

陽子さん、こんにちは。
Yōko san. Konnichiwa.
Yoko, hi! (Good afternoon!)

ああ、広さん。こんにちは。
Ā, Hiroshi-san. Konnichiwa.
Oh, Hiroshi. Hi! (Good afternoon!)

じゃあ、また。さようなら。
Jā, mata. Sayōnara.
Okay, see you! Bye!

ええ。じゃあ、また。さようなら。
Ē. Jā, mata. Sayōnara.
Yep. See you! Bye!

EXPRESSING GRATITUDE AND APOLOGIES

To thank someone most elaborately and politely, say どうもありがとうございます
Dōmo arigatō gozaimasu (*Thank you very much*). To thank quickly your friend or
subordinate, you can just say ありがとう **Arigatō** (*Thanks*). The reply to thanking is

いいえ **Īe** (*no*) or ぜんぜん **Zenzen** (*not at all*), which means something like *Don't mention it*, *It is nothing*, or *No problem*. You can also reply with どういたしまして **Dōitashimashite** (*You are welcome*).

To apologize nicely, say どうもすみません **Dōmo sumimasen** (*I am very sorry*) or すみません **Sumimasen** (*I am sorry*). In an informal context, you can also say ごめんなさい **Gomennasai** (*I'm sorry*). A typical reply to an apology is いいえ **Īe** (*Not a big deal*).

By now, you must know that どうも **dōmo** is an adverb used to emphasize your seriousness for either thanking or apologizing. Actually, どうも **dōmo** alone can be used to thank quickly, yet respectfully.

Oral Practice

 TRACK 15

Practice thanking and apologizing by reading the following sentences out loud.

どうもありがとうございます。
Dōmo arigatō gozaimasu.
Thank you very much.

いいえ。ぜんぜん。
Īe. Zenzen.
Don't mention it. It is nothing.

どうも。
Dōmo.
Thank you.

いいえ。
Īe.
Don't mention it.

どうもすみません。
Dōmo sumimasen.
I am very sorry.

いいえ。
Īe.
It's not a big deal.

Written Practice 8

What would you say in each of the following situations? Choose the most appropriate Japanese phrase and write its letter in the blank.

a. はじめまして。 Hajimemashite.

b. ごめんなさい。 Gomennasai.

c. おはようございます。 Ohayō gozaimasu.

d. どうもありがとうございます。 Dōmo arigatō gozaimasu.

e. じゃあ、また。さようなら。 Jā, mata. Sayōnara.

1. At a party, you met someone for the first time. You want to introduce yourself. _____

2. Your friend came to your house and spent some time with you. Now she is about to leave. _____

3. At the library, you dropped your papers all over the floor, but some stranger helped you pick them up. _____

4. It is 10 A.M., and you are walking to class on campus. Suddenly, you recognize your teacher walking in front of you. _____

5. You just spilled your coffee in your friend's living room. _____

QUIZ

Circle the letter of the phrase that can fill in the blank most appropriately.

1. スミスさん_____学生 です。

   Sumisu-san _____ gakusei desu.

   (a) じゃ ja   (c) は wa

   (b) じゃあ jā   (d) では de wa

2. ブラウンさんは日本人_____ありません。

   Buraun-san wa Nihon-jin _____ arimasen.

   (a) じゃあ jā   (c) じゃ ja

   (b) も mo   (d) は wa

3. 私は_____です。

   Watashi wa _____ desu.

(a) アメリカ人 Amerika-jin   (c) イギリス Igirisu

(b) 先生 sensei   (d) アメリカ Amerika

4. 私は＿＿＿です。

Watashi wa ＿＿＿ desu.

(a) 山田 Yamada   (c) あの人 ano hito

(b) 陽子ちゃん Yōko-chan   (d)田中さん Tanaka-san

5. スミスさんは学生です。ブラウンさん＿＿＿学生です。

Sumisu-san wa gakusei desu. Buraun-san ＿＿＿ gakusei desu.

(a) は wa   (c) じゃ ja

(b) も mo   (d) じゃあ jā

6. スミスさんはアメリカ人です。ブラウンさん＿＿＿イギリス人です。

Sumisu-san wa Amerika-jin desu. Buraun-san ＿＿＿ Igirisu-jin desu.

(a) じゃ ja   (c) は wa

(b) も mo   (d) じゃあ jā

7. ＿＿＿はカフェテリアです。

＿＿＿ wa kafeteria desu.

(a) あの ano   (c) あれ are

(b) この kono   (d) その sono

8. ＿＿＿人は弁護士です。

＿＿＿ hito wa bengoshi desu.

(a) あの ano   (c) あれ are

(b) これ kore   (d) それ sore

9. ＿＿＿。山田です。よろしく。

＿＿＿ Yamada desu. Yoroshiku.

(a) さようなら Sayōnara   (c) はじめまして Hajimemashite

(b) ありがとう Arigatō   (d) こちらこそ Kochira koso

10. どうも＿＿＿。

Dōmo ＿＿＿

(a) さようなら Sayōnara

(b) はじめまして Hajimemashite

(c) よろしく Yoroshiku

(d) すみません sumimasen

CHAPTER 3

Asking Questions

In this chapter you'll learn:

The Question Particle か **ka**
Asking Who is it?
Asking What is it?
Asking Where is it?
The Japanese-Speaking World

The Question Particle か ka

Regardless whether a question is expecting an answer with "Yes" or "No" or an answer with some content information, all Japanese questions end in the question particle か **ka**. The question mark "?" is not supposed to be used in the Japanese orthography system, but it is actually very commonly used in Japanese novels and magazines. In this book, the question mark is used only in the cases where its presence will clarify the interpretation.

YES-NO QUESTIONS

In Chapter 2 you learned how to make a statement sentence, for example:

あの人は山田さんです。
Ano hito wa Yamada-san desu.
That person is Ms. Yamada.

You can easily convert a statement to a yes-no question just by adding the question particle か **ka** at the end. Make sure to use the rising intonation when you say it. For example:

あの人は山田さんですか。
Ano hito wa Yamada-san desu ka.
Is that person Ms. Yamada?

Unlike in English, there is no need to invert the subject noun and the verb in Japanese.

EXPRESSING AGREEMENT WITH はい HAI AND DISAGREEMENT WITH いいえ ĪE

はい **hai** shows agreement and いいえ **ie** shows disagreement. When the question is a simple affirmative Yes-No question, はい **hai** and いいえ **ie** correspond to *Yes* and *No*, respectively. Your answer to a Yes-No question can be just はい **Hai** (*Yes*) or いいえ **Ie** (*No*), but it can also be the slightly longer:

はい、そうです。
Hai, sō desu.
Yes, it is.

or

いいえ、ちがいます。
Ie, chigaimasu.
No, it isn't.

It can also be a full sentence like:

はい、私は日本人です。
Hai, watashi wa Nihon-jin desu.
Yes, I'm Japanese.

or

いいえ、私は日本人じゃありません。
Īe, watashi wa Nihon-jin ja arimasen.
No, I'm not Japanese.

When the question is negative, はい **hai** and いいえ **īe** do not match with *Yes* and *No* in English. Say はい **hai** if you agree, and say いいえ **īe** if you disagree. See the section "Answering a Negative Question with はい hai and いいえ īe" in Chapter 10 for examples of such cases.

Oral Practice

 TRACK 16

Practice asking the following yes-no questions by reading the questions and answers out loud.

あれは犬ですか。
Are wa inu desu ka.
Is that a dog?

いいえ。
Īe.
No.

あなたは日本人ですか。
Anata wa Nihon-jin desu ka.
Are you Japanese?

いいえ、ちがいます。
Īe, chigaimasu.
No, I'm not.

あメリカ人ですか。
Amerika-jin desu ka.
Are you an American?

はい、そうです。
Hai, sō desu.
Yes, I am.

あの人はマイクさんですか。
Ano hito wa Maiku-san desu ka.
Is that person Mike?

はい、あの人はマイクさんです。
Hai, ano hito wa Maiku-san desu.
Yes, that person is Mike.

これはボールペンですか。
Kore wa bōrupen desu ka.
Is this a ballpoint pen?

いいえ、それはボールペンじゃありません。
Īe, sore wa bōrupen ja arimasen.
No, it is not a ballpoint pen.

Asking *Who is it?*

Let's learn how to ask the identity of the people around us, using the question word だれ/どなた **dare/donata** (*who*), as well as how to answer such a question.

THE QUESTION WORD だれ DARE

The Japanese counterpart for *who* is だれ **dare**. To ask a question using だれ **dare**, start from a typical statement sentence, but just place だれ **dare** at the position where you would expect the answer to be, and add the question particle か **ka** at the end of it. For example:

あの人はだれですか。
Ano hito wa dare desu ka.
Who is that person?

The answer to such a question can be very simple, consisting of just the name along with the copular verb です **desu**, for example:

マイクさんです。
Maiku-san desu
(He) is Mike.

Or, it can be a full-sentence, as in:

あの人はマイクさんです。
Ano hito wa Maiku-san desu.
That person is Mike.

THE QUESTION WORD どなた DONATA

If you want to show respect to the person you are inquiring about, use どなた **donata** instead of だれ **dare**. You can also use 方 **kata** instead of 人 **hito** (*person*) to make your speech polite. Remember that 方 **kata** cannot be used independently, but must follow some demonstrative adjective such as あの **ano** (*that*), as in:

あの方はどなたですか。
Ano kata wa donata desu ka.
Who is that person over there?

ACKNOWLEDGING INFORMATION

Whenever your conversation partner provides you with some information, you should acknowledge it by saying ああ、そうですか **Ā, sō desu ka**, which means *Oh, really?*, *Oh, is that so?*, or *Oh, I see.* You can also say just ああ **Ā** (*Oh*) with a falling intonation, if you feel like you are saying ああ、そうですか **Ā, sō desu ka** too many times. If you do not give such acknowledgements, your conversation partner will think that you are not paying attention or are upset for some reason.

CORE FAMILY MEMBERS

The following table lists basic terms for core family members.

父	chichi	*one's own father*
お父さん	otōsan	*someone else's father*
母	haha	*one's own mother*

お母さん	okāsan	*someone else's mother*
兄	ani	*one's own older brother*
お兄さん	onīsan	*someone else's brother*
姉	ane	*one's own older sister*
お姉さん	onēsan	*someone else's older sister*
弟	otōto	*one's own younger brother*
弟さん	otōtosan	*someone else's younger brother*
妹	imōto	*one's own younger sister*
妹さん	imōtosan	*someone else's younger sister*

As you can see, there are two terms for each: the longer version, which is the polite form, and the shorter version, which is the plain form. For example, *mother* is either お母さん **okāsan** or 母 **haha** in Japanese. For referring to someone else's family, you need to use the polite form. For referring to your own family in front of other people, you need to use the plain form. The plain form and polite form are also referred to as the humble form and the respectful form (see Chapter 20).

Note that the polite forms shown previously, for example, お母さん **okāsan** and お父さん **otōsan**, can also be used for addressing one's own older family members. For example, if you want to get attention from your mother at home, you can call her out with お母さん! **Okāsan!** (*Mom!*). To address your younger family members, use their first names or nicknames.

OTHER PEOPLE

The following are useful terms that show human relationships other than family.

先生	sensei	*teacher*
学生	gakusei	*student*
同僚	dōryō	*colleague*
上司	jōshi	*superior (boss)*
友達	tomodachi	*friend*
ボーイフレンド	bōifurendo	*boyfriend*
ガールフレンド	gārufurendo	*girlfriend*

INDICATING "WHOSE" WITH THE PARTICLE の NO

To specify *whose*, just take the person's name or a pronoun and add the particle の **no**, as in マイクさんの **Maiku-san no** (*Mike's*) or 私の **watashi no** (*my*). As you can see, の **no** in this use is similar to the apostrophes in English. You can use の **no** for specifying the owner of things, as in:

マイクさんの本	Maiku-san no hon	*Mike's book*
私のかばん	Watashi no kaban	*My bag*

You can also use の **no** for specifying human relationship more precisely, as below:

マイクさんのお母さん	Maiku-san no okāsan	*Mike's mother*
私の母	watashi no haha	*my mother*
私の学生	watashi no gakusei	*My student*

マイクさんのお母さんのお兄さんの友達
Miaku-san no okāsan no onīsan no tomodachi
Mike's mother's older brother's friend

Oral Practice

 TRACK 17

Practice asking about people by reading the following questions and answering them out loud.

あの人はだれですか。
Ano hito wa dare desu ka.
Who is that person over there?

陽子さんの妹さんです。
Yōko-san no imōtosan desu.
(She) is Yoko's younger sister.

ああ、そうですか。
Ā, sō desu ka.
Oh, really?

あの人はだれですか。
Ano hito wa dare desu ka.
Who is that person over there?

私の妹です。
Watashi no imōto desu.
(She) is my younger sister.

ああ、そうですか。
Ā, sō desu ka.
Oh, I see.

あの方はどなたですか。
Ano kata wa donata desu ka.
Who is that person over there?

私の先生です。
Watashi no sensei desu.
(He) is my teacher.

あの先生はどなたですか。
Ano sensei wa donata desu ka.
Who is that teacher?

ホワイト先生です。
Howaito sensei desu.
(He/she) is Professor White.

Written Practice 1

For each of the given people, create a question that asks about his/her identity following the example.

あの人 ano hito (*that person*)

<u>あの人はだれですか。</u> *Ano hito wa dare desu ka.*

1. あの女の人 ano onna no hito (*that woman*)

   _____

2. あの学生 ano gakusei (*that student*)

   _____

3. あの先生 ano sensei (*that teacher*)

_____

4. あの方 ano kata (*that person*)

_____

Asking *What is it?*

Now, let's learn how to ask about the identity of things and animals around us using the question word 何 **nani/nan** (*what*).

THE QUESTION WORD 何 NANI/NAN

To find out the identity of things and animals, use the question word 何 **nani/nan** (*what*). This word is pronounced as **nani** independently, but is pronounced as **nan** in some contexts. For example, when followed by です **desu** (*to be*), it is pronounced as **nan**. You can ask the identity of animals, things in the room, buildings in the town, foods at the restaurant, college major, hobby, and so forth, with 何ですか **nan desu ka** (*What is (it)?*). For example:

あの建物は何ですか。 —郵便局です。
Ano tatemono wa nan desu ka. —Yūbinkyoku desu.
What is that building over there? —It is a post office.

あの山は何ですか。 —富士山です。
Ano yama wa nan desu ka. —Fujisan desu.
What is that mountain? —Mt. Fuji.

専攻は何ですか。 —文学です。
Senkō wa nan desu ka. —Bungaku desu.
What is (your) major? —Literature.

趣味は何ですか。 —テニスです。
Shumi wa nan desu ka. —Tenisu desu.
What is (your) favorite pastime activity (hobby)? —Tennis.

ASKING "WHICH"

For asking "which", use the question word どれ **dore** (*which one*) or どの **dono** + Noun (*which* + Noun).

図書館はどれですか。
Toshokan wa dore desu ka.
Which one is the library?

図書館はどの建物ですか。
Toshokan wa dono tatemono desu ka.
Which building is the library?

For people and locations, do not use どれ **dore** but use どの **dono** + Noun.

田中さんはどの人ですか。
Tanaka-san wa dono hito desu ka.
Which person is Mr. Tanaka?

See Chapter 13 for more about questions with "which."

Oral Practice

 TRACK 18

Practice asking the identity of things and answering it out loud.

あれは何ですか。
Are wa nan desu ka.
What is that over there?

あれはリスです。
Are wa risu desu.
That's a squirrel.

それは何ですか。
Sore wa nan desu ka.
What is that?

これはカメラです。
Kore wa kamera desu.
This is a camera.

これは何ですか。
Kore wa nan desu ka.
What is this?

それは英和辞典です。
Sore wa eiwa-jiten desu.
That is an English-Japanese dictionary.

Written Practice 2

Following the example, create a question whose answer should be the given sentence.

Question: それは何ですか。 *Sore wa nan desu ka.* _____

Answer: これはうなぎです。
Kore wa unagi desu.
This is an eel.

1. Question: _____
   Answer: これはカメラです。
   Kore wa kamera desu.
   This is a camera.

2. Question: _____
   Answer: あの建物は銀行です。
   Ano tatemono wa ginkō desu.
   That building is a bank.

3. Question: _____
   Answer: 専攻は数学です。
   Senkō wa sūgaku desu.
   (My) major is math.

4. Question: _____
   Answer: 趣味はテニスです。
   Shumi wa tenisu desu.
   (My) favorite pastime activity is tennis.

5. Question: _____
   Answer: あの人は田中さんです。
   Ano hito wa Tanaka-san desu.
   That person is Mr. Tanaka.

Asking *Where is it?*

Now, let's learn how to ask about the location of people and things using the question word どこ **doko** (*where*) as well as how to answer such a question using a variety of relative location terms.

THE QUESTION WORD どこ DOKO

The question word that means *where* is どこ **doko** in Japanese. This word is particularly useful when you are traveling in Japan. If you are looking for a 郵便局 **yūbinkyoku** (*post office*), for example, you can simply ask:

郵便局はどこですか。
Yūbinkyoku wa doko desu ka.
Where is the post office?

DEMONSTRATIVE PRONOUNS FOR LOCATIONS

In some cases, you can answer a question with どこ **doko** using a demonstrative pronoun for location, ここ **koko** (*here*), そこ **soko** (*there near you*), or あそこ **asoko** (*over there*), as you point at the location. For example:

銀行はどこですか。—あそこです。
Ginkō wa doko desu ka. — Asoko desu.
Where is the bank? — (It) is over there.

私のめがねはどこですか。 —そこです。
Watashi no megane wa doko desu ka. —Soko desu.
Where are my eyeglasses? — (They) are there (right by you).

本はどこですか。—ここです。
Hon wa doko desu ka. — Koko desu.
Where is the book? —(It) is right here.

TERMS FOR RELATIVE LOCATION

If the answer to a question with *where* cannot be formed by a simple word like あそこ **asoko** (*over there*), you can use some of the relative location words listed in the following table. Some of them may sound like English prepositions, but they are all nouns.

前	mae	*front*
後ろ	ushiro	*behind*
近く	chikaku	*vicinity, near*
隣	tonari	*next to*
間	aida	*between (. . . and . . .)*
横	yoko	*side*
中	naka	*inside*
右	migi	*right*
左	hidari	*left*
上	ue	*above*
下	shita	*below*
東	higashi	*east*
西	nishi	*west*
南	minami	*south*
北	kita	*north*

These terms cannot pinpoint any location just by themselves. In order to make sense, you need to add a reference item such as 銀行 **ginkō** (*bank*) and 机 **tsukue** (*desk*), and the particle の **no**, right before them. For example:

| 銀行の前 | ginkō no mae | *in front of the bank* |
| 机の右 | tsukue no migi | *to the right of the desk* |

間 **aida** requires two reference items conjoined by the particle と **to** (see Chapter 5 for the particle と **to**).

銀行と図書館の間
Ginkō to toshokan no aida
between the bank and the library

Oral Practice

 TRACK 19

Practice stating the location of things out loud.

郵便局は銀行の前です。
Yūbinkyoku wa ginkō no mae desu.
The post office is in front of the bank.

辞書は机の上です。
Jisho wa tsukue no ue desu.
The dictionary is on the desk.

横浜は東京の近くです。
Yokohama wa Tōkyō no chikaku desu.
Yokohama is near Tokyo.

大学は3番通りの北です。
Daigaku wa San-ban-dōri no kita desu.
The university is north of Third Street.

INDICATING THE STARTING POINT AND ENDING POINT WITH THE PARTICLE から KARA AND まで MADE

The particle から **kara** (*from*) and the particle まで **made** (*up to*) specify the starting point and the ending point, respectively. They can be locations. For example:

うちから学校まで	uchi kara gakkō made	*from home to school*
東京から大阪まで	Tōkyō kara Ōsaka made	*from Tokyo to Osaka*

They can also be used for other notions such as time, page, and diversity. For example:

2時から3時まで
2-ji kara 3-ji made
from 2 o'clock to 3 o'clock

23ページから35ページまで
23-pēji kara 35-pēji made
from page 23 to page 35

子供から大人まで
kodomo kara otona made
(anyone) from children to adults

食べ物から家具まで
tabemono kara kagu made
(anything ranging) from foods to furniture

THE QUESTION WORD どちら DOCHIRA

In a polite context, どこ **doko** is replaced by どちら **dochira**, which means *which way* or *which direction*, but can also mean *where* in some context. For example, if you want to ask someone where Professor Yamada is, say:

山田先生はどちらですか。
Yamada sensei wa dochira desu ka.
Where is Professor Yamada?

If you want to ask someone where he is from or where he came from, you can say どちらからですか **Dochira kara desu ka.**

スミスさんはどちらからですか 。 —イギリスからです。
Sumisu-san wa dochira kara desu ka. —Igirisu kara desu.
Mr. Smith, where are you from? —I'm from England.

If you want to ask more specifically where the person was born politely, you can say:

ご出身はどちらですか。
Go-shusshin wa dochira desu ka.
Where were you born?

Written Practice 3

In each of the following situations, what would you say? Create a sentence using all the items in the parentheses.

You want to find out where the post office is.

{どこ doko, 郵便局 yūbinkyoku, か ka, です desu, は wa}

郵便局はどこですか。 *Yūbinkyoku wa doko desu ka.*
_____

1. You want to ask where your book is.

   {本 hon, どこ doko, は wa, か ka, です desu}
   _____

2. You want to say that the book is on the table.

   {本 hon, 上 ue, テーブル tēburu, は wa, の no, です desu}
   _____

3. You want to ask where Mr. Tanaka is.

   {田中さん Tanaka-san, です desu, は wa, か ka, どちら dochira}
   _____

4. You just met Mr. Yan for the first time. You want to ask him where he is from.

   {ヤンさん Yan-san, から kara, です desu, か ka, は wa, どちら dochira}
   _____

The Japanese-Speaking World

Japanese is generally considered to be one of the top ten most influential languages in the world in terms of the number of primary/secondary speakers and socioeconomic and sociocultural factors. Japanese is spoken as an official language in Japan.

The total area of Japan is 380,000 km², which is about 1/25 of the total area of the United States, smaller than the state of California, and about the same size as the state of Montana. Japan's population is about 128 million, which is a little over one-third of the population in the United States. Considering the fact that more than two-thirds of the land in Japan is mountainous, you can imagine how crowded Japan is.

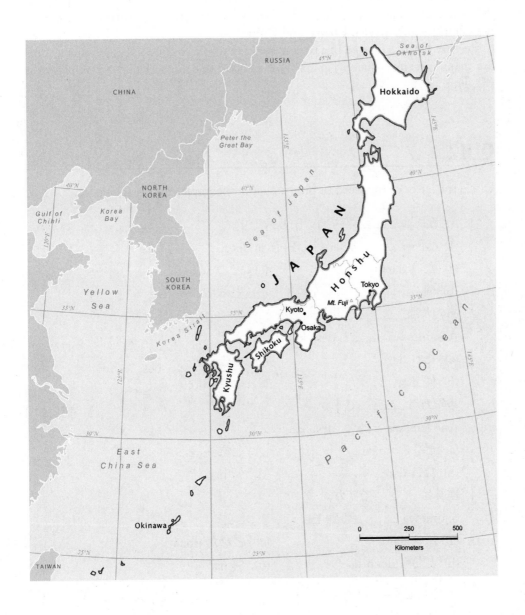

Japan consists of four major islands, which are 本州 **Honshū** (*Honshu*), 北海道 **Hokkaidō** (*Hokkaido*), 九州 **Kyūshū** (*Kyushu*), and 四国 **Shikoku** (*Shikoku*), and several thousand small islands, which are in a chain from northeast to southwest. The length of Japan is about 3,000 km, and its north end is located near 45° N. L., which is the same latitude as Montreal, Canada, and its south end is located near 20° N. L., which is the same latitude as the southern part of Florida. Japan's closest neighbors include Korea, Russia, and China.

Because Japan is located in a region where multiple continental plates meet, there are many volcanoes there. Japan's most famous volcano and highest mountain is Mt. Fuji.

QUIZ

Circle the letter of the word or phrase that best completes each sentence.

1. A: あれは_____ですか。B: リスです。

   A: Are wa _____ desu ka. B: Risu desu.
   - (a) だれ dare
   - (b) 何 nan
   - (c) どこ doko
   - (d) どちら dochira

2. あの人は_____ですか。

   Ano hito wa _____ desu ka.
   - (a) だれ dare
   - (b) 何 nan
   - (c) どこ doko
   - (d) どれ dore

3. あの方は_____ですか。

   Ano kata wa _____ desu ka.
   - (a) どなた donata
   - (b) だれ dare
   - (c) どれ dore
   - (d) 何 nan

4. 趣味は_____ですか。

   Shumi wa _____ desu ka.
   - (a) だれ dare
   - (b) どちら dochira
   - (c) どなた donata
   - (d) 何 nan

5. A: _____ は何ですか。B: 文学です。

   A: _____ wa nan desu ka. B: Bungaku desu.

   (a) 専攻 senkō   (c) あの人 ano hito

   (b) 学校 gakkō   (d) あの建物 ano tatemono

6. あの人は私の _____ です。

   Ano hito wa watashi no _____ desu.

   (a) お母さん okāsan   (c) お兄さん onīsan

   (b) リス risu   (d) 母 haha

7. あの人は鈴木さんの _____ です。

   Ano hito wa Suzuki-san no _____ desu.

   (a) お母さん okāsan   (c) 兄 ani

   (b) 父 chichi   (d) 母 haha

8. 辞書は机の _____ です。

   Jisho wa tsukue no _____ desu.

   (a) 学生 gakusei   (c) 上 ue

   (b) どこ doko   (d) 建物 tatemono

9. A: ヤンさんはどちらからですか。B: 上海 _____ です。

   A: Yan-san wa dochira kara desu ka. B: Shanhai _____ desu.

   (a) の no   (c) から kara

   (b) どこ doko   (d) まで made

10. あの人は高橋さん _____ 友達です。

    Ano hito wa Takahashi-san _____ tomodachi desu.

    (a) の no   (c) から kara

    (b) は wa   (d) まで made

CHAPTER 4

Describing People and Things

In this chapter you'll learn:

Some Useful Adjectives
Asking How is it?
Creating a Modifier Using a Noun and the Particle の **no**
Using the Numbers One to Ten

Some Useful Adjectives

In English, an adjective can be used as a prenominal modifier (a modifier placed right before a noun that it modifies), as in *an **old** building*, or as a sentence predicate

(a predicate placed at the end of a sentence), as in *This is old*. This situation also holds in Japanese. Japanese adjectives can be used as a prenominal modifier, as in:

| 古い建物 | furui tatemono | *an old building* |

or, as a sentence predicate, as in:

| これは古いです。 | Kore wa furui desu. | *This is old.* |

I-TYPE AND NA-TYPE ADJECTIVES

All the Japanese adjectives end in either い **i** or な **na** when used as a prenominal modifier, as you can see in the following examples:

古い建物	furui tatemono	*an old building*
新しい建物	atarashii tatemono	*new building*
きれいな建物	kirei na tatemono	*beautiful building*
立派な建物	rippa na tatemono	*splendid building*

An adjective that ends in い **i** at a prenominal position is called an i-type adjective, and an adjective that ends in な **na** at a prenominal position is called a na-type adjective. In the above examples, 古い **furui** (*old*) and 新しい **atarashii** (*new*) are i-type, and きれいな **kirei na** (*beautiful*) and 立派な **rippa na** (*splendid*) are na-type. You need to know this distinction because these two types of adjectives conjugate differently. In fact, い **i** and な **na** are an inflection part and the part without い **i** or な **na** is the *stem* of the adjective. The following table lists some useful adjectives:

I-Type (Stem + い i)			Na-type (Stem + な na)		
明るい	akarui	*bright*	便利な	benri na	*convenient*
新しい	atarashii	*new*	不便な	fuben na	*inconvenient*
古い	furui	*old*	意地悪な	ijiwaru na	*nasty, mean*
広い	hiroi	*spacious*	きれいな	kirei na	*pretty*
忙しい	isogashii	*busy*	まじめな	majime na	*serious*
かわいい	kawaii	*cute*	立派な	rippa na	*splendid*
厳しい	kibishii	*strict*	静かな	shizuka na	*quiet*
きたない	kitanai	*dirty*	モダンな	modan na	*modern*
おもしろい	omoshiroi	*interesting*	ユニークな	yunīku na	*unique*
おいしい	oishii	*delicious*	安全な	anzen na	*safe*

せまい	semai	*not spacious, narrow*	元気な	genki na	*healthy*
高い	takai	*expensive, high*	簡単な	kantan na	*easy*
うるさい	urusai	*noisy*			
やさしい	yasashii	*kind*			
安い	yasui	*cheap*			
いい	ii	*good*			
大きい	ōkii	*big*			
小さい	chīsai	*small*			
おかしい	okashii	*funny*			

NOTE: 大きい *ōkii*, 小さい *chīsai*, and おかしい *okashii* are slightly irregular: they are i-type adjectives, but they have additional prenominal modifier forms, which are 大きな *ōki na*, 小さな *chīsa na*, and おかしな *okashi na*, respectively. Also note that some scholars consider that there is a third type of adjectives, those followed by の *no*. In this book, they are considered as a part of nouns to avoid confusion.

CONJUGATING ADJECTIVES IN THE POLITE PRESENT TENSE

Adjectives conjugate in the present tense in the polite style as summarized in the following table:

	Adjectives in the Polite Present Form	
	I-type (Stem + い i) EX: 古い furui (*old*)	Na-type (Stem + な na) EX: 静かな shizuka na (*quiet*)
Affirmative	Stem + いです Stem + i desu EX: 古いです。Furui desu. *(It) is old.*	Stem + です Stem + desu EX: 静かです。shizuka desu. *(It) is quiet.*
Negative	Stem + くありません Stem + ku arimasen EX: 古くありません。 Furuku arimasen. *(It) is not old.*	Stem + じゃありません Stem + ja arimasen EX: 静かじゃありません。 Shizuka ja arimasen. *(It) is not quiet.*

Note that ありません **arimasen** in the negative forms in the above table can be ないです **nai desu**, and じゃ **ja** in the negative forms in the above table can be では **dewa**. Also note that いい **ii** (*good*) is irregular, and its negative form is よくありません **yoku arimasen** (or よくないです **yoku nai desu**).

Oral Practice

 TRACK 20

Practice saying the following statements out loud, paying attention to the type and the form of adjectives.

山田先生は厳しい先生です。
Yamada sensei wa kibishii sensei desu.
Professor Yamada is a strict teacher.

山田先生は厳しいです。
Yamada sensei wa kibishii desu.
Professor Yamada is strict.

田中先生は厳しくありません。
Tanaka sensei wa kibishiku arimasen.
Professor Tanaka is not strict.

田中先生は厳しくないです。
Tanaka sensei wa kibishiku nai desu.
Professor Tanaka is not strict.

この部屋は静かな部屋です。
Kono heya wa shizuka na heya desu.
This room is a quiet room.

この部屋は静かです。
Kono heya wa shizuka desu.
This room is quiet.

あの部屋は静かじゃありません。
Ano heya wa shizuka ja arimasen.
That room is not quiet.

あの部屋は静かじゃないです。
Ano heya wa shizuka ja nai desu.
That room is not quiet.

この本はいいです。
Kono hon wa ii desu.
This book is good.

あの本はよくありません。
Ano hon wa yoku arimasen.
That book is not good.

CONFIRMING WITH THE PARTICLE ね NE

To seek an agreement from your conversation partner about what you want to say, just add the particle ね **ne** at the end of your statement. The reply to it can be ええ、そうですね **Ē, sō desu ne** (*Yes, it is*) if the listener agrees with the statement, but そうですか **Sō desu ka?** (*Is it so?*) with a falling-rising intonation if he/she disagrees with it. For example:

今日はいい天気ですね。—ええ、そうですね。
Kyō wa ii tenki desu ne. —Ē, sō desu ne.
Today's weather is nice, isn't it? — Yes, it is.

日本語は簡単ですね。 —そうですか。
Nihon-go wa kantan desu ne. —Sō desu ka?
Japanese is easy, isn't it? —Is it?

EMPHASIZING WITH THE PARTICLE よ YO

The particle よ **yo** can be optionally placed at the end of a statement in a conversational context. Its function is to emphasize the statement by showing the speaker's enthusiasm.

日本語は簡単ですよ。
Nihon-go wa kantan desu yo.
Japanese is easy, you know?

スミス先生はやさしいですよ。
Sumisu sensei wa yasashii desu yo.
Professor Smith is kind, I tell you!

However, you must be careful not to overuse よ **yo** because it could give an imposing and assertive impression depending on the content and the context of your statement as well as your intonation and the tone of your voice.

Written Practice 1

Fill in the blanks using some of the given adjectives. Make sure to conjugate them appropriately. You may use the same adjective more than once.

(きれいな kirei na, きびしい kibishii, 難しい muzukashii)

1. 英語は＿＿＿＿＿＿＿ですよ。
   Eigo wa ＿＿＿＿＿＿＿＿＿ desu yo.
   English is . . .

2. あの花は＿＿＿＿＿＿ですね。
   Ano hana wa ＿＿＿＿＿＿＿＿ desu ne.
   That flower is . . .

3. 田中先生は＿＿＿＿＿＿です。
   Tanaka sensei wa ＿＿＿＿＿＿＿＿ desu.
   Professor Tanaka is . . .

4. この部屋は＿＿＿＿＿＿ありませんね。
   Kono heya wa ＿＿＿＿＿＿＿＿ arimasen ne.
   This room isn't . . .

5. 日本語は＿＿＿＿＿＿ありませんね。
   Nihon-go wa ＿＿＿＿＿＿＿＿ arimasen ne.
   Japanese isn't . . .

Asking *How is it?*

In this section, you will learn how to ask about the state or the condition of people and things using the question words どんな **donna** and どう **dō**. You will also learn how to answer such a question using adjectives and degree adverbs.

THE QUESTION WORDS どんな DONNA AND どう DŌ

To ask about the state or the property of people and things, use the question word どんな **donna** (*what kind of*) or どう **dō** (*how*) depending on where it is placed in the sentence: どんな **donna** is placed right before a noun; どう **dō** is placed as a predicate, preceding です **desu** (*to be*). For example:

田中さんはどんな人ですか。
Tanaka-san wa donna hito desu ka.
What kind of person is Mr. Tanaka?

日本語のクラスはどうですか。
Nihon-go no kurasu wa dō desu ka.
How is (your) Japanese class?

In a polite context, you can use いかが **ikaga** instead of どう **dō**. (See Chapter 20.)

DEGREE ADVERBS

Use degree adverbs to express the degree of some property described by adjectives. Some degree adverbs such as とても **totemo** (*very much*), まあまあ **māmā** (*more or less, relatively*), and ちょっと **chotto** (*a little bit*) must be used with an adjective in the affirmative form. Also remember that ちょっと **chotto** (*a little bit*) is used with an adjective that expresses an unfavorable meaning such as *dirty* or *ugly*. By contrast, まあまあ **māmā** (*more or less*) must be used with an adjective with a favorable meaning such as *clean* or *beautiful*. とても **totemo** (*very much*) can be used with either favorable or unfavorable properties. For example:

英語のテストはとても難しいです。
Eigo no tesuto wa totemo muzukashii desu.
English tests are very hard.

数学のテストはとても簡単です。
Sūgaku no tesuto wa totemo kantan desu.
Math tests are very easy.

山田さんはまあまあやさしいです。
Yamada-san wa māmā yasashii desu.
Ms. Yamada is relatively kind.

田中さんはちょっと意地悪です。
Tanaka-san wa chotto ijiwaru desu.
Mr. Tanaka is a little bit nasty.

By contrast, あまり **amari** ([*not*] *very much*) and ぜんぜん **zenzen** ([*not*] *at all*) must be used with an adjective in the negative form, regardless of whether the adjective represents a favorable or unfavorable property.

英語のテストはあまり難しくありません。
Eigo no tesuto wa amari muzukashiku arimasen.
English tests are not very hard.

数学のテストはあまり簡単じゃありません。
Sūgaku no tesuto wa amari kantan ja arimasen.
Math tests are not very easy.

父はぜんぜん厳しくありません。
Chichi wa zenzen kibishiku arimasen.
My father is not strict at all.

このコーヒーはぜんぜんおいしくありません。
Kono kōhī wa zenzen oishiku arimasen.
This coffee is not delicious at all.

Oral Practice

 TRACK 21

Practice asking the state of things and people paying attention to the choice of the question words and the degree adverbs.

どんな犬ですか。
Donna inu desu ka.
What kind of dog is it?

とてもかわいい犬です。
Totemo kawaii inu desu.
(It) is a very cute dog.

そのステーキはどうですか。
Sono sutēki wa dō desu ka.
How is that steak?

まあまあおいしいです。
Māmā oishii desu.
(It) is more or less delicious.

日本語は難しいですか。
Nihon-go wa muzukashii desu ka.
Is Japanese difficult?

いいえ、ぜんぜん難しくありません。
Īe, zenzen muzukashiku arimasen.
No, it is not difficult at all.

あのレストランはどうですか。
Ano resutoran wa dō desu ka.
How is that restaurant?

ちょっと高いです。
Chotto takai desu.
A little bit expensive.

Written Practice 2

Complete the answer to each question appropriately, paying attention to the degree adverbs and whether the adjective should be in the affirmative form or in the negative form.

1. 日本語は難しいですか。—はい、とても _____。

   Nihongo wa muzukashii desu ka. —Hai, totemo _____.

   Is Japanese difficult? —Yes, . . .

2. あの映画はおもしろいですか。—いいえ、あまり _____。

   Ano eiga wa omoshiroi desu ka. —Īe, amari _____.

   Is that movie interesting? —No, . . .

3. 明日は忙しいですか。—はい、ちょっと _____。

   Ashita wa isogashii desu ka. —Hai, chotto _____.

   Are you busy tomorrow? —Yes, . . .

4. この本は高いですか。—いいえ。まあまあ _____。

   Kono hon wa takai desu ka. —Īe. Māmā _____.

   Is this book expensive? —No. . . .

THE CONJUNCTIONS それに SORENI AND でも DEMO

For mentioning multiple properties of some item in separate sentences, connect the sentences appropriately using the conjunction それに **soreni** (*furthermore, in addition*) or でも **demo** (*but*) depending on the context. If you are mentioning an additional property, use それに **soreni**. If you are mentioning a conflicting or contrasting property, use でも **demo**. For example:

あの部屋はとても明るいです。それに、まあまあ広いです。
Ano heya mo totemo akarui desu. Soreni, māmā hiroi desu.
That room is very bright. Furthermore, it is relatively spacious.

この部屋はまあまあ広いです。でも、あまり明るくありません。
Kono heya wa māmā hiroi desu. Demo, amari akaruku arimasen.
This room is relatively spacious. But it is not very bright.

Written Practice 3

Complete the following sentences based on the facts around you. You may use multiple sentences using the conjunction それに **soreni** (*in addition*) or でも **demo** (*but*).

1. 私の母は_____。

   Watashi no haha wa _____.

   My mother is . . .

2. 私の父は_____。

   Watashi no chichi wa _____.

   My father is . . .

3. 私の部屋は_____。

   Watashi no heya wa _____.

   My room is . . .

4. 日本語は_____。

   Nihon-go wa _____.

   The Japanese language is . . .

Creating a Modifier Using a Noun and the Particle の no

In Chapter 3, you saw that the particle の **no** can be used to mean *...'s* as in:

山田さんのお母さん	Yamada-san no okāsan	*Ms. Yamada's mother*
マイクさんの本	Maiku-san no hon	*Mike's book*

or to specify the reference item for relative location, as in:

銀行のとなり	ginkō no tonari	*next to the bank*

You can create more variety of modifiers using a noun and the particle の **no**, for example:

日本語の本	Nihon-go no hon	*a Japanese book*
日本語の学生	Nihon-go no gakusei	*a student of Japanese language*
日本人の学生	Nihon-jin no gakusei	*a Japanese student*
アメリカの大学	Amerika no daigaku	*a university in the United States*
アメリカの車	Amerika no kuruma	*an American car*

You can have multiple modifiers in the form of noun + の **no**, as in:

日本の大学の数学の学生
Nihon no daigaku no sūgaku no gakusei
A student of mathematics at a university in Japan

Remember that the ultimate item being modified must be placed at the very end of the phrase. Don't be misled by the word order found in English translations.

Written Practice 4

Using the words provided, translate the following English phrases into Japanese. Use the particle の **no** as many times as you need. Pay attention to the word order.

1. Mike's book   _____
2. Mike's Japanese language book   _____
3. Mike's Japanese friend   _____
4. a student of Japanese   _____
5. Mike's friend's Japanese book   _____

マイクさん Maiku-san (*Mike*)   本 hon (*book*)   友達 tomodachi (*friend*)

学生 gakusei (*student*)   日本語 Nihon-go (*Japanese language*)

日本人 Nihon-jin (*Japanese person*)

Using the Numbers One to Ten

Let's learn how to count from one to ten in Japanese as well as how to read telephone numbers.

THE NUMBERS ONE TO TEN

You can count from one to ten in Japanese as follows:

1	いち ichi		6	ろく roku
2	に ni		7	なな nana or しち shichi
3	さん san		8	はち hachi
4	よん yon or し shi		9	きゅう kyū or く ku
5	ご go		10	じゅう jū

Note that the number 4 is an unlucky number in Japan because one of its pronunciations, し **shi**, is also the pronunciation of the word 死 **shi**, which means *death*.

READING TELEPHONE NUMBERS

When reading a telephone number, 4, 7, and 9 are usually pronounced as よん **yon**, なな **nana**, and きゅう **kyū** rather than as し **shi**, しち **shichi**, and く **ku**, respectively. The number 0 is pronounced as either ゼロ **zero** or れい **rei**.

Oral Practice

 **TRACK 22**

Read the following telephone numbers out loud.

03–5542–1354
zero san – go go yon ni – ichi san go yon

056–798–8292
zero go roku – nana kyū hachi – hachi ni kyū ni

0182–69–1143
zero ichi hachi ni – roku kyū – ichi ichi yon san

QUIZ

Circle the letter of the word or phrase that best completes each sentence.

1. 高橋さんの部屋は＿＿＿＿部屋ですか。

   Takahashi-san no heya wa ＿＿＿＿ heya desu ka.

   (a) どう dō   (c) どんな donna

   (b) だれ dare   (d) どこ doko

2. あの部屋は静かです。この部屋も＿＿＿＿部屋ですね。

   Ano heya wa shizuka desu. Kono heya mo ＿＿＿＿ heya desu ne.

   (a) 静か shizuka   (c) 広い hiroi

   (b) 静かな shizuka na   (d) きれいな kirei na

3. この犬は＿＿＿＿犬です。

   Kono inu wa ＿＿＿＿ inu desu.

   (a) かわいい kawaii   (c) かわいな kawai na

   (b) かわいいな kawaii na (d) かわい kawai

4. 日本語はあまり＿＿＿＿ありません。

   Nihon-go wa amari ＿＿＿＿ arimasen.

   (a) 難しい muzukashii   (c) 難しく muzukashiku

   (b) 難しいじゃ muzukashii ja (d) 難しくない muzukashiku nai

5. 日本語はまあまあ＿＿＿＿。

   Nihon-go wa māmā ＿＿＿＿.

   (a) 難しいです muzukashii desu

   (b) 難しくありません muzukashiku arimasen

   (c) 簡単です kantan desu

   (d) 簡単じゃありません kantan ja arimasen

6. 兄はちょっと意地悪＿＿＿＿。

   Ani wa chotto ijiwaru ＿＿＿＿.

   (a) です desu

   (b) じゃありません ja arimasen

   (c) ではありません de wa arimasen

   (d) じゃないです ja nai desu

7. あのレストランはきれいです。それに、＿＿＿＿ です。

Ano resutoran wa kirei desu. Soreni, ＿＿＿＿ desu.

(a) せまい semai   (c) きたない kitanai

(b) おいしい oishii   (d) うるさい urusai

8. あのレストランはきれいです。でも、＿＿＿＿ です。

Ano resutoran wa kirei desu. Demo, ＿＿＿＿ desu.

(a) うるさい urusai   (c) おいしいoishii

(b) 静か shizuka   (d) 広い hiroi

9. スミスさんは＿＿＿＿ です。

Sumisu-san wa ＿＿＿＿ desu.

(a) 日本語のアメリカ Nihon-go no Amerika

(b) 日本語の学生 Nihon-go no gakusei

(c) 学生の日本語 gakusei no Nihon-go

(d) 学生のアメリカ gakusei no Amerika

10. あれは＿＿＿＿ です。

Are wa ＿＿＿＿ desu.

(a) 車の姉の友達 kuruma no ane no tomodachi

(b) 姉の車の友達 ane no kuruma no tomodachi

(c) 姉の友達の車 ane no tomodachi no kuruma

(d) 友達の車の姉 tomodachi no kuruma no ane

CHAPTER 5

Expressing Existence and Location

In this chapter you'll learn:

The Verbs います **imasu** *and* あります **arimasu**
Expressing What Exists
Expressing What You Have
Expressing the Location of People and Things
Using the Numbers Eleven to Ninety-Nine

The Verbs います imasu and あります arimasu

To talk about existence, regardless of whether expressing what exists or where it exists, use the verb います **imasu** (*exist*) or あります **arimasu** (*exist*). For an item that can move by itself, for example, a person or an animal, use います **imasu**; for an item that cannot move by itself, for example, a book, a building, or a tree, use あります **arimasu**. In any case, the item is marked by the particle が **ga** and its location is marked by the particle に **ni**.

THE PARTICLE が GA IN EXISTENTIAL SENTENCES

In a sentence that expresses the existence of something as in "X exists," the item that exists (X) is the subject and is marked by the particle subject が **ga**; as in:

大きい建物があります。
Ōkii tatemono ga arimasu.
There is a big building.

高い木があります。
Takai ki ga arimasu.
There is a tall tree.

かわいい犬がいます。
Kawaii inu ga imasu.
There is a cute dog.

(For more about the particle が **ga** as the subject particle, see Chapter 7.)

SPECIFYING THE LOCATION OF EXISTENCE WITH THE PARTICLE に NI

The location of existence is marked by the particle に **ni** in a sentence with the verb います **imasu** (*exist*) or あります **arimasu** (*exist*). As long as the verb is placed at the end of the sentence, the order between the subject noun and the location noun does not matter. Both of the following sentences mean *There is a dog over there.*

あそこに犬がいます。
Asoko ni inu ga imasu.

犬があそこにいます。
Inu ga asoko ni imasu.

THE PARTICLE CLUSTER には NI WA

Some particles such as は **wa** and も **mo** can follow another particle, creating a cluster of particles such as には **ni wa** and にも **ni mo**. For example, you can say, あそこには犬がいます **Asoko ni wa inu ga imasu** (*There is a dog over there*) if あそこ **asoko** is the location of the existence and also the topic of the sentence. However, note that the first particle may be occasionally deleted and that the subject particle が **ga** and the direct object particle を **o** (see Chapter 7) must be deleted if they are followed by another particle such as は **wa**. For example, even if the subject noun is also the topic of the sentence, it is wrong to say がは **ga wa**. If the *dog* is the subject of the sentence and also the topic of the sentence, just mark it with は **wa**, as in, 犬はあそこにいます **Inu wa asoko ni imasu** (*The dog is over there*). As you can see in these two example sentences, what the sentence expresses slightly changes depending on what is the topic of the sentence. The nature of the topic particle は **wa** is discussed in Chapter 2, and the difference between the following two constructions will be discussed in the following sections in this chapter:

YにはXがいます。
Y ni wa X ga imasu.
There is an X in Y.

XはYにいます。
X wa Y ni imasu.
X is at Y.

Expressing What Exists

Let's look at the construction YにはXがいます/あります **Y ni wa X ga imasu/arimasu.** (*There is an X in Y.*) If you want to express what exists at the cafeteria, then think that your statement will be about "at the cafeteria" and start your statement with このカフェテリアには **kono kafeteria ni wa**, where both the location particle and the topic particle co-exit. At this point, it is assumed that your conversation partner is also familiar with the cafeteria you are talking about and that what will be said shortly after このカフェテリアには **kono kafeteria ni wa** provides a piece of new information. For example, in the following sentence, the new piece of information expressed by the sentence is the existence of てんぷらうどん **tenpura udon** (*noodles with tempura*) at that cafeteria.

このカフェテリアにはてんぷらうどんがあります。
Kono kafeteria ni wa tenpura udon ga arimasu.
This cafeteria has tempura noodles.

It is very abstract, but the point is to start the sentence with the location treated as the topic of the sentence if you want to express what exists in there, and the item that exists must be marked by が **ga**. The following are additional examples. Go through each of them thinking about what the topic of the sentence (old shared information) is and what the new piece of information is.

うちの庭には桜の木があります。
Uchi no niwa ni wa sakura no ki ga arimasu.
In my garden, there is a cherry tree.

駅のとなりにはきれいなレストランがあります。
Eki no tonari ni wa kirei na resutoran ga arimasu.
Next to the train station, there is a pretty restaurant.

空港には警察官がいます。
Kūkō ni wa keisatsukan ga imasu.
There are police officers at the airport.

LISTING MULTIPLE ITEMS WITH THE PARTICLE と TO

You can list multiple items in the same sentence using the particle と **to**. Place と **to** after each item except the last one.

このかばんの中には傘と財布があります。
Kono kaban no naka ni wa kasa to saifu ga arimasu.
In this bag, there are an umbrella and a wallet.

私の部屋にはベッドとソファーとテーブルがあります。
Watashi no heya ni wa beddo to sofā to tēburu ga arimasu.
In my room, there is a bed, a sofa, and a table.

日本語のクラスにはアメリカ人と中国人と韓国人がいます。
Nihon-go no kurasu ni wa Amerika-jin to Chūgoku-jin to Kankoku-jin ga imasu.
In the Japanese language class, there are Americans, Chinese, and Koreans.

NOTE: と *to can be used only for nouns. For listing verbs and adjectives, use their te-forms (Chapter 9).*

Written Practice 1

Following the example, form a grammatical sentence by using the given items in each set. You will need to add some verbs and particles.

{サンドイッチ sandoitchi (*sandwich*), ハンバーガー hambāgā (*hamburger*), このカフェテリアには kono kafeteria ni wa (*at this cafeteria*)}

このカフェテリアにはサンドイッチとハンバーガーがあります。

Kono kafeteria ni wa sandoitchi to hambāgā ga arimasu.

1. (駅のとなりには eki no tonari ni wa (*next to the train station*), 銀行 ginkō (*bank*))

   _____

2. (猫 neko (*cat*), 犬 inu (*dog*), うちには uchi ni wa (*at home*))

   _____

3. (机の上には tsukue no ue ni wa (*on the desk*), 鉛筆 enpitsu (*pencil*), 辞書 jisho (*dictionary*), 消しゴム keshigomu (*eraser*))

   _____

4. (日本語のクラスには Nihon-go no kurasu ni wa (*in the Japanese class*), アメリカ人 Amerika-jin (*Americans*), 中国人 Chūgoku-jin (*Chinese*), 韓国人 Kankoku-jin (*Koreans*))

   _____

Expressing What You Have

The verb います **imasu** and あります **arimasu** express not only what and who exist but also what human relationships, schedules, and plans one has. In such cases, the topic can be a person or date. For example:

私は兄がいます。
Watashi wa ani ga imasu.
I have an older brother.

姉は中国人の友達がいます。
Ane wa Chūgoku-jin no tomodachi ga imasu.
My older sister has a Chinese friend.

今日は日本語のクラスがあります。
Kyō wa Nihon-go no kurasu ga arimasu.
(I) have a Japanese class today.

Note: *It is also possible to add the particle* に *ni after the person.*

私には兄がいます。
Watashi ni wa ani ga imasu.
I have an older brother.

姉には中国人の友達がいます。
Ane ni wa Chūgoku-jin no tomodachi ga imasu.
My older sister has a Chinese friend.

To express what you don't have, use the negative forms of います **imasu** and あります **arimasu**, which are いません **imasen** and ありません **arimasen**, respectively.

山田さん(に)は兄弟がいません。
Yamada-san (ni) wa kyōdai ga imasen.
Ms. Yamada doesn't have any siblings.

私(に)は友達がいません。
Watashi (ni) wa tomodachi ga imasen.
I don't have any friends.

弟(に)はお金がありません。
Otōto (ni) wa o-kane ga arimasen.
My younger brother doesn't have any money.

時間がありません。
Jikan ga arimasen.
(We) don't have time.

今日はクラスがありません。
Kyō wa kurasu ga arimasen.
(I) don't have a class today.

Oral Practice

 TRACK 23

Practice asking the following questions and answering them.

山田さんは兄弟がいますか。
Yamada-san wa kyōdai ga imasu ka.
Do you have any siblings, Ms. Yamada?

いいえ、いません。
Īe, imasen.
No, I don't.

今、時間がありますか。
Ima, jikan ga arimasu ka.
Do you have (free) time now?

はい、あります。
Hai, arimasu.
Yes, I do.

今日は仕事がありますか。
Kyō wa shigoto ga arimasu ka.
Do you have to work today?

いいえ、ありません。
Īe, arimasen.
No, I don't.

先生。明日はクイズがありますか。
Sensei. Ashita wa kuizu ga arimasu ka.
Professor. Do we have a quiz tomorrow?

もちろん、ありますよ。
Mochiron arimasu yo.
Of course we do.

Written Practice 2

Complete the following sentences appropriately.

1. 山田さんは ＿＿＿＿＿＿＿＿＿＿＿＿＿＿＿＿＿＿＿＿＿＿＿。

   Yamada-san wa ＿＿＿＿＿＿＿＿＿＿＿＿＿＿＿＿＿＿＿.

   Do you have any siblings, Ms. Yamada?

2. 今日は＿＿＿＿＿＿＿＿＿＿＿＿＿＿＿＿＿＿＿＿＿＿＿。

   Kyō wa ＿＿＿＿＿＿＿＿＿＿＿＿＿＿＿＿＿＿＿＿＿.

   Do you have classes today?

3. 今、＿＿＿＿＿＿＿＿＿＿＿＿＿＿＿＿＿＿＿＿＿＿＿＿。

   Ima, ＿＿＿＿＿＿＿＿＿＿＿＿＿＿＿＿＿＿＿＿＿＿.

   Do you have time now?

4. 私は_____。

Watashi wa_____.

I don't have money.

Expressing the Location of People and Things

When talking about the location of people and things, use the construction:

XはYにいます/あります
X wa Y ni imasu/arimasu.
X is at Y.

Earlier in this chapter, you learned that a sentence like the following expresses what exists.

ソファーのうしろには犬がいます。
Sofā no ushiro ni wa inu ga imasu.
There is a dog behind the sofa.

What if people already know that there is a dog, a specific dog, but they just don't know where it is? That is, what if you just want to express the location of the dog? You can do so just by changing the topic in the above sentence: as you and your conversational partner already know the specific dog, make it a topic, so its location can serve as a new piece of information about that dog. For example:

犬はソファーのうしろにいます。
Inu wa sofā no ushiro ni imasu.
The dog is behind the sofa.

As discussed earlier in this chapter, the subject particle が **ga** had to be deleted when followed by the topic particle は **wa**. Recall that the copular verb です **desu** can also express the location of things and people (see Chapter 3). So the previous sentence can be rephrased as:

犬はソファーのうしろです。
Inu wa sofā no ushiro desu.
The dog is behind the sofa.

USING THE VERB いらっしゃいます IRASSHAIMASU TO SHOW RESPECT

For your social superior such as your teacher and your boss, or simply people who are older than you are, use いらっしゃいます **irasshaimasu** instead of います **imasu**. For example:

先生は図書館にいらっしゃいます。
Sensei wa toshokan ni irasshaimasu.
The teacher is at the library.

You should also use いらっしゃいます **irasshaimasu** for someone else's mother. However, do not use it for your own mother because she is a member of your in-group.

山田さんのお母さんはあそこにいらっしゃいます。
Yamada-san no okāsan wa asoko ni irasshaimasu.
Ms. Yamada's mother is over there.

母はあそこにいます。
Haha wa asoko ni imasu.
My mother is over there.

NOTE: *There is another form, called the humble form, used for one's in-group in this context, which will be explained in Chapter 20.*

Oral Practice

 TRACK 24

Practice asking the location of people and things and answering them.

郵便局はどこにありますか。
Yūbinkyoku wa doko ni arimasu ka.
Where is the post office?

郵便局はレストランと銀行の間にあります。
Yūbinkyoku wa resutoran to ginkō no aida ni arimasu.
The post office is between the restaurant and the bank.

陽子さんはどこにいますか。
Yōko-san wa doko ni imasu ka.
Where is Yoko?

陽子さんは友達のうちにいます。
Yōko-san wa tomodachi no uchi ni imasu.
Yoko is at her friend's house.

先生はどちらにいらっしゃいますか。
Sensei wa dochira ni irasshaimasu ka.
Where is the teacher?

先生は図書館にいらっしゃいます。
Sensei wa toshokan ni irasshaimasu.
The teacher is at the library.

お母さんはどちらにいらっしゃいますか。
Okāsan wa dochira ni irasshaimasu ka.
Where is your mother?

母は今うちにいます。
Haha wa ima uchi ni imasu.
My mother is at home now.

Written Practice 3

Make a question that asks where each of the following people and things is.

銀行 ginkō

銀行はどこにありますか。 Ginkō wa doko ni arimasu ka.

1. 郵便局 yūbinkyoku

2. 陽子さん Yōko-san

3. 陽子さんのお母さん Yōko-san no okāsan

4. 母 haha

_____

5. 日本語の辞書 Nihon-go no jisho

_____

Using the Numbers Eleven to Ninety-Nine

In this section, you will learn how to count from eleven to ninety-nine in Japanese. You will also learn how to express people's age as well as the quantity of a variety of things using appropriate counters.

THE NUMBERS ELEVEN TO NINETY-NINE

Counting from eleven to ninety-nine is very simple. Eleven is じゅういち **jūichi**, which is actually じゅう **jū** (10) plus いち **ichi** (1). Similarly, twelve is じゅうに **jūni**, and the rest will follow the same pattern up to 19. Twenty is にじゅう **nijū**, which is like two of じゅう **jū** (10). Twenty-one is にじゅういち **nijūichi**, which is like two of じゅう **jū** (10) plus いち **ichi** (1). Once you know how to say the numbers up to 21, you can say any number up to 99 by applying the same logic: how many of tens plus what. Thus, 99 is きゅうじゅうきゅう **kyūjūkyū** (99). The following table lists some numbers from eleven to ninety-nine.

11	じゅういち jūichi		20	にじゅう nijū
12	じゅうに jūni		21	にじゅういち nijūichi
13	じゅうさん jūsan		30	さんじゅう sanjū
14	じゅうよん jūyon		40	よんじゅう yonjū
	(or じゅうし jūshi)		50	ごじゅう gojū
15	じゅうご jūgo		60	ろくじゅう rokujū
16	じゅうろく jūroku		70	ななじゅう nanajū
17	じゅうなな jūnana		80	はちじゅう hachijū
	(or じゅうしち jūshichi)		90	きゅうじゅう kyūjū
18	じゅうはち jūhachi		99	きゅうじゅうきゅう kyūjūkyū
19	じゅうきゅう jūkyū			
	(or じゅうく jūku)			

STATING YOUR AGE

To say your age, simply add 歳 **sai** after the number. For example, *25 years old* is 25 歳 **nijūgo-sai**. (An exception to this rule is if you are 20 years old, which is pronounced as はたち **hatachi**.) To ask someone else's age, say 何歳ですか **Nan-sai desu ka** or more politely, おいくつですか **O-ikutsu desu ka**.

Oral Practice

 TRACK 25

Practice asking about age and answering it by reading the following sentences out loud.

> マイクさんは何歳ですか。
> Maiku-san wa nan-sai desu ka.
> *Mike, how old are you?*

> 私は29歳です。
> Watashi wa nijūkyū-sai desu.
> *I'm 29.*

> マイクさんのお父さんはおいくつですか。
> Maiku-san no otōsan wa o-ikutsu desu ka.
> *Mike, how old is your father?*

> 父は65歳です。
> Chichi wa rokujūgo-sai desu.
> *My father is 65.*

> おじいさんはおいくつですか。
> Ojīsan wa o-ikutsu desu ka.
> *How old is your grandfather?*

> 祖父は99歳です。
> Sofu wa kyūjūkyū-sai desu.
> *My grandfather is 99 years old.*

THE COUNTERS 枚 MAI, 本 HON, 人 NIN, AND つ TSU

One of the astonishing features of Japanese counting system is the fact that they use a counter after the number for counting almost everything and the counter varies depending on the shape, size, and type of the item you are counting. Also note that some counters cause minor sound changes or exceptional pronunciations.

For counting flat-shaped items such as sheets of paper, tickets, and towels, use the counter 枚 **mai**. For counting cylindrically shaped long items such as pens, bananas, and cigarettes, use the counter 本 **hon**. For counting people, use the counter 人 **nin**. (Note that the first two are irregular.) For counting medium-size objects such as apples and candies as well as some other non-animate items, use the native counter つ **tsu**, which follows native Japanese number words.

Number	Flat item	Cylindrical/long items	People	Medium-size items
1	いちまい ichi-mai	いっぽん ip-pon	ひとり hito-ri	ひとつ hito-tsu
2	にまい ni-mai	にほん ni-hon	ふたり futa-ri	ふたつ futa-tsu
3	さんまい san-mai	さんぼん san-bon	さんにん san-nin	みっつ mit-tsu
4	よんまい yon-mai	よんほん yon-hon	よにん yo-nin	よっつ yot-tsu
5	ごまい go-mai	ごほん go-hon	ごにん go-nin	いつつ itsu-tsu
6	ろくまい roku-mai	ろっぽん rop-pon	ろくにん roku-nin	むっつ mut-tsu
7	ななまい nana-mai	ななほん nana-hon	ななにん nana-nin (or しち にん shichi-nin)	ななつ nana-tsu
8	はちまいhachi-mai	はっぽん hap-pon (or はちほん hachi-hon)	はちにんhachi-nin	やっつ yat-tsu
9	きゅうまいkyū-mai	きゅうほんkyū-hon	きゅうにん kyū-nin (or くにん ku-nin)	ここのつ kokono-tsu
10	じゅうまい jū-mai	じゅっぽんjup-pon	じゅうにん jū-nin	とお tō

USING A NUMBER PHRASE IN A SENTENCE

When using a number phrase in a sentence, place it right after the item the number applies to and the particle associated with the item.

私は姉が2人います。
Watashi wa ane ga futa-ri imasu.
I have two older sisters.

私は姉が2人と、兄が1人と、弟が1人います。
Watashi wa ane ga futa-ri to, ani ga hito-ri to, otōto ga hito-ri imasu.
I have two older sisters, one older brother, and one younger brother.

There are other places you can put the number phrase in a sentence, but this position is very common and unmarked.

USING たくさん TAKUSAN AND 少し SUKOSHI TO EXPRESS QUANTITY

Instead of using the number phrases, you can also use たくさん **takusan** or 少し **sukoshi** to express the amount and quantity. Unlike English words such as *many, much, a little, a few, etc.*, たくさん **takusan** and 少し **sukoshi** can be used for either countable or uncountable items. たくさん **takusan** means *a large amount/quantity* and 少し means *a small amount/quantity*. You can place these words where you usually see number phrases in a sentence.

クッキーがたくさんあります。ケーキも少しあります。
Kukkī ga takusan arimasu. Kēki mo sukoshi arimasu.
There are a lot of cookies. There are some cakes, too.

数学の宿題がたくさんあります。英語の宿題も少しあります。
Sūgaku no shukudai ga takusan arimasu. Eigo no shukudai mo sukoshi arimasu.
I have a lot of math homework. I also have some English homework.

私は中国人の友達がたくさんいます。
Watashi wa Chūgoku-jin no tomodachi ga takusan imasu.
I have many Chinese friends.

韓国人の友達も少しいます。
Kankoku-jin no tomodachi mo sukoshi imasu.
I also have some Korean friends.

お砂糖は？―ああ、少しお願いします。
O-satō wa? — Ā, sukoshi onegai shimasu.
How about sugar? —Oh, a little bit, please.

Written Practice 4

Fill in the blanks with appropriate particles, if necessary.

1. 私は兄＿＿＿＿1人＿＿＿＿います。

   Watashi wa ani＿＿＿＿ hito-ri＿＿＿＿ imasu.

   I have one older brother.

2. 山田さんはお兄さん＿＿＿＿1人＿＿＿＿、お姉さん＿＿＿＿2人＿＿＿＿
   います。

   Yamada-san wa onīsan＿＿＿＿ hito-ri＿＿＿＿, onēsan＿＿＿＿ futa-ri＿＿＿＿
   imasu.

   Ms. Yamada has one older brother and two older sisters.

3. 鉛筆＿＿＿＿3本＿＿＿＿、消しゴム＿＿＿＿1つ＿＿＿＿、ペン＿＿＿＿
   2本＿＿＿＿あります。

   Enpitsu ＿＿＿＿ san-bon ＿＿＿＿, keshigomu ＿＿＿＿ hito-tsu ＿＿＿＿,
   pen ＿＿＿＿ ni-hon ＿＿＿＿ arimasu.

   There are three pencils, one eraser, and two pens.

4. ８０円の切手＿＿＿＿2枚＿＿＿＿、６０円の切手＿＿＿＿3枚＿＿＿＿
   あります。

   Hachijū-en no kitte ＿＿＿＿ ni-mai ＿＿＿＿, rokujū-en no kitte ＿＿＿＿
   san-mai ＿＿＿＿ arimasu.

   There are two 80-yen stamps and three 60-yen stamps.

5. DVD＿＿＿＿少し＿＿＿＿、CD＿＿＿＿たくさん＿＿＿＿あります。

   DVD ＿＿＿＿ sukoshi ＿＿＿＿, CD ＿＿＿＿ takusan ＿＿＿＿ arimasu.

   There are some DVDs and many CDs.

QUESTION WORDS WITH COUNTERS

For asking the quantity or amount of some items, use the question word with the appropriate counter, for example:

何枚	nan-mai	(*how many* for flat items)
何本	nan-bon	(*how many* for long items)
何人	nan-nin	(*how many* for people)
いくつ	iku-tsu	(*how many* for medium-size objects, etc.)

Use them in question sentences, as in:

この箱の中に折り紙が何枚ありますか。
Kono hako no naka ni origami ga nan-mai arimasu ka.
How many (sheets of) origami paper are there in this box?

学生は何人いますか。
Gakusei ga nan-nin imasu ka.
How many students are there?

今日はクラスがいくつありますか。
Kyō wa kurasu ga ikutsu arimasu ka.
How many classes do you have today?

QUIZ

Circle the letter of the word or phrase that best completes each sentence.

1. あそこに高い建物が＿＿＿＿。

   Asoko ni takai tatemono ga ＿＿＿＿ .
   (a) あります arimasu
   (c) いらっしゃいます irasshaimasu
   (b) います imasu
   (d) です desu

2. あそこにかわいい犬が＿＿＿＿。

   Asoko ni kawaii inu ga ＿＿＿＿ .
   (a) あります arimasu
   (c) いらっしゃいます irasshaimasu
   (b) います imasu
   (d) です desu

3. 陽子さんのお母さんは どちらに＿＿＿＿か。

   Yōko-san no okāsan wa dochira ni ＿＿＿＿ ka.

   (a) あります arimasu   (c) いらっしゃいます irasshaimasu

   (b) います imasu   (d) です desu

4. 郵便局はどこ＿＿＿＿か。

   Yūbinkyoku wa doko ＿＿＿＿ ka.

   (a) あります arimasu   (c) いらっしゃいます irasshaimasu

   (b) にいます ni imasu   (d) です desu

5. 今、時間＿＿＿＿ありますか。

   Ima, jikan ＿＿＿＿ arimasu ka.

   (a) が ga   (c) に ni

   (b) から kara   (d) と to

6. 今日はクラスが ＿＿＿＿か。

   Kyō wa kurasu ga ＿＿＿＿ ka.

   (a) あります arimasu   (c) いらっしゃいます irasshaimasu

   (b) います imasu   (d) です desu

7. かばんの中＿＿＿＿鉛筆があります。

   Kaban no naka ＿＿＿＿ enpitsu ga arimasu.

   (a) が ga   (c) はに wa ni

   (b) には ni wa   (d) もに mo ni

8. 私は日本人の友達が＿＿＿＿います。

   Watashi wa Nihon-jin no tomodachi ga ＿＿＿＿ imasu.

   (a) 3枚 san-mai   (c) 3人 san-nin

   (b) 4本 yon-hon   (d) 2つ futa-tsu

9. マイクさんは＿＿＿＿ですか。

   Maiku-san wa ＿＿＿＿ desu ka.

   (a) 何本 nan-bon   (c) 何枚 nan-mai

   (b) 何歳 nan-sai   (d) 何人 nan-nin

10. かばんの中には 切手が2枚と消しゴム＿＿＿＿1つあります。

    Kaban no naka ni wa kitte ga ni-mai to keshigomu ＿＿＿＿ hito-tsu arimasu.

    (a) は wa   (c) が ga

    (b) と to   (d) に ni

PART ONE TEST

Circle the letter of the word or phrase that corresponds to the English or that best completes each sentence.

1. one's own older sister
   - (a) お姉さん onēsan
   - (b) 母 haha
   - (c) 姉 ane
   - (d) 妹 imōto

2. nurse
   - (a) 教師 kyōshi
   - (b) 看護師 kangoshi
   - (c) 医者 isha
   - (d) 弁護士 bengoshi

3. left
   - (a) 右 migi
   - (b) 上 ue
   - (c) 左 hidari
   - (d) 下 shita

4. south
   - (a) 南 minami
   - (b) 西 nishi
   - (c) 東 higashi
   - (d) 北 kita

5. はじめまして。田中です。_____ 。

   Hajimemashite. Tanaka desu. _____ .
   - (a) すみません sumimasen
   - (b) こちらこそ kochira koso
   - (c) よろしく yoroshiku
   - (d) どうも dōmo

6. 父は医者じゃ_____ 。

   Chichi wa isha ja _____ .
   - (a) です desu
   - (b) あります arimasu
   - (c) ありません arimasen
   - (d) ございます gozaimasu

7. 陽子さんは_____人です。

   Yōko-san wa _____ hito desu.
   - (a) きれい kirei
   - (b) きれいじゃありません kirei ja arimasen
   - (c) きれいだ kirei da
   - (d) きれいな kirei na

8. _____ 車は田中さんの車です。

   _____ kuruma wa Tanaka-san no kuruma desu.

   (a) これ Kore   (c) あれ Are

   (b) その Sono   (d) それ Sore

9. ヤンさんは上海からです。チェンさん _____ 上海からです。

   Yan-san wa Shanhai kara desu. Chen-san _____ Shanhai kara desu.

   (a) は wa   (c) に ni

   (b) も mo   (d) と to

10. あの _____ は何ですか。

    Ano _____ wa nan desu ka.

    (a) 男の人 otoko no hito   (c) 建物 tatemono

    (b) 先生 sensei   (d) 専攻 senkō

11. あの女の方は _____ ですか。

    Ano onna no kata wa _____ desu ka.

    (a) どなた donata   (c) どれ dore

    (b) だれ dare   (d) 何 nan

12. 銀行は _____ ですか。

    Ginkō wa _____ desu ka.

    (a) どこに doko ni   (c) どこ doko

    (b) だれ dare   (d) どなた donata

13. 学校は郵便局の _____ です。

    Gakkō wa yūbinkyoku no _____ desu.

    (a) ここ koko   (c) となり tonari

    (b) どこ doko   (d) そこ soko

14. 図書館のカフェテリアは _____ ですか。

    Toshokan no kafeteria wa _____ desu ka.

    (a) どう dō   (c) どんな donna

    (b) だれ dare   (d) 何歳 nan-sai

15. 日本語はあまり _____ 。

    Nihon-go wa amari _____ .

    (a) 難しいです muzukashii desu

    (b) 難しくありません muzukashiku arimasen

    (c) 簡単です kantan desu

    (d) いいです ii desu

16. 陽子さんの部屋はきれいです。それに、_____ です。

    Yōko-san no heya wa kirei desu. Soreni, _____ desu.

    (a) せまい semai   (c) きたない kitanai

    (b) 明るい akarui   (d) うるさい urusai

17. 私のアパートは広いです。でも、_____ です。

    Watashi no apāto wa hiroi desu. Demo, _____ desu.

    (a) うるさい urusai   (c) 新しい atarashii

    (b) 静か shizuka   (d) きれい kirei

18. ブラウンさんは _____ です。

    Buraun-san wa _____ desu.

    (a) 学生の文学 gakusei no bungaku

    (b) 文学の学生 bungaku no gakusei

    (c) 文学のアメリカ人 bungaku no Amerika-jin

    (d) 学生のアメリカ gakusei no Amerika

19. 先生の部屋には大きいテレビが _____ 。

    Sensei no heya ni wa ōkii terebi ga _____ .

    (a) あります arimasu

    (b) います imasu

    (c) いらっしゃいます irasshaimasu

    (d) です desu

20. テーブルの下には猫が_____ 。

Tēburu no shita ni wa neko ga _____ .

(a) あります arimasu   (c) いらっしゃいます irasshaimasu

(b) います imasu   (d) です desu

21. 先生は図書館に_____ 。

Sensei wa toshokan ni _____ .

(a) あります arimasu   (c) いらっしゃいます irasshaimasu

(b) います imasu   (d) です desu

22. 今日はクラスが_____ 。

Kyō wa kurasu ga _____ .

(a) ありません arimasen   (c) いらっしゃいません irasshaimasen

(b) いません imasen   (d) じゃありません ja arimasen

23. ペンが_____あります。

Pen ga _____ arimasu.

(a) 2枚 ni-mai   (c) 2人 futa-ri

(b) 2本 ni-hon   (d) 2つ futa-tsu

24. マイクさんのおじいさんは_____ですか。

Maiku-san no ojīsan wa _____ desu ka.

(a) 何本 nan-bon   (c) おいくつ o-ikutsu

(b) 何歳 nan-sai   (d) 何 nan

25. 犬と猫_____リスがいます。

Inu to neko _____ risu ga imasu.

(a) に ni   (c) が ga

(b) と to   (d) も mo

PART TWO

TALKING
ABOUT ACTIONS

CHAPTER 6

Expressing Coming and Going

In this chapter you'll learn:

Japanese Verb Forms
Verbs of Coming and Going
Making Suggestions and Invitations
Useful Particles
Using the Numbers 100 to 99,999

Japanese Verb Forms

A Japanese verb is always placed at the end of the sentence, and it conjugates based on the speech style, tense, and whether it is affirmative or negative. It may appear that there are many verb forms in Japanese, but most of them can be derived easily from one of the several very basic forms, just by adding one or more suffixes. In this section, you will learn three important notions required for understanding the basic verb forms, namely, the plain/polite distinction, the present/past tense, and the affirmative/negative distinction.

THE PLAIN AND POLITE VERB FORMS

Japanese verbs have a short form called the plain form, which is used in an informal conversational context, and a long form called the polite form, which is used in a neutral or polite conversational context. For example, the verb that means to go in Japanese is 行く **iku** in the plain present affirmative form and 行きます **ikimasu** in the polite present affirmative form. That is, you can say 行く **iku** in an informal conversation whereas you must say 行きます **ikimasu** in a neutral/polite conversational context. However, the plain form is not just the form used in an informal context. It is also the form that must be used in certain grammatical constructions, even in a neutral/polite conversational context.

The Stem Form and the Polite Suffix The polite form of a verb discussed above is actually the combination of the stem form and the polite suffix. For example, the stem form of the verb 行く **iku** is 行き **iki**, and ます **masu** is the polite suffix in the present affirmative form. The polite present negative suffix is ません **masen**. For example:

行きます	ikimasu	*(I) will go (there).*
行きません	ikimasen	*(I) won't go (there).*

The stem form is often called "pre-*masu* form" because it is the form that precedes ます **masu**. The stem form is used not only before the polite suffix, but also before other variety of suffixes and auxiliaries, many of which are introduced in Chapter 14.

THE PRESENT AND PAST VERB FORMS

Japanese verbs have present and past tense forms. 行く **iku** and 行きます **ikimasu** discussed above are both in the present tense form, and the former is in the plain form and the latter is in the polite form. Their past counter parts are 行った **itta** and 行きました **ikimashita**, respectively.

The present tense expresses a habitual action or a future action. Thus, the term "present tense" is a little misleading, and so it is also called "non-past tense." The past tense expresses an action that took place in the past. (See Chapter 8 for more about past tense and Chapter 12 for additional meanings of present and past tense.)

THE AFFIRMATIVE AND NEGATIVE VERB FORMS

Unlike English verbs, Japanese verbs conjugate based on whether they are affirmative or negative. 行く **iku** is affirmative, and its negative counterpart is 行かない **ikanai**. 行きます **ikimasu** is also affirmative and its negative counterpart is 行きません **ikimasen**.

In dictionaries, verbs are listed in the plain present affirmative form. For example, the verb "to go" is listed as 行く **iku** in a Japanese dictionary. Accordingly, the plain present affirmative form is also called a *dictionary form*.

Verbs of Coming and Going

The verbs of coming and going are frequently used for describing one's daily activities. 行く **iku** means *to go*, 来る **kuru** means *to come*, and 帰る **kaeru** means *to return*. When one goes back to his base place such as his home, dorm, or office, the verb 帰る **kaeru** must be used.

POLITE PRESENT FORMS

The following are the polite present forms of the verbs of coming and going:

	Polite Present Affirmative	**Polite Present Negative**
行く iku (*go*)	行きます ikimasu	行きません ikimasen
来る kuru (*come*)	来ます kimasu	来ません kimasen
帰る kaeru (*return*)	帰ります kaerimasu	帰りません kaerimasen

For the mechanism of conjugating verbs, see Chapter 7. As mentioned earlier in this chapter, the present tense actually expresses a future action or a habitual action.

明日行きます。
Ashita ikimasu.
I will go there tomorrow.

よく行きます。
Yoku ikimasu.
I often go there.

PLACES YOU OFTEN GO

The following are places people frequently go to study, to work, or to do other things:

高校	kōkō	*high school*
大学	daigaku	*university, college*
クラス	kurasu	*class*
会社	kaisha	*company*
郵便局	yūbinkyoku	*post office*
病院	byōin	*hospital*
銀行	ginkō	*bank*
スーパー	sūpā	*supermarket*

INDICATING DESTINATION WITH THE PARTICLE に NI

The particle に **ni** has many functions. One of them is to mark the location of existence when used with an existential verb, as discussed in Chapter 5. Another function is to mark the destination when used with a verb of coming and going, as in the following examples:

私はニューヨークに行きます。
Watashi wa Nyūyōku ni ikimasu.
I'll go to New York.

友達がニューヨークに来ます。
Tomodachi ga Nyūyōku ni kimasu.
My friend will come to New York.

私はうちに帰ります。
Watashi wa uchi ni kaerimasu.
I'll go home.

SOME TIME EXPRESSIONS

The following words can specify some current or future time:

今日	kyō	*today*
今晩	konban	*tonight*
明日	ashita	*tomorrow*
あさって	asatte	*the day after tomorrow*
今週	konshū	*this week*
来週	raishū	*next week*
来月	raigetsu	*next month*
来年	rainen	*next year*
週末	shūmatsu	*weekend*

These words are used in a sentence as shown here:

今日、クラスに行きます。
Kyō, kurasu ni ikimasu.
I'll go to class today.

来週はクラスに行きません。
Raishū wa kurasu ni ikimasen.
I won't go to class next week.

SOME FREQUENCY ADVERBS

The following frequency adverbs are useful for describing daily activities including coming and going:

よく	yoku	*often, frequently*
いつも	itsumo	*always*
たいてい	taitei	*usually*
時々	tokidoki	*sometimes*
あまり(...ない)	amari(...nai)	*(not . . .) often*
ぜんぜん(...ない)	zenzen(...nai)	*(not . . .) at all*
毎日	mainichi	*every day*

毎週	maishū	*every week*
毎月	maitsuki	*every month*
毎年	maitoshi, mainen	*every year*

NOTE: あまり *amari* and ぜんぜん *zenzen* must be used with a verb in the negative form.

兄はあまり病院に行きません。
Ani wa amari byōin ni ikimasen.
My older brother doesn't go to the hospital very often.

姉はよく銀行に行きます。
Ane wa yoku ginkō ni ikimasu.
My older sister often goes to the bank.

INDICATING DIRECTION WITH THE PARTICLE へ E

If the verb expresses coming or going, に **ni** and へ **e** can be used interchangeably to mark where they are going. They give a slightly different nuance: へ **e** sounds like "toward" (*direction*) whereas に **ni** sound like "to" (*destination*). However, most native speakers do not easily detect such a difference. The pronunciation of the particle へ is exceptional: the letter へ **he** is read as **e** if it represents this direction-marking particle.

Oral Practice

 TRACK 26

Practice asking the following questions and answering them.

今日はクラスに行きますか。
Kyō wa kurasu ni ikimasu ka.
Will you go to class today?

いいえ、行きません。
Īe, ikimasen.
No, I won't.

チェンさんはよく中国へ帰りますか。
Chen-san wa yoku Chūgoku e kaerimasu ka
Do you often go back to China, Mr. Chen?

はい、毎年帰ります。
Hai, maitoshi kaerimasu.
Yes, I go back there every year.

スミスさんの弟さんはよく日本に来ますか。
Sumisu-san no otōtosan wa yoku Nihon ni kimasu ka.
Does your younger brother come to Japan often?

いいえ、あまり来ません。
Īe, amari kimasen.
No, he doesn't come very often.

Written Practice 1

Using the items in each set, form a grammatical sentence.

1. (父は chichi wa, 行きます ikimasu, に ni, 毎日 mainichi, 会社 kaisha)

   _____

2. (うち uchi, 今日は kyō wa, に ni, 帰りません kaerimasen)

   _____

3. (週末は shūmatsu wa, へ e, 京都 Kyōto, 行きます ikimasu)

   _____

4. (田中さんは Tanaka-san wa, うち uchi, 来ません kimasen, に ni, あまり amari)

   _____

5. (行きます ikimasu, 母は haha wa, 時々 tokidoki, に ni, 病院 byōin)

   _____

Making Suggestions and Invitations

In this section, you will learn how to make suggestions and invitations. In addition, you will learn some vocabulary words that denote fun places you can go with your friends.

MAKING A SUGGESTION WITH . . . ませんか MASEN KA

For making a suggestion nicely, use a negative question. For example, レストランに行きませんか **Resutoran ni ikimasen ka** means *Why don't we go to a restaurant?* Depending on the context, it may mean *Why don't you . . .* instead of *why don't we . . .* For example, うちに来ませんか **Uchi ni kimasen ka** means *Why don't you come to my house?*

FUN PLACES TO GO

The following are some fun places to go with your friends.

映画館	eigakan	*movie theater*
美術館	bijutsukan	*art museum*
公園	kōen	*park*
動物園	dōbutsuen	*zoo*
遊園地	yūenchi	*theme park, amusement park*
デパート	depāto	*department store*
レストラン	resutoran	*restaurant*
本屋	hon'ya	*bookstore*

EXPRESSING EXHORTATION WITH . . . ましょう MASHŌ

To say *Let's do . . .* , use the polite volitional form ましょう **mashō**. Take a verb in the polite affirmative present form, and replace ます **masu** with ましょう **mashō**. For example, 帰りましょう **kaerimashō** means *Let's go home.*

Oral Practice

 TRACK 27

Practice making the following suggestions and answering them by reading the following sentences out loud.

今晩レストランに行きませんか。
Konban resutoran ni ikimasen ka.
How about going to a restaurant tonight?

ええ、行きましょう。
Ē, ikimashō.
Yes, let's go there.

来週いっしょに美術館に行きませんか。
Raishū isshoni bijutsukan ni ikimasen ka.
How about going to the art museum together next week?

ええ、行きましょう。
Ē, ikimashō.
Yes, let's go there.

明日うちに来ませんか。
Ashita uchi ni kimasen ka.
Why don't you come to my house tomorrow?

ええ、行きます。
Ē, ikimasu.
Yes, I will.

寮に帰りませんか。
Ryō ni kaerimasen ka.
Why don't we go back to the dorm?

ええ、帰りましょう。
Ē, kaerimashō.
Yes, let's do so.

Useful Particles

In this section, you will learn some usages of the particle で **de** and と **to**.

INDICATING TRANSPORTATION WITH THE PARTICLE で DE

The particle で **de** specifies the surrounding condition of the given action. For example, it can specify the form of transportation for a coming or going action, as in:

京都に車で行きます。
Kyōto ni kuruma de ikimasu.
I'll go to Kyoto by car.

大学には毎日自転車で来ます。
Daigaku ni wa mainichi jitensha de kimasu.
I come to the college by bicycle every day.

The particle で **de** can also specify other types of surrounding conditions of an action.

友達の結婚式に着物で行きます。
Tomodachi no kekkonshiki ni kimono de ikimasu.
I'll go to my friend's wedding in kimono.

一人で美術館に行きます。
Hitori de bijutsukan ni ikimasu.
I go to the art museum by myself.

今晩家族でレストランに行きます。
Konban kazoku de resutoran ni ikimasu.
Tonight, I will go to the restaurant with my family.

FORMS OF TRANSPORTATION

Here are some useful terms to specify the forms of transportation.

電車	densha	*train*
地下鉄	chikatetsu	*subway*
車	kuruma	*car*
バス	basu	*bus*
タクシー	takushī	*taxi*
自転車	jitensha	*bicycle*
飛行機	hikōki	*airplane*
フェリー	ferī	*ferry*

If one walks, use 歩いて **aruite**, which is the te-form of the verb 歩く **aruku** (*walk*), instead of using the particle で **de**. See Chapter 9 for the te-form.

私は毎日歩いて会社に行きます。
Watashi wa mainichi aruite kaisha ni ikimasu.
I go to my company on foot every day.

INDICATING A PARTNER WITH THE PARTICLE と TO

The particle と **to** can be used for listing nouns, as discussed in Chapter 5, but it can also mark the accompanying action performer.

私は来週ボーイフレンドと京都に行きます。
Watashi wa raishū bōifurendo to Kyōto ni ikimasu.
I will go to Kyoto with my boyfriend next week.

毎日犬と公園に行きます。
Mainichi inu to kōen ni ikimasu.
I go to the park with my dog every day.

Written Practice 2

Choose the appropriate particle in the parentheses.

1. 父は母 (に, と) レストラン (に, と) 行きます。
   Chichi wa haha (ni, to) resutoran (ni, to) ikimasu.
2. 私は電車 (に, で) 会社 (に, で) 行きます。
   Watashi wa densha (ni, de) kaisha (ni, de) ikimasu.
3. 明日は友達 (へ, と) 京都 (へ, と) 行きます。
   Ashita wa tomodachi (e, to) Kyōto (e, to) ikimasu.
4. 毎日、妹 (へ, と) 歩いてうち (に, と) 帰ります。
   Mainichi, imōto (e, to) aruite uchi (ni, to) kaerimasu.
5. 飛行機 (に, で) フロリダ (に, で) 行きます。
   Hikōki (ni, de) Furorida (ni, de) ikimasu.

Using the Numbers 100 to 99,999

In this section, you will learn how to say the numbers from 100 to 99,999 in Japanese as well as how to ask prices of merchandises at stores.

THE NUMBERS 100 TO 99,999

To count over 100, you need to know the following digit words.

100	ひゃく	hyaku	*hundred*
1,000	せん	sen	*thousand*
10,000	まん	man	*ten thousand*

Unlike English, Japanese has a specific digit word that means *ten thousand*. When the above digit words are preceded by numbers, some combinations cause a minor sound change, as you can see in the following table:

100	ひゃく hyaku	1,000	せん sen	10,000	いちまん ichiman
200	にひゃく nihyaku	2,000	にせん nisen	20,000	にまん niman
300	さんびゃく sanbyaku	3,000	さんぜん sanzen	30,000	さんまん sanman
400	よんひゃく yonhyaku	4,000	よんせん yonsen	40,000	よんまん yonman
500	ごひゃく gohyaku	5,000	ごせん gosen	50,000	ごまん goman
600	ろっぴゃく roppyaku	6,000	ろくせん rokusen	60,000	ろくまん rokuman
700	ななひゃく nanahyaku	7,000	ななせん nanasen	70,000	ななまん nanaman
800	はっぴゃく happyaku	8,000	はっせん hassem	80,000	はちまん hachiman
900	きゅうひゃく kyūhyaku	9,000	きゅうせん kyūsen	90,000	きゅうまん kyūman

Note: *10,000 is* いちまん **ichiman** *rather than just* まん **man**.

Apply the same logic you applied for counting from 1 to 99 in Chapter 5. You can easily and correctly tell that 201 is にひゃくいち **nihyaku-ichi**, 2,301 is にせんさんびゃくいち **nisen-sanbyaku-ichi**, 19,800 is いちまんきゅうせんはっぴゃく **ichiman-kyūsen-happyaku**, and 99,999 is きゅうまんきゅうせんきゅうひゃくきゅうじゅうきゅう **kyūman-kyūsen-kyūhyaku-kyūjū-kyū**.

Written Practice 3

Write the pronunciation of the following numbers in hiragana or romaji.

| | 77,600 | ななまんななせんろっぴゃく | nanaman-nanasen-roppyaku |

1. 352 _____
2. 1,200 _____
3. 2,990 _____
4. 35,000 _____
5. 89,037 _____

THE QUESTION WORD いくら IKURA

For asking the price, use the question word いくら **ikura** (*how much*).

このかばんはいくらですか。
Kono kaban wa ikura desu ka.
How much is this bag?

THE COUNTER 円 EN

The currency unit in Japan is *yen*, which is actually written as 円 and pronounced as **en** in Japanese. You can place it at the end of the price, as in 100 円 **hyaku-en**. Dollar is ドル **doru** in Japanese.

Oral Practice

 TRACK 28

Practice asking the price and answering them.

このペンはいくらですか。
Kono pen wa ikura desu ka.
How much is this pen?

100円です。
Hyaku-en desu.
100 yen.

このカメラはいくらですか。
Kono kamera wa ikura desu ka.
How much is this camera?

35,900円です。
Sanman-gosen-kyūhyaku-en desu.
It is 35,900 yen.

あのラジオはいくらですか。
Ano rajio wa ikura desu ka.
How much is that radio?

25ドルです。
Nijūgo-doru desu.
25 dollars.

1ドルは今、何円ですか。
Ichi-doru wa ima, nan-en desu ka
How much yen it is for a dollar now?

1ドルは88円です。
Ichi-doru wa hachijū-hachi-en desu.
One dollar is 88 yen.

QUIZ

Circle the letter of the word or phrase that best completes each sentence.

1. よく美術館_____行きます。

   Yoku bijutsukan _____ ikimasu.

   (a) へ e   (c) と to

   (b) で de   (d) も mo

2. 中国にはだれ_____行きますか。

   Chūgoku ni wa dare _____ ikimasu ka.

   (a) に ni   (c) へ e

   (b) で de   (d) と to

3. 大阪には車_____行きます。

   Ōsaka ni wa kuruma _____ ikimasu.

   (a) に ni   (c) と to

   (b) で de   (d) へ e

4. 私は明日病院に _____ 。

   Watashi wa ashita byōin ni _____ .

   (a) 行きました ikimashita   (c) 行きませんでした ikimasen deshita

   (b) 行きます ikimasu   (d) 帰りました kaerimashita

5. 私は来週うちに_____ 。

   Watashi wa raishū uchi ni _____ .

   (a) 行きます ikimasu   (c) 来ます kimasu

   (b) 帰ります kaerimasu   (d) 行きません ikimasen

6. 私はあまりデパートに _____ 。

   Watashi wa amari depāto ni _____ .

   (a) 行きます ikimasu   (c) 行きません ikimasen

   (b) 帰ります kaerimasu   (d) 行きました ikimashita

7. 今晩私といっしょにレストランに_____ 。

   Konban watashi to issho ni resutoran ni _____ .

   (a) 行きます ikimasu   (c) 行きませんか ikimasen ka

   (b) 行きません ikimasen   (d) 来ませんか kimasen ka

8. 明日は＿＿＿＿＿へ行きますか。

Ashita wa ＿＿＿＿＿ e ikimasu ka.

(a) 自転車 jitensha   (c) だれ dare

(b) どこ doko   (d) 何 nani

9. そのペンは＿＿＿＿＿ですか。

Sono pen wa ＿＿＿＿＿ desu ka.

(a) 円 en   (c) いくら ikura

(b) ドル doru   (d) だれ dare

10. このペンは５０＿＿＿＿＿です。

Kono pen wa 50 ＿＿＿＿＿ desu.

(a) 本 hon   (c) 枚 mai

(b) 円 en   (d) 人 nin

CHAPTER 7

Expressing
What You Do

In this chapter you'll learn:

Verb Conjugation
Verbs of Activities
Verbs of Giving and Receiving
Colors
More About Using Numbers

Verb Conjugation

Compared with English, Japanese verbs conjugate quite systematically. There are only two major irregular verbs, which are する **suru** (*to do*) and くる **kuru** (*to come*).

Other verbs are all regular verbs except several verbs whose one or two forms undergo a slight sound change. (The copular verb です **desu** (*to be*), which is discussed in Chapter 2, "Identifying People and Things," patterns extremely differently, and will not be included in the discussion of verb conjugation in this chapter.) There are two kinds of regular verbs, and they are called ru-verbs and u-verbs.

RU-VERBS

Most forms of ru-verbs are created after dropping **ru** from their dictionary form (the plain present affirmative form) and adding something. That's why they are called ru-verbs. Take the verb 食べる **taberu** (*to eat*), for example. Its negative counterpart is 食べない **tabenai**, which is the output of dropping the **ru** at the end and adding **nai**. Its polite counterpart is 食べます **tabemasu**, which is the output of dropping **ru** and adding **masu**. Note that the vowel before **ru** is always **i** or **e** if the verb is a ru-verb.

The following table lists some examples of ru-verbs in their dictionary form (the plain present affirmative form), the plain present negative form, and the polite present affirmative form.

Plain Present Affirmative (dictionary form)	Plain Present Negative	Polite Present Affirmative
食べる taberu (*eat*)	食べない tabenai	食べます tabemasu
寝る neru (*sleep*)	寝ない nenai	寝ます nemasu
見る miru (*look*)	見ない minai	見ます mimasu

U-VERBS

Most forms of u-verbs are created after dropping **u** from their dictionary form and adding something. That's why they are called u-verbs. For example, take the verb かえる **kaeru** (*to return*). Its negative counterpart is **kaeranai**, which is the output of dropping the **u** at the end and adding **anai**. Its polite counterpart is かえります **kaerimasu**, which is the output of dropping **u** and adding **imasu**. The u-verbs end in one of the following nine hiragana letters:

る ru	く ku	ぐ gu	う u	つ tsu
す su	む mu	ぬ nu	ぶ bu	

The following table summarizes the patterns of these nine kinds of u-verbs.

Plain Present Affirmative (dictionary form)	Plain Present Negative	Polite Present Affirmative
帰る kaeru (*return*)	帰らない kaeranai	帰ります kaerimasu
書く kaku (*write*)	書かない kakanai	書きます kakimasu
泳ぐ oyogu (*swim*)	泳がない oyoganai	泳ぎます oyogimasu
買う kau (*buy*)	買わない kawanai	買います kaimasu
待つ matsu (*wait*)	待たない matanai	待ちます machimasu
話す hanasu (*speak*)	話さない hanasanai	話します hanashimasu
飲む nomu (*drink*)	飲まない nomanai	飲みます nomimasu
死ぬ shinu (*die*)	死なない shinanai	死にます shinimasu
遊ぶ asobu (*play*)	遊ばない asobanai	遊びます asobimasu

Notice that **w** is inserted before the suffix **anai** if the last syllable of the dictionary form is just the vowel **u**, without any preceding consonant, which is represented by the hiragana う **u,** as you can see in the conjugation of 買う **kau**. Also notice that **ts** in the last syllable of the verb in the dictionary form becomes **t** when followed by the vowel **a**, and **ch** when followed by the vowel **i**, as you can see in the conjugation of 待つ **matsu** (*wait*). In addition, **s** in the last syllable of the verb in the dictionary form becomes **sh** when followed by the vowel **i**, as shown in the conjugation of 話す **hanasu** (*speak*).

Indeterminacy of Eru/Iru-Ending Verbs Although both 食べる **taberu** (*to eat*) and かえる **kaeru** (*to return*) end in **eru**, the former is a ru-verb and the latter is a u-verb. If a verb ends in **eru** or **iru**, you cannot tell whether it is a ru-verb or a u-verb just by looking at the dictionary forms. You must remember which one each time you see a verb that ends in **eru** or **iru**. By contrast, if a verb doesn't end in **eru** or **iru**, it is always a u-verb.

Written Practice 1

Circle the verbs that can only be u-verbs. For this exercise, do not think about the meaning of the verbs, but concentrate on the form of the verbs.

たたく tataku   ねる neru   もらう morau   かかる kakaru
いる iru   はこぶ hakobu   おとす otosu   たのむ tanomu
きる kiru   かつ katsu   しぬ shinu   こぐ kogu

IRREGULAR VERBS

The major irregular verbs are する **suru** (*to do*) and 来る **kuru** (*to come*). They pattern like shown.

Plain Present Affirmative (dictionary form)	Plain Present Negative	Polite Present Affirmative
する suru	しない shinai	します shimasu
来る kuru	来ない konai	来ます kimasu

SOME SLIGHTLY IRREGULAR VERBS

The verb ある **aru** (*to exist*) is an u-verb, but its plain present negative form is ない **nai** rather than あらない **aranai**. The verb いらっしゃる **irassharu** (*to exist*) is an u-verb, but its polite present affirmative form is いらっしゃいます **irasshaimasu** rather than いらっしゃります **irassharimasu**.

Written Practice 2

Following the example, conjugate the verbs. *Hint*: These verbs do not end in **iru** or **eru** sequence, so they are u-verbs.

      かく kaku (*write*)   かかない kakanai   かきます kakimasu

1. もつ motsu (*hold*)   _____   _____
2. かす kasu (*lend*)   _____   _____
3. とる toru (*take*)   _____   _____
4. のむ nomu (*drink*)   _____   _____
5. かう kau (*buy*)   _____   _____

Written Practice 3

Following the example, conjugate the verbs. In this exercise, all the verbs end in る **ru**. *Hint*: Some of these verbs end in **eru** or **iru** sequence, and whether it is a ru-verb or a u-verb is specified. Others are irregular verbs.

たべる (ru-verb)   たべない tabenai   たべます tabemasu

1. かえる kaeru (*return*) u-verb   _____   _____
2. かえる kaeru (*change*) ru-verb   _____   _____
3. みる miru (*look*) ru-verb   _____   _____
4. する suru (*do*) irregular   _____   _____
5. くる kuru (*come*) irregular   _____   _____
6. はいる hairu (*enter*) u-verb   _____   _____

MAKING THE POLITE PRESENT NEGATIVE FORMS OF VERBS

Once you know how to make the polite present affirmative form of verbs, it is extremely easy to make their polite present negative form. As in Chapter 6, the negative counterpart of the suffix ます **masu** is ません **masen**, so you can just replace ます **masu** with ません **masen**:

食べます tabemasu   食べません tabemasen

Oral Practice

 TRACK 29

Practice asking a question and answering to it negatively.

食べますか。
Tabemasu ka.
Will you eat?

いいえ、食べません。
Īe, tabemasen.
No, I won't.

飲みますか。
Nomimasu ka.
Will you drink?

いいえ、飲みません。
Īe, nomimasen.
No, I won't.

帰りますか。
Kaerimasu ka.
Will you go home?

いいえ、帰りません。
Īe, kaerimasen.
No, I won't.

Verbs of Activities

In this section, you will learn many useful verbs that denote everyday activities such as eating, reading, and shopping as well as the particles that are needed to express the details of these actions.

SOME USEFUL ACTION VERBS

The following are some useful verbs that describe your daily activities:

食べる taberu (*eat*)	ru-verb
寝る neru (*sleep*)	ru-verb
飲む nomu (*drink*)	u-verb
作る tsukuru (*make*)	u-verb
書く kaku (*write*)	u-verb
見る miru (*look*)	ru-verb
読む yomu (*read*)	u-verb
聞く kiku (*listen*)	u-verb
話す hanasu (*speak*)	u-verb

SOME USEFUL VERBS CREATED WITH する SURU

Many verbs were created by adding the verb する **suru** (*to do*) at the end of a Chinese compound, as in the following examples:

勉強する	benkyō suru	*to study*
運転する	unten suru	*to drive*
練習する	renshū suru	*to practice*
留学する	ryūgaku suru	*to study abroad*

There are also many verbs created from non-Chinese loans in the same way, as in コピーする **kopī suru** (*to make a copy*) and キャンセルする **kyanseru suru** (*to cancel*).

THE SUBJECT PARTICLE が GA

Regardless of whether it is English or Japanese, every verb can take a subject noun in the sentence. In English, the subject is not marked by anything, but you can identify it by the position in the sentence: the subject is the noun or the noun phrase that occurs before the verb. The subject can be a person, an animal, a thing, or a concept. For example, the underlined parts in the following English sentences are subjects:

Joan came here yesterday.

He took a picture of the flower.

My dog is cute.

My car broke on me.

Education is important for children.

The subject is marked by the particle が **ga** in Japanese, as in:

山田さんが来ます。
Yamada-san ga kimasu.
Ms. Yamada will come.

If the subject is also the topic of the sentence at the same time, it is marked by the topic particle は **wa** and the particle が **ga** is deleted.

山田さんは来ます。
Yamada-san wa kimasu.
As for Ms. Yamada, (she) will come.

THE DIRECT OBJECT PARTICLE を O

The direct object is the noun or the noun phrase that occurs right after the verb. Only some verbs can take a direct object. They are called transitive verbs. For example, the verb "to make" is a transitive verb, and it makes sense when *someone makes something*, and the latter "something" is the direct object. By contrast, the verb "to go" is not a transitive verb, but is an intransitive verb. It cannot be directly followed by a noun. For example, you can say *He will go to Tokyo*, but you cannot say *He will go Tokyo*. In Japanese, the direct object is marked by the particle を **o**, as in the following examples:

すしを食べます。
Sushi o tabemasu.
(I) will eat sushi.

新聞を読みます。
Shinbun o yomimasu.
(I) will read newspaper.

田中さんを招待します。
Tanaka-san o shōtai shimasu.
(I) will invite Mr. Tanaka.

Because nouns are clearly marked by particles in Japanese, the word order in a Japanese sentence is flexible as long as the verb is at the end of the sentence. So, both of the following sentences are grammatical, meaning *my sister will make tempura*, although the first one is somewhat more unmarked than the second one:

姉がてんぷらを作ります。
Ane ga tenpura o tsukurimasu.

てんぷらを姉が作ります。
Tenpura o ane ga tsukurimasu.

Written Practice 4

Choose the appropriate particle in the parentheses in the following passage. *Hint:* Don't be misled by the word order.

今日は友達 (が, を) 来ます。晩ご飯 (が, を) 姉 (が, を) 作ります。兄 (が, を) ワイン (が, を) 買います。
Kyō wa tomodachi (ga, o) kimasu. Bangohan (ga, o) ane (ga, o) tsukurimasu. Ani (ga, o) wain (ga, o) kaimasu.
Today, my friend will come. My older sister will make dinner. My older brother will buy wine.

INDICATING THE LOCATION OF ACTIVITY WITH THE PARTICLE で DE

The particle で **de** can mark the location of activities. For example:

週末は図書館で勉強します。
Shūmatsu wa toshokan de benkyō shimasu.
I study at the library on weekends.

明日は田中さんのうちで晩ご飯を食べます。
Ashita wa Tanaka-san no uchi de bangohan o tabemasu.
I will have dinner at Mr. Tanaka's house tomorrow.

For marking the location of existence, use the particle に **ni** (see Chapter 5).

INDICATING TOOLS, MEANS, AND METHODS WITH THE PARTICLE で DE

The particle で **de** in general expresses how the action is performed, and as a result, it can mark the tools, means, and method used for the given action, in addition to the forms of transportation (discussed in Chapter 6) and the location of the activity (discussed in the above section). The following are some examples:

はしで食べます。
Hashi de tabemasu.
I eat with chopsticks.

筆で手紙を書きます。
Fude de tegami o kakimasu.
I write a letter with a brush.

テレビで映画を見ます。
Terebi de eiga o mimasu.
I watch a movie on TV.

オンラインで本を買います。
Onrain de hon o kaimasu.
I buy a book online.

日本語で話しましょう。
Nihon-go de hanashimashō.
Let's talk in Japanese.

Written Practice 5

Translate the following sentences into Japanese, using the given words. You must add some items and conjugate some verbs.

1. *I will study Japanese.*
   (日本語 Nihon-go, 勉強する benkyō suru)

   _____

2. *I read the newspaper at the library every day.*
   (新聞 shinbun, 図書館 toshokan, 読む yomu, 毎日 mainichi)

   _____

3. *I eat sushi with chopsticks.*
   (はし hashi, すし sushi, 食べる taberu)

   _____

4. *A student will come here tomorrow.*
   (学生 gakusei, 来る kuru, 明日 ashita, ここ koko)

   _____

THE CONJUNCTION それから SOREKARA

The conjunction それから **sorekara** relates two sentences that express chronologically ordered or non-ordered events, meaning either *(and) then* or *in addition*, depending on the context.

> 今日はクラスに行きます。それから、図書館に行きます。
> Kyō wa kurasu ni ikimasu. Sorekara, toshokan ni ikimasu.
> *Today, I'll go to class. Then, I'll go to the library.*

> 週末はたいてい掃除をします。それから、洗濯をします。
> Shūmatsu wa taitei sōji o shimasu. Sorekara, sentaku o shimasu.
> *On weekends, I usually clean. In addition, I do laundry.*

Verbs of Giving and Receiving

The verbs of giving and receiving have several forms that are used differently depending on who is giving the item to whom. (In this section, the past tense suffix ました **mashita** is used in many of the example sentences, although it is formally introduced in the next chapter.)

THE VERB TO GIVE

There are two verbs that mean *to give*. One is あげる **ageru** and the other is くれる **kureru**. くれる **kureru** is used in the following three contexts:

- When the item is given to the speaker
- When the item is given to the speaker's in-group member by the speaker's out-group member
- When the item is given to the speaker's in-group member by the speaker's less close in-group member

In all other cases, あげる **ageru** is used.

These verbs are replaced by different verbs depending on the formality of the context. くれる **kureru** is replaced by 下さる **kudasaru** if the giver is the speaker's social superior or one from whom the speaker feels distant. あげる **ageru** is replaced by 差し上げる **sashiageru** if the recipient is the speaker's social superior or one from whom the speaker feels distant. By contrast, if the recipient is the speaker's very intimate subordinate such as his children, younger siblings, and pets, あげる **ageru** may be replaced by やる **yaru**, but it is not required.

INDICATING A RECIPIENT WITH THE PARTICLE に NI

The recipient is marked by the particle に **ni** in a sentence with a verb of giving, discussed in the above section. For example:

母が私にきれいなネックレスをくれました。
Haha ga watashi ni kirei na nekkuresu o kuremashita.
My mother gave me a pretty necklace.

私は母にスカーフをあげました。
Watashi wa haha ni sukāfu o agemashita.
I gave my mother a scarf.

Oral Practice

 TRACK 30

Practice using the verbs of giving by reading the following sentences out loud. Pay attention to who is giving the item to whom and what verb is being used.

父が 私に時計をくれました。
Chichi ga watashi ni tokei o kuremashita.
My father gave me a watch.

スミスさんが母に花をくれました。
Simisu-san ga haha ni hana o kuremashita.
Mr. Smith gave my mother a flower.

先生が私に辞書を下さいました。
Sensei ga watashi ni jisho o kudasaimashita.
My teacher gave me a dictionary.

父は母にスカーフをあげました。
Chichi wa haha ni sukāfu o agemashita.
My father gave my mother a scarf.

私も母にスカーフをあげました。
Watashi mo haha ni sukāfu o agemashita.
I also gave a scarf to my mother.

私は鈴木社長にワインを差し上げました。
Watashi wa Suzuki shachō ni wain o sashiagemashita.
I gave President Suzuki (a bottle of) wine.

私は犬にステーキをやりました。
Watashi wa inu ni sutēki o yarimashita.
I gave a steak to my dog.

Written Practice 6

Choose the appropriate option in the parentheses.

1. 父は私にお小遣いを(あげます・くれます)。

    Chichi wa watashi ni okozukai o (agemasu, kuremasu).

    My father gives me an allowance.

2. 私は母にネックレスを (あげます・くれます) 。

    Watashi wa haha ni nekkuresu o (agemasu, kuremasu).

    I will give my mother a necklace.

3. 山田さんはよく妹にチョコレートを (あげます・くれます) 。

    Yamada-san wa yoku imōto ni chokorēto o (agemasu, kuremasu).

    Ms. Yamada often gives my younger sister chocolate.

4. 先生に花を (差し上げます・下さいます) 。

    Sensei ni hana o (sashiagemasu, kudasaimasu).

    I'll give the teacher a flower.

5. 毎年、先生は私に本を (差し上げます・下さいます) 。

    Maitoshi, sensei wa watashi ni hon o (sashiagemasu, kudasaimasu).

    Every year, my teacher gives me a book.

6. 犬にケーキを (くれました・やりました) 。

    Inu ni kēki o (kuremashita, yarimashita).

    I gave a cake to my dog.

THE VERB TO RECEIVE

The verb that means *to receive* is もらう **morau** in Japanese. The subject noun of this verb must be the receiver of the item and also must be the speaker or someone who the speaker feels closer to than to the giver. もらう **morau** is replaced by 頂く **itadaku** when the speaker wishes to show respect to the giver.

INDICATING THE SOURCE OF RECEIVING WITH THE PARTICLE に NI

The person from whom the item is received is marked by the particle から **kara** or by the particle に **ni**. For example:

私は祖母にお小遣いをもらいました。
Watashi wa sobo ni o-kozukai o moraimashita.
I received some allowance from my grandmother.

祖父から財布をもらいました。
Sofu kara saifu o moraimashita.
I received a wallet from my grandfather.

先生に辞書を頂きました。
Sensei ni jisho o itadakimashita.
I received a dictionary from my teacher.

As you can see, the particle に **ni** can mark the recipient when used with the verbs あげる **ageru** and くれる **kureru** and also the source of receiving when used with the verb もらう **morau**, which appears contradictory. So, you must carefully consider what is the verb for interpreting the meaning of に **ni**.

INDICATING THE OCCASION WITH THE PARTICLE に NI

The particle に **ni** marks the occasion of giving and receiving, as illustrated in the following sentences:

祖父が入学のお祝いに時計をくれました。
Sofu ga nyūgaku no o-iwai ni tokei o kuremashita.
My grandfather gave me a watch in celebration of my school admission.

誕生日のプレゼントにハンドバッグをもらいました。
Tanjōbi no purezento ni handobaggu o moraimashita.
I received a handbag for my birthday present.

出産祝いに陽子さんに赤ちゃんの服をあげました。

Shussan-iwai ni Yōko-san ni akachan no fuku o agemashita.

I gave Yoko baby clothes to celebrate the birth of her baby.

Written Practice 7

Choose the most appropriate option in the parentheses.

1. 私はボーイフレンドに花を(くれました, もらいました)。

    Watashi wa bōifurendo ni hana o (kuremashita, moraimashita.)

2. 私はボーイフレンドに財布を (あげました、 くれました) 。

    Watashi wa bōifurendo ni saifu o (agemashita, kuremashita).

3. 先生から本を (下さいました・頂きました) 。

    Sensei kara hon o (kudasaimashita, itadakimashita).

4. 入学のお祝いに祖父が私に時計を (くれました, もらいました) 。

    Nyūgaku no o-iwai ni sofu ga watashi ni tokei o (kuremashita, moraimashita).

Colors

The following words are nouns and adjectives for colors.

Color	Noun	Adjective
red	赤 aka	赤い akai
blue	青 ao	青い aoi
black	黒 kuro	黒い kuroi
yellow	黄色 kiiro	黄色い kiiroi
white	白 shiro	白い shiroi
green	緑 midori	— (緑の midori no)
purple	紫 murasaki	— (紫の murasaki no)
brown	茶色 chairo	茶色い chairoi
grey	灰色 haiiro	— (灰色の haiiro no)

Written Practice 8

Match the Japanese color words with their meaning.

1. 赤 aka   a. green
2. 緑 midori   b. black
3. 白 shiro   c. red
4. 青 ao   d. blue
5. 黒 kuro   e. white

More About Using Numbers

In this section, you will learn additional counters, 匹 **hiki**, 冊 **satsu**, and 台 **dai**, and will also learn how to create ordinal numbers using the suffix 目 **me**.

THE COUNTERS 匹 HIKI, 冊 SATSU, AND 台 DAI

The counter 匹 **hiki** is used for small or medium-size animals such as fish, insects, dogs, cats, and monkeys. (For larger animals such as elephants and cows, the counter 頭 **tō** is usually used.) The counter 冊 **satsu** is used for counting bound items such as books, magazines, and notebooks. The counter 台 **dai** is used for counting machines or mechanical items such as cars, trucks, and copiers.

うちには金魚が5匹います。
Uchi ni wa kingyo ga go-hiki imasu.
There are five goldfish at my house.

本を2冊買います。
Hon o ni-satsu kaimasu.
I'll buy two books.

車が一台あります。
Kuruma ga ichi-dai arimasu.
There is one car.

As you can see in the following table, 匹 **hiki** and 冊 **satsu** cause some irregular sound changes.

Number	Animals	Books	Machines
1	いっぴき ip-piki	いっさつ is-satsu	いちだい ichi-dai
2	にひき ni-hiki	にさつ ni-satsu	にだい ni-dai
3	さんびき san-biki	さんさつ san-satsu	さんだい san-dai
4	よんひき yon-hiki	よんさつ yon-satsu	よんだい yon-dai
5	ごひき go-hiki	ごさつ go-satsu	ごだい go-dai
6	ろっぴき rop-piki	ろくさつ roku-satsu	ろくだい roku-dai
7	ななひき nana-hiki	ななさつ nana-satsu	ななだい nana-dai
8	はっぴき hap-piki	はっさつ has-satsu	はちだい hachi-dai
9	きゅうひき kyū-hiki	きゅうさつ kyū-satsu	きゅうだい kyū-dai
10	じゅっぴき jup-piki	じゅっさつ jus-satsu	じゅうだい jū-dai

Note that there are some variations in the pronunciation of number phrases depending on the speaker's dialect and age.

THE DISTRIBUTIVE SUFFIX ずつ ZUTSU

The suffix ずつ **zutsu** follows a number phrase such as 5人 **go-nin** (*five people*) and 3つ **mit-tsu** (*three pieces*), and means *each* or *at a time*.

子供が飴を3つずつもらいます。
Kodomo ga ame o mit-tsu zutsu moraimasu.
Children will receive three candies each.

学生が2人ずつ来ます。
Gakusei ga futari zutsu kimasu.
Two students will come at a time.

部屋には机が2つずつあります。
Heya ni wa tsukue ga futa-tsu zutsu arimasu.
There are two desks in each room.

毎日、漢字を5つずつ勉強します。
Mainichi, kanji o itsu-tsu zutsu benkyō shimasu.
I study five kanji each day.

USING 目 ME TO EXPRESS ORDINAL NUMBERS

Ordinal numbers express the position in the order, such as *first*, *second*, and *third*. In Japanese, ordinal numbers can be easily created by adding 目 **me** to a number phrase with a counter. For example, 3つ **mit-tsu** means *three pieces*, but 3つ目 **mit-tsu-me** means *the third piece*. The following are additional examples:

3人目の学生は日本人です。
San-nin-me no gakusei wa Nihon-jin desu.
The third student is Japanese.

2つ目の交差点まで歩きます。
Futa-tsu-me no kōsaten made arukimasu.
I will walk up to the second intersection.

QUIZ

Circle the letter of the word or phrase that best completes each sentence.

1. 明日だれ＿＿＿＿ここ＿＿＿＿来ますか。

   Ashita dare ＿＿＿＿ koko ＿＿＿＿ kimasu ka.

   (a) が ga, に ni   (c) が ga, で de

   (b) を o, に ni   (d) に ni, が ga

2. 姉はよくカフェテリア ＿＿＿＿ 新聞＿＿＿＿ 読みます。

Ane wa yoku kafeteria ＿＿＿＿ shinbun ＿＿＿＿ yomimasu.

(a) が ga, を o   (c) で de, が ga

(b) に ni, を o   (d) で de, を o

3. 父と私はうち＿＿＿＿ 英語＿＿＿＿ 話します。

Chichi to watashi wa uchi ＿＿＿＿ eigo ＿＿＿＿ hanashimasu.

(a) で de, を o   (c) に ni, を o

(b) を o, で de   (d) が ga, を o

4. 晩ご飯を食べます。それから、＿＿＿＿＿＿＿＿＿＿＿。

Bangohan o tabemasu. Sorekara, ＿＿＿＿＿＿＿＿＿＿ .

(a) 母は日本人です Haha wa Nihon-jin desu

(b) テレビを見ます Terebi o mimasu

(c) 山田さんはあそこです Yamada-san wa asoko desu

(d) 車が3台あります Kuruma ga san-dai arimasu

5. 結婚のお祝い＿＿＿＿ 田中さん＿＿＿＿ 花瓶をあげます。

Kekkon no o-iwai ＿＿＿＿ Tanaka-san ＿＿＿＿ kabin o agemasu.

(a) で de, に ni   (c) から kara, に ni

(b) に ni, から kara   (d) に ni, に ni

6. 私は母にハンドバッグを ＿＿＿＿ 。

Watashi wa haha ni handobaggu o ＿＿＿＿ .

(a) くれます kuremasu   (c) 下さいます kudasaimasu

(b) あげます agemasu   (d) 差し上げます sashiagemasu

7. 私はよく父にお金を ＿＿＿＿ 。

Watashi wa yoku chichi ni o-kane o ＿＿＿＿ .

(a) くれます kuremasu   (c) もらいます moraimasu

(b) 下さいます kudasaimasu   (d) 差し上げます sashiagemasu

8. 先生は私に本を ＿＿＿＿ 。

Sensei wa watashi ni hon o ＿＿＿＿ .

(a) 下さいました kudasaimashita

(b) あげました agemashita

(c) くれました kuremashita

(d) 頂きました itadakimashita

9. 学生が＿＿＿来ました。

Gakusei ga ＿＿＿ kimashita.

(a) 3人ずつ san-nin zutsu   (c) 2冊 ni-satsu

(b) 2枚目の ni-mai-me no   (d) 2冊目の ni-satsu-me no

10. トマトは＿＿＿です。

Tomato wa ＿＿＿ desu.

(a) 白い shiroi   (c) 黒い kuroi

(b) 青い aoi   (d) 赤い akai

CHAPTER 8

Talking About the Past

In this chapter you'll learn:

The Past Tense Forms in the Polite Style
Indefinite Pronouns and Negative Pronouns
Some Useful Particles
Talking About Experiences
Describing People and Things More Specifically
Some Absolute Time Expressions

The Past Tense Forms in the Polite Style

The past tense expresses what one did or how something was at a specific time in the past.

VERBS IN THE POLITE PAST FORM

It is very easy to convert a verb in the present tense in the polite style to the past tense counterpart. Just change ます **masu** and ません **masen** to ました **mashita** and ませんでした **masendeshita**, respectively.

スミスさんは病院に行きます。
Sumisu-san wa byōin ni ikimasu.
Mr. Smith will go to the hospital.

スミスさんは病院に行きました。
Sumisu-san wa byōin ni ikimashita.
Mr. Smith went to the hospital.

山田さんはクラスに行きません。
Yamada-san wa kurasu ni ikimasen.
Ms. Yamada will not go to class.

山田さんはクラスに行きませんでした。
Yamada-san wa kurasu ni ikimasendeshita.
Ms. Yamada did not go to class.

SOME RELATIVE TIME EXPRESSIONS FOR THE PAST

The following words are useful for referring to some relative time in the past.

昨日	kinō	*yesterday*
おととい	ototoi	*the day before yesterday*
前	mae	*before*
先週	senshū	*last week*
2週間前	ni-shūkan mae	*two weeks ago*
先月	sengetsu	*last month*

2ヶ月前	ni-kagetsu mae	*two months ago*
去年	kyonen	*last year*
3年前	san-nen mae	*three years ago*

Written Practice 1

Translate the following passage into English.

昨日はクラスには行きませんでした。* うちにいました。テレビでおもしろい
映画を見ました。それから、本を読みました。

Kinō wa kurasu ni wa ikimasendeshita.* Uchi ni imashita. Terebi de omoshiroi
eiga o mimashita. Sorekara, hon o yomimashita.

_____

_____

THE COPULAR VERB IN THE POLITE PAST FORM

The past tense form of the copular verb です **desu** is でした **deshita**. The past tense
form of the negative copular verb じゃありません **ja arimasen** (or ではありません
de wa arimasen) is じゃありませんでした **ja arimasendeshita** (or ではありません
でした **de wa arimasendeshita**). Regardless of whether affirmative or negative, the
past tense form of the copular verb in the polite style ends in でした **deshita**, as you
can see in the following examples:

兄はこの高校の学生でした。
Ani wa kono kōkō no gakusei deshita.
My brother was a student of this high school.

私はこの高校の学生じゃありませんでした。
Watashi wa kono kōkō no gakusei ja arimasendeshita.
I was not a student of this high school.

---

*For the use of は **wa** in the first Japanese sentence in Written Practice 1, see Chapter 5, "The
Particle Cluster には **ni wa**," and Chapter 12, "Indicating Contrast and the Scope of Negation
with the Particle は **wa**."

ADJECTIVES IN THE POLITE PAST FORM

Adjectives conjugate in the past tense in the polite form as summarized in the following table.

	Past-Tense of Adjectives in the Polite Form	
	I-type	**Na-type**
Affirmative	Stem + かったです Stem + katta desu EX: 古かったです。 furukatta desu. *(It) was old.*	Stem + でした Stem + deshita EX: きれいでした。 kirei deshita. *(It) was pretty.*
Negative	Stem + くありませんでした Stem + ku arimasendeshita EX: 古くありませんでした。 furuku arimasendeshita. *(It) was not old.* Or stem + くなかったです Stem + ku nakatta desu EX: 古くなかったです。 Furuku nakatta desu. *(It) was not old.*	Stem + じゃありませんでした Stem + ja arimasendeshita* EX: きれいじゃありませんでした。 kirei ja arimasendeshita. *(It) was not pretty.* Or stem + じゃなかったです* Stem + ja nakatta desu* EX: きれいじゃなかったです。 Kirei ja nakatta desu. *(It) was not pretty.*

Written Practice 2

Convert the following sentences into the past tense following the example.

兄は学生です。 Ani wa gakusei desu

兄は学生でした。 Ani wa gakusei deshita.

1. 本を読みます。 Hon o yomimasu.

---

*じゃ **ja** in the negative forms in the above table can be では **dewa**.

2. このかばんは高いです。 Kono kaban wa takai desu.

_____

3. レストランは静かです。 Resutoran wa shizuka desu.

_____

4. 部屋はきれいじゃありません。 Heya wa kirei ja arimasen.

_____

5. クラスには行きません。 Kurasu ni wa ikimasen.

_____

Indefinite Pronouns and Negative Pronouns

In daily-life conversations, we frequently use words such as *something* or *nothing*. Words such as *something, someone,* or *somewhere* are called indefinite pronouns, and words such as *nothing, nobody,* or *nowhere* are called negative pronouns.

INDEFINITE PRONOUNS

Indefinite pronouns in Japanese are generally composed of a question word and the particle か **ka**. Recall the question words you learned in Chapter 3:

何 nani (*what*)   だれ dare (*who*)   どこ doko (*where*)

These question words can be converted to indefinite pronouns once you add か **ka**.

何か	nanika	*something*
だれか	dareka	*someone*
どこか	dokoka	*somewhere*

Suppose you thought that something small moved near the bush in the distance. If you are sure that there is something although you don't know what, you can say:

あそこに何かいます。
Asoko ni nanika imasu.
There is something over there.

Suppose you are not sure whether there is something or not, you can ask:

あそこに何かいますか。
Asoko ni nanika imasu ka.
Is there anything over there?

Don't be misled by the alternation between *something* and *anything* in English translations in the above two sentences. In English questions, *anything* is usually used instead of *something*, but in Japanese, we can use the same indefinite pronoun in both question sentences and statement sentences.

The particle が **ga** and を **o** are usually deleted when they follow an indefinite pronoun, but other particles such as に **ni**, で **de**, and と **to** are usually not deleted, as you can see in the following examples:

あそこにだれかいますか。
Asoko ni dareka imasu ka.
Is there anyone over there?

だれか見ましたか。
Dareka mimashita ka.
Did you see anyone?

だれかに会いましたか。
Dareka ni aimashita ka.
Did you meet anyone?

夏休みはどこかに行きましたか。
Natsu-yasumi wa dokoka ni ikimashita ka.
Did you go anywhere during the summer vacation?

だれかと話しましたか。
Dareka to hanashimashita ka.
Did you talk with anyone?

どこかで会いましたか。
Dokoka de aimashita ka.
Did they meet somewhere?

Written Practice 3

Translate the following questions into Japanese. *Hint:* In general, you don't have to translate the English word *you* into Japanese.

1. Did you eat something? _____
2. Did you do anything? _____
3. Did you go anywhere? _____
4. Did anyone come? _____

NEGATIVE PRONOUNS

To say *nothing* or *not . . . anything*, use the question words and add the particle も **mo** after them and their associated particle. The verb must be in the negative form. The particle が **ga** and を **o** must be deleted when followed by も **mo**, although other particles usually stay. For example:

だれもいません。
Dare mo imasen.
There is no one.

だれとも話しませんでした。
Dare to mo hanashimasendeshita.
I didn't talk with anyone.

何も食べませんでした。
Nani mo tabemasendeshita.
I did not eat anything.

どこにも行きませんでした。
Doko ni mo ikimasendeshita.
I didn't go anywhere.

Written Practice 4

Following the example, answer the questions in the negative.

> Question: どこかに行きましたか。 Dokoka ni ikimashita ka.
> Answer: <u>いいえ、どこにも行きませんでした。 Īe, doko ni mo</u>
> <u>ikimasendeshita.</u>

1. Question: 何か食べましたか。Nanika tabemashita ka.

   Answer: _____

2. Question: 何かしましたか。 Nanika shimashita ka.

   Answer: _____

3. Question: どこかに行きましたか。 Dokoka ni ikimashita ka.

   Answer: _____

4. Question: だれか来ましたか。 Dareka kimashita ka.

   Answer: _____

5. Question: だれかと話しましたか。 Dareka to hanashimashita ka.

   Answer: _____

Oral Practice

 TRACK 31

Practice asking and answering questions by reading the following sentences out loud.

だれかに言いましたか。
Dareka ni iimashita ka.
Did you tell anyone (about it)?

いいえ、だれにも言いませんでした。
Īe, dare ni mo iimasendeshita.
No, I didn't tell anyone.

だれか来ましたか。
Dareka kimashita ka.
Did anyone come?

いいえ、だれも来ませんでした。
Īe, dare mo kimasendeshita.
No, no one came.

日本で何か買いましたか。
Nihon de nanika kaimashita ka.
Did you buy anything in Japan?

はい。着物と人形を買いました。
Hai. Kimono to ningyō o kaimashita.
Yes. I bought a kimono and a doll.

どこかで晩ご飯を食べませんか。
Dokoka de bangohan o tabemasen ka.
Shall we eat dinner somewhere?

ええ、いいですよ。
Ē, ii desu yo.
Yes, sure!

週末、私の車でどこかに行きませんか。
Shūmatsu, watashi no kuruma de dokoka ni ikimasen ka.
How about going somewhere in my car on the weekend?

週末はちょっと忙しいです。
Shūmatsu wa chotto isogashii desu.
I'm a little busy on weekends.

Some Useful Particles

In this section, you will learn an additional function of the particle で **de** as well as the usage of the particle や **ya**.

INDICATING REASONS WITH THE PARTICLE で DE

The particle で **de** can express reasons and causes, showing how the given action takes place or how the given state holds. For example:

雪でバスが来ませんでした。
Yuki de basu ga kimasendeshita.
The bus didn't come due to (heavy) snow.

このレストランはおいしいパンで有名です。
Kono resutoran wa oishii pan de yūmei desu.
This restaurant is famous for delicious bread.

兄は宿題で忙しいです。
Ani wa shukudai de isogashii desu.
My brother is busy with homework.

MAKING A PARTIAL LIST WITH THE PARTICLE や YA

Unlike the particle と **to**, which plainly lists items as discussed in Chapter 5, the particle や **ya** lists items implying that the list is not exhaustive and there are additional items.

昨日はビールやワインを飲みました。
Kinō wa bīru ya wain o nomimashita.
I drank beer, wine, and other drinks yesterday.

フランスや、スペインや、イタリアに行きました。
Furansu ya, Supein ya, Itaria ni ikimashita.
I went to France, Spain, Italy, etc.

日本語や、中国語を勉強しました。
Nihon-go ya, Chūgoku-go o benkyō shimashita.
I studied Japanese, Chinese, etc.

Remember that both と **to** and や **ya** are used only for nouns.

Talking About Experiences

In this section, you will learn how to express your experiences in Japanese using the verb ある **aru.**

EXPRESSING A PAST EXPERIENCE WITH THE VERB ある ARU

For telling someone what experience you have had, use the verb ある **aru** (*to exist, to have*) in the present tense. You may wonder why we use the present tense for expressing our experience, but we can think of an experience as something like a personal memory that we currently hold and possess. Then, the use of present tense with the main verb ある **aru** becomes not counterintuitive. For the subject of ある **aru**, create a nominal phrase using a verb in the plain past (see the next sub-section) and add the abstract noun こと **koto**. Here, you need to use the past tense. The purpose of using こと **koto** is to nominalize the verb so it can be placed where a noun is usually placed. For example, the following sentence shows that you have had the experience of eating eel:

> うなぎを食べたことがあります。
> Unagi o tabeta koto ga arimasu.
> *I have had eel (before).*

Unlike a simple past sentence, which was discussed earlier in this chapter, the main concern of the above sentence with ある **aru** is not on what one did or didn't do at some specific time in the past, but is on what experience one has.

NOTE: *If you use a verb in the plain present tense before* ことがあります *koto ga arimasu, it expresses what you sometimes do.*

> 仕事でホンコンに行くことがあります。
> Shigoto de Honkon ni iku koto ga arimasu.
> *I have occasion to go to Hong Kong on business.*

VERBS IN THE PLAIN PAST FORM

Forming a verb in the plain past affirmative form from its dictionary form is slightly complicated. The conjugation pattern depends on the verb class and the verb ending. The rules are summarized in the following table.

Verb Class	The ending syllable of the dictionary form	Replace last syllable with:	Example
Ru-verb	る **ru**	た **ta**	見る **miru** → 見た **mita**
U-verb	る **ru**, つ **tsu**, or う **u** (う **u**: **u** which is syllabic by itself and is not preceded by a consonant)	った **tta**	とる **toru** → とった **totta** 待つ **matsu** → 待った **matta** 買う **kau** → 買った **katta**
	む **mu**, ぬ **nu**, or ぶ **bu**	んだ **nda**	飲む **nomu** → 飲んだ **nonda** 死ぬ **shinu** → 死んだ **shinda** とぶ **tobu** → とんだ **tonda**
	く **ku**	いた **ita**	書く **kaku** → 書いた **kaita**
	ぐ **gu**	いだ **ida**	泳ぐ **oyogu** → 泳いだ **oyoida**
	す **su**	した **shita**	おす **osu** → おした **oshita**

Irregular cases include:

する suru (*to do*)	した shita
来る kuru (*to come*)	来た kita
行く iku (*to go*)	行った itta

Oral Practice

 **TRACK 32**

Practice forming the plain past affirmative forms from the dictionary forms by reading the following out loud.

食べる taberu (*eat*)	食べた tabeta
見る miru (*look*)	見た mita
寝る neru (*sleep*)	寝た neta

作る tsukuru (*make*)   作った tsukutta

待つ matsu (*wait*)   待った matta

買う kau (*buy*)   買った katta

飲む nomu (*drink*)   飲んだ nonda

読む yomu (*read*)   読んだ yonda

死ぬ shinu (*die*)   死んだ shinda

遊ぶ asobu (*play*)   遊んだ asonda

聞く kiku (*listen*)   聞いた kiita

泳ぐ oyogu (*swim*)   泳いだ oyoida

話す hanasu (*speak*)   話した hanashita

する suru (*do*)   した shita

来る kuru (*come*)   来た kita

行く iku (*go*)   行った itta

Oral Practice

 TRACK 33

Practice asking and answering the questions about experiences by reading the following sentences out loud.

友達とけんかをしたことがありますか。
Tomodachi to kenka o shita koto ga arimasu ka.
Have you ever fought with your friend?

いいえ、ありません。
Īe, arimasen.
No, I haven't.

クレジットカードをなくしたことがありますか。
Kurejitto-kādo o nakushita koto ga arimasu ka.
Have you ever lost your credit card?

はい、一度あります。
Hai, ichi-do arimasu.
Yes, I have once.

日本語で手紙を書いたことがありますか。
Nihon-go de tegami o kaita koto ga arimasu ka.
Have you ever written a letter in Japanese?

まだ、ありません。
Mada, arimasen.
No, not yet.

Written Practice 5

Following the examples, create question sentences that ask whether someone has the experience of doing the following activities.

お酒を飲む o-sake o nomu (*to drink sake*)

お酒を飲んだことがありますか。 O-sake o nonda koto ga arimasu ka.

1. 黒澤の映画を見る Kurosawa no eiga o miru (*to watch Kurosawa's film*)

    _____

2. アラスカに行く Arasuka ni iku (*to go to Alaska*)

    _____

3. 着物を着る kimono o kiru (*to wear kimono*) *Hint*: 着る **kiru** is a ru-verb

    _____

4. 留学する ryūgaku suru (*to study abroad*)

    _____

Describing People and Things More Specifically

You learned how to describe people and things using adjectives in Chapter 4, for example:

陽子さんはきれいです。
Yōko-san wa kirei desu.
Yoko is pretty.

However, you can describe people and things more specifically by adding a noun and the particle が **ga**, right before the adjective, to indicate to what part or aspect the property applies. Let's look at the following construction:

XはYがZです
X wa Y ga Z desu
X is Z in terms of Y.

If you want to say that Yoko is pretty as far as her hair is concerned, rather than saying she is pretty over all, you can say:

陽子さんは髪がきれいです。
Yōko-san wa kami ga kirei desu.
Yoko has pretty hair.

The above sentence is a statement about Yoko, whereas the following sentence is a statement about Yoko's hair:

陽子さんの髪はきれいです。
Yōko-san no kami wa kirei desu.
Yoko's hair is pretty.

By using XはYがZです **X wa Y ga Z desu**, you can describe a variety of people and things. They are exemplified in the following subsections.

DESCRIBING PEOPLE'S APPEARANCES

The following are useful phrases for describing the appearance of people:

背が高い	se ga takai	*tall*
背が低い	se ga hikui	*short*
髪が長い	kami ga nagai	*have long hair*
髪が短い	kami ga mijikai	*have short hair*
目が大きい	me ga ōkii	*have big eyes*
目がきれいな	me ga kirei na	*have pretty eyes*
口が小さい	kuchi ga chīsai	*have a small mouth*
やせている	yasete iru	*skinny*
ふとっている	futotte iru	*fat*

For example, you can say:

兄は背が高いです。
Ani wa se ga takai desu.
My older brother is tall.

僕のガールフレンドは目がきれいです。
Boku no gārufurendo wa me ga kirei desu.
My girlfriend has beautiful eyes.

姉は髪が長いです。
Ane wa kami ga nagai desu.
My sister has long hair.

DESCRIBING PLACES

You can use XはYがZです **X wa Y ga Z desu** for describing many countries and cities:

日本は魚がおいしいです。
Nihon wa sakana ga oishii desu.
As for Japan, fish are delicious.

イギリスは建物が古いです。
Igirisu wa tatemono ga furui desu.
As for England, their buildings are old.

中国は自転車が多いです。
Chūgoku wa jitensha ga ōi desu.
As for China, there are a lot of bicycles.

DESCRIBING SKILLS AND TALENTS

The following are useful phrases for describing the skills and talent of people:

上手な	jōzu na	*good at . . .*
得意な	tokui na	*good at . . .*
うまい	umai	*good at . . .*
下手な	heta na	*bad at . . .*
苦手な	nigate na	*bad at . . .*

For speaking one's own skills, use 得意な **tokui na** rather than 上手な **jōzu na** or うまい **umai**. The following examples show how you can describe skills and talents of people:

山田さんはスキーが上手です。
Yamada-san wa sukī ga jōzu desu.
Ms. Yamada is good at skiing.

私はゴルフが得意です。
Watashi wa gorufu ga tokui desu.
I'm good at golf.

兄はうたが下手です。
Ani wa uta ga heta desu.
My older brother is bad at singing.

弟は目がいいです。
Otōto wa me ga ii desu.
My younger brother has good eyesight.

祖父は耳が悪いです。
Sofu wa mimi ga warui desu.
My grandfather cannot hear well. (*Literally: My grandfather has bad ears.*)

田中さんは頭がいいです。
Tanaka-san wa atama ga ii desu.
Mr. Tanaka is smart.

PREFERENCES AND DESIRES

One's likes and dislikes as well as desire are typically expressed by verbs in English. For example, *to like, to love, to hate,* and *to want* are verbs in English. By contrast, they are more commonly expressed by adjectives in Japanese. The following are some examples:

好きな	suki na	*to like*
大好きな	daisuki na	*to like very much*
嫌いな	kirai na	*to hate*
ほしい	hoshii	*to want*

These adjectives can be used in sentences in the form of XはYがZです **X wa Y ga Z desu**, as shown here.

私は桃が好きです。
Watashi wa momo ga suki desu.
I like peaches.

妹はアイスクリームが大好きです。
Imōto wa aisukurīmu ga daisuki desu.
My younger sister loves ice cream.

弟は猫が嫌いです。
Otōto wa neko ga kirai desu.
My younger brother hates cats.

私は新しいプリンターがほしいです。
Watashi wa atarashii purintā ga hoshii desu.
I want a new printer.

NOTE: ほしい *hoshii cannot be used for actions. To say you want to do something, use the suffix* たい *tai, which will be discussed later in this chapter.*

THE NOMINALIZERS の NO AND こと KOTO

To express the activity that you like or you are good at using a verb, you must, first, nominalize the verb by adding the particle の **no** or the abstract noun こと **koto** (*thing*). The verb must be in the plain form in this case. For example, if you like *running*, say:

私は走るのが好きです。
Watashi wa hashiru no ga suki desu.

or

私は走ることが好きです。
Watashi wa hashiru koto ga suki desu.

The following are additional examples:

父はお酒を飲むのが好きです。
Chichi wa o-sake o nomu no ga suki desu.
My father likes drinking sake.

母は友達としゃべるのが好きです。
Haha wa tomodachi to shaberu no ga suki desu.
My mother likes chatting with her friends.

兄はうたをうたうことが好きです。
Ani wa uta o utau koto ga suki desu.
My older brother likes singing songs.

In this construction, の **no** and こと **koto** can be used interchangeably, although they cannot always be used interchangeably in other contexts.

THE SUFFIX たい TAI

To say you want to do something, use the verb in the stem form (pre-masu form) and add the suffix たい **tai**, as in 食べたい **tabe-tai** (*to want to eat*). The output is an i-type adjective, and you can use it just like other i-type adjectives. For example:

日本で働きたいです。
Nihon de hataraki-tai desu.
I want to work in Japan.

医者になりたいです。
Isha ni nari-tai desu.
I want to become a doctor.

大きい家に住みたいです。
Ōkii ie ni sumi-tai desu.
I want to live in a big house.

友達とフランスに行きたいです。
Tomodachi to Furansu ni iki-tai desu.
I want to go to France with my friend.

When the verb has a direct object, it can be marked either by を **o** (direct object marker) or by が **ga** (subject marker).

魚が食べたいです。
Sakana ga tabe-tai desu.
I want to eat fish.

魚を食べたいです。
Sakana o tabe-tai desu.
I want to eat fish.

The difference between the above two sentences is very subtle: the first sentence sounds like expressing what you want to eat, whereas the second sentence sounds like expressing what you want to do.

Written Practice 6

Complete the following sentences using information about yourself.

1. 私は＿＿＿＿＿が好きです。よく、＿＿＿＿＿を食べます。

   Watashi wa ＿＿＿＿＿＿＿＿＿ ga suki desu. Yoku, ＿＿＿＿＿＿＿＿＿
   o tabemasu.

2. 私は＿＿＿＿＿が得意です。

   Watashi wa ＿＿＿＿＿＿＿＿＿ ga tokui desu.

3. 私は＿＿＿＿＿がほしいです。それから、＿＿＿＿＿もほしいです。

   Watashi wa ＿＿＿＿＿＿＿＿＿ ga hoshii desu. Sorekara, ＿＿＿＿＿
   mo hoshii desu.

4. 私は今＿＿＿＿＿たいです。

   Watashi wa ima ＿＿＿＿＿＿＿＿＿ tai desu.

Some Absolute Time Expressions

In this section, you will learn how to express time, dates, etc. in Japanese.

EXPRESSING TIME WITH 時 JI AND 分 FUN

To express time, use 時 **ji** (*o'clock*) and 分 **fun** (*minutes*):

2時35分   ni-ji sanjūgo-fun   *2:35*

午前 **gozen** is A.M. and 午後 **gogo** is P.M., but unlike in English they are placed at the beginning of the time phrase:

| 午前6時15分 | gozen roku-ji jūgo-fun | 6:15 *A.M.* |
| 午後10時22分 | gogo jū-ji nijūni-fun | 10:22 *P.M.* |

The notion of *quarter* is not used in Japanese, but *half* is represented by 半 **han**:

| 午後3時半 | gogo san-ji han | *3:30 P.M.* |

The number phrases with 時 **ji** and 分 **fun** often go through a minor sound change. The following list shows how they are actually pronounced.

1時	ichi-ji	*one o'clock*
2時	ni-ji	*two o'clock*
3時	san-ji	*three o'clock*
4時	yo-ji	*four o'clock*
5時	go-ji	*five o'clock*
6時	roku-ji	*six o'clock*
7時	shichi-ji	*seven o'clock*
8時	hachi-ji	*eight o'clock*
9時	ku-ji	*nine o'clock*
10時	jū-ji	*ten o'clock*
11時	jūichi-ji	*eleven o'clock*
12時	jūni-ji	*twelve o'clock*

1分	ip-pun	*one minute*
2分	ni-fun	*two minutes*
3分	san-pun	*three minutes*
4分	yon-pun	*four minutes*
5分	go-fun	*five minutes*
6分	rop-pun	*six minutes*
7分	nana-fun	*seven minutes*
8分	hap-pun (hachi-fun)	*eight minutes*
9分	kyū-fun	*nine minutes*
10分	jup-pun	*ten minutes*

Oral Practice

 TRACK 34

Practice asking and answering questions about time by reading the following sentences out loud.

すみません。今、何時ですか。
Sumimasen. Ima, nan-ji desu ka.
Excuse me. What time is it now?

今、2時35分です。
Ima, ni-ji sanjūgo-fun desu.
It is 2:35 now.

日本語のクラスは何時から何時までですか。
Nihon-go no kurasu wa nan-ji kara nan-ji made desu ka.
From what time to what time is Japanese class?

9時35分から、10時30分までです。
Ku-ji sanjūgo-fun kara, jū-ji sanjup-pun made desu.
It is from 9:35 to 10:30.

何時の飛行機ですか。
Nan-ji no hikōki desu ka.
What time is your flight?

午後5時25分です。
Gogo go-ji nijūgo-fun desu.
5:25 P.M.

THE DAYS OF THE WEEK

The days of a week in Japanese are as follows:

月曜日	Getsuyōbi	*Monday*
火曜日	Kayōbi	*Tuesday*
水曜日	Suiyōbi	*Wednesday*
木曜日	Mokuyōbi	*Thursday*
金曜日	Kinyōbi	*Friday*

| 土曜日 | Doyōbi | *Saturday* |
| 日曜日 | Nichiyōbi | *Sunday* |

THE MONTHS OF THE YEAR

The twelve months are expressed with numbers along with 月 **gatsu**. Note that the rarely used pronunciation of 4, し **shi**, is used before 月 **gatsu**.

1月	Ichi-gatsu	*January*
2月	Ni-gatsu	*February*
3月	San-gatsu	*March*
4月	Shi-gatsu	*April*
5月	Go-gatsu	*May*
6月	Roku-gatsu	*June*
7月	Shichi-gatsu	*July*
8月	Hachi-gatsu	*August*
9月	Ku-gatsu	*September*
10月	Jū-gatsu	*October*
11月	Jūichi-gatsu	*November*
12月	Jūni-gatsu	*December*

THE DAYS OF THE MONTH

The days of the month are expressed by a number followed by the ordinal counter, 日 **nichi**. However, there are numerous irregular forms.

1日	tsuitachi	*the first*
2日	futsu-ka	*the second*
3日	mik-ka	*the third*
4日	yok-ka	*the fourth*
5日	itsu-ka	*the fifth*
6日	mui-ka	*the sixth*

7日	nano-ka	*the seventh*
8日	yō-ka	*the eighth*
9日	kokono-ka	*the ninth*
10日	tō-ka	*the tenth*
11日	jūichi-nichi	*the eleventh*
12日	jūni-nichi	*the twelfth*
13日	jūsan-nichi	*the thirteenth*
14日	jūyok-ka	*the fourteenth*
15日	jūgo-nichi	*the fifteenth*
16日	jūroku-nichi	*the sixteenth*
17日	jūshichi-nichi	*the seventeenth*
18日	jūhachi-nichi	*the eighteenth*
19日	jūku-nichi	*the nineteenth*
20日	hatsu-ka	*the twentieth*
21日	nijūichi-nichi	*the twenty-first*
22日	nijūni-nichi	*the twenty-second*
23日	nijūsan-nichi	*the twenty-third*
24日	nijūyok-ka	*the twenty-fourth*
25日	nijūgo-nichi	*the twenty-fifth*
26日	nijūroku-nichi	*the twenty-sixth*
27日	nijūshichi-nichi	*the twenty-seventh*
28日	nijūhachi-nichi	*the twenty-eighth*
29日	nijūku-nichi	*the twenty-ninth*
30日	sanjū-nichi	*the thirtieth*
31日	sanjūichi-nichi	*the thirty-first*

YEARS

The ordinal counter for years is 年 **nen**.

1年	ichi-nen	*(year) 1*
2年	ni-nen	*(year) 2*

3年	san-nen	(year) 3
4年	yo-nen	(year) 4
5年	go-nen	(year) 5
6年	roku-nen	(year) 6
7年	nana-nen	(year) 7
8年	hachi-nen	(year) 8
9年	kyū-nen	(year) 9
10年	jū-nen	(year) 10
1998年	sen-kyūhyaku-kyūjūhachi-nen	(year) 1998
2007年	nisen-nana-nen	(year) 2007

There are two systems for expressing the year in Japan: the Western system based on the Christian era, and the Japanese system based on the reigns of emperors. When a new emperor ascends the throne, a new era name is created, and it is used until the next new emperor ascends the throne. For example, the year Emperor Heisei ascended the throne was 平成1年 **Heisei ichi-nen**, which is more commonly called 平成元年 **Heisei gannen**, in the Japanese system and 1989年 **sen-kyūhyaku-hachijū-kyū-nen** in the Western system. Accordingly, the following year was 平成2年 **Heisei ni-nen** in the Japanese system and 1990年 **sen-kyūhyaku-kyūjū-nen** in the Western system. The previous era was *Shōwa*. The *Shōwa* era began in 1926 and ended in 1989.

EXPRESSING ABSOLUTE TIME WITH THE PARTICLE に NI

The time of an event is marked by the particle に **ni** in a sentence if the time phrase expresses an absolute time such as *Monday*, *27th*, or *3 P.M.* On the other hand, the particle に **ni** is unnecessary if the time phrase expresses a relative time such as *yesterday* and *next month*. For example:

田中さんは3時に来ました。
Tanaka-san wa san-ji ni kimashita.
Mr. Tanaka came at 3 o'clock.

月曜日にスミスさんに会いました。
Getsuyōbi ni Sumisu-san ni aimashita.
I met Mr. Smith on Monday.

来月イタリアに行きます。
Raigetsu Itaria ni ikimasu.
I'll go to Italy next month.

THE QUESTION WORD いつ ITSU

The question word いつ **itsu** is used for asking *when*, and the expected answer can be either absolute time or relative time expressions. いつ **itsu** does not have to be marked by the particle に **ni**.

いつアメリカに来ましたか。
Itsu Amerika ni kimashita ka.
When did you come to the US?

For asking *what time*, use 何時 **nan-ji** (*what o'clock*) instead of いつ **itsu** (*when*).

昨日は何時にねましたか。
Kinō wa nan-ji ni nemashita ka.
What time did you go to bed yesterday?

You can also use other phrases such as 何曜日 **nan-yōbi** (*which day of the week*) or 何月 **nan-gatsu** (*which month*).

Oral Practice

 TRACK 35

Practice asking and answering questions about time by reading the following sentences out loud.

誕生日はいつですか。
Tanjōbi wa itsu desu ka.
When is your birthday?

12月3日です。
Jūni-gatsu mik-ka desu.
It is December 3rd.

いつスミスさんに会いましたか。
Itsu Sumisu-san ni aimashita ka.
When did you see Mr. Smith?

おとといに会いました。
Ototoi aimashita.
I met him the day before yesterday.

今日は何日ですか。
Kyō wa nan-nichi desu ka.
What date is it today?

今日は13日です。
Kyō wa jūsan-nichi desu.
Today is 13th.

何曜日ですか。
Nanyōbi desu ka.
What day is it?

水曜日です。
Suiyōbi desu.
Wednesday.

QUIZ

Circle the letter of the word or phrase that best completes each sentence.

1. 母は昨日スーパーに＿＿＿＿。

   Haha wa kinō sūpā ni ＿＿＿＿ .

   (a) 行く iku   (c) 行きます ikimasu

   (b) 行かない ikanai   (d) 行きました ikimashita

2. 昨日は＿＿＿＿。

   Kinō wa ＿＿＿＿ .

   (a) 忙しいいかったです isogashiikatta desu

   (b) 忙しかったです isogashikatta desu

   (c) 忙しいです isogashii desu

   (b) 忙しい isogashii

3. 先週のテストはとても＿＿＿＿。

   Senshū no tesuto wa totemo ＿＿＿＿ .

   (a) 簡単かったです kantankatta desu

   (b) 簡単です kantan desu

   (c) 簡単でした kantan deshita

   (d) 簡単なです kantan na desu

4. 昨日は＿＿＿＿行きましたか。

Kinō wa ＿＿＿＿ ikimashita ka.

(a) どこかに dokoka ni   (c) どこ doko

(b) どこにか doko ni ka   (d) どこにも doko ni mo

5. 昨日は＿＿＿＿行きませんでした。

Kinō wa ＿＿＿＿ ikimasen deshita.

(a) どこかに dokoka ni   (c) どこ doko

(b) どこにか doko ni ka   (d) どこにも doko ni mo

6. アニメを＿＿＿＿がありますか。

Anime o ＿＿＿＿ ga arimasu ka.

(a) 見ます mimasu   (c) 見た mita

(b) 見る miru   (d) 見たこと mita koto

7. ＿＿＿＿ほしいです。

＿＿＿＿ hoshii desu.

(a) 食べるのが taberu no ga   (c) 車が kuruma ga

(b) 食べるのを taberu no o   (d) 車を kuruma o

8. ＿＿＿＿たいです。

＿＿＿＿ tai desu.

(a) 魚が sakana ga

(b) 魚が食べる sakana ga taberu

(c) 魚が食べ sakana ga tabe

(d) 魚を sakana o

9. 日本語を＿＿＿＿好きです。

Nihon-go o ＿＿＿＿ suki desu.

(a) 話し hanashi   (c) 話すが hanasu ga

(b) 話すのが hanasu no ga   (d) 話すこと hanasu koto

10. すし＿＿＿＿さしみを食べました。

Sushi ＿＿＿＿ sashimi o tabemashita.

(a) や ya   (c) で de

(b) を o   (d) が ga

CHAPTER 9

Using the Te-Form

In this chapter you'll learn:

Te-Form
Listing Actions and Properties Using the Te-Form
Requesting with the Te-Form + ください **kudasai**
Giving Directions
Te-Form + いる **iru**

Te-Form

The verbs and adjectives in the te-form end in て **te** or で **de**, as in 食べて **tabete** (*eat*), 飲んで **nonde** (*drink*), 高くて **takakute** (*expensive*), きれいで **kirei de** (*pretty*), and 学生で **gakusei de**. The most basic function of the te-form is to show that the verb or the adjective is followed by an additional verb or adjective in the same sentence, representing a meaning like *do something, and . . .* or *to be someway/something,*

and . . . For example, in the following sentence, all the verbs are in the te-form, except for the last verb:

昨日は、晩ご飯を食べて、テレビを見て、ねました。
Kinō wa, bangohan o tabete, terebi o mite, nemashita.
Yesterday, I ate supper, watched TV, and went to bed.

The time of all the actions is expressed by the last verb. For example, unlike in the above sentence, all the actions expressed in the following sentence will take place in the future.

今日は、晩ご飯を食べて、テレビを見て、ねます。
Kyō wa, bangohan o tabete, terebi o mite, nemasu.
Today, I will eat supper, watch TV, and go to bed.

The same logic applies to the adjectives in the te-form. For example:

山田さんは頭がよくて、きれいで、やさしいです。
Yamada-san wa atama ga yokute, kirei de, yasashii desu.
Ms. Yamada is smart, pretty, and kind.

去年の日本語のクラスは、宿題が多くて、テストが難しくて、大変でした。
Kyonen no Nihon-go no kurasu wa, shukudai ga ōkute, tesuto ga muzukashikute, taihen deshita.
Last year's Japanese class had a lot of homework and difficult tests, and it was a lot of work.

CREATING A VERB IN THE TE-FORM

A verb in the te-form can be created very easily from the plain past affirmative form introduced in Chapter 8. Just change the final syllable た **ta** and だ **da** to て **te** and で **de**, respectively. For example, the plain past affirmative form of 食べる **taberu** (*eat*) is 食べた **tabeta**, and its te-form is 食べて **tabete**.

Oral Practice

 TRACK 36

Practice saying the plain present affirmative form, its past counterpart, and its te-form of each verb many times.

食べる taberu (*eat*)   食べた tabeta   食べて tabete
見る miru (*look*)   見た mita   見て mite

寝る neru (*sleep*)	寝た neta	寝て nete
作る tsukuru (*make*)	作った tsukutta	作って tsukutte
待つ matsu (*wait*)	待った matta	待って matte
買う kau (*buy*)	買った katta	買って katte
飲む nomu (*drink*)	飲んだ nonda	飲んで nonde
読む yomu (*read*)	読んだ yonda	読んで yonde
死ぬ shinu (*die*)	死んだ shinda	死んで shinde
遊ぶ asobu (*play*)	遊んだ asonda	遊んで asonde
聞く kiku (*listen*)	聞いた kiita	聞いて kiite
泳ぐ oyogu (*swim*)	泳いだ oyoida	泳いで oyoide
話す hanasu (*speak*)	話した hanashita	話して hanashite
する suru (*do*)	した shita	して shite
来る kuru (*come*)	来た kita	来て kite
行く iku (*go*)	行った itta	行って itte

The te-form of the copular verb is で **de**. For example, the te-form of 学生です **gakusei desu** is 学生で **gakusei de**.

CREATING AN ADJECTIVE IN THE TE-FORM

The te-form of an i-type adjective is created by adding くて **kute** at the end of its stem. For example, the te-form of 高い **takai** is 高くて **takakute**. The te-form of a na-type adjective is created by adding で **de** at the end of its stem. For example, the te-form of きれいな **kirei na** (*pretty*) is きれいで **kirei de**. The te-form of いい **ii** is よくて **yokute**, which is slightly irregular.

Oral Practice

 TRACK 37

Practice saying the following adjectives in the polite present affirmative form and in the te-form.

高いです takai desu (*expensive*)	高くて takakute
安いです yasui desu (*cheap*)	安くて yasukute
きれいです kirei desu (*pretty*)	きれいで kirei de

大きいです ōkii desu (*big*)	大きくて ōkikute
おいしいです oishii desu (*delicious*)	おいしくて oishikute
静かです shizuka desu (*quiet*)	静かで shizuka de
おもしろいです omoshiroi desu (*interesting*)	おもしろくて omoshirokute
便利です benri desu (*convenient*)	便利で benri de

CREATING A NEGATIVE TE-FORM

You can form verbs in the negative te-form by replacing い **i** at the end of the plain present negative form with くて **kute**. For example, the plain present negative form of the verb 食べる **taberu** is 食べない **tabenai**, and its negative te-form is 食べなくて **tabenakute**. That is, you are treating the plain present negative form just like an i-type adjective. The same logic applies to the copular verb and adjectives. (Their plain present negative forms will be introduced in Chapter 11.) The following table summarizes it:

Plain present negative form	Negative te-form
食べない tabenai	食べなくて tabenakute
高くない takakunai	高くなくて takakunakute
静かじゃない shizuka ja nai	静かじゃなくて shizuka ja nakute
学生じゃない gakusei ja nai	学生じゃなくて gakusei ja nakute

The following are some example sentences with verbs and adjectives in the negative te-form:

母が来なくて、困りました。
Haha ga konakute, komarimashita.
My mother didn't come, and I was upset.

高くなくて、おいしくて、とてもいいです。
Takakunakute, oishikute, totemo ii desu.
It is not expensive, but it is delicious and very good.

Verbs have another negative te-form, namely, the plain present negative plus で **de**, like 食べないで **tabenai de**. The negative te-form of a verb that ends in なくて **nakute** (e.g., 食べなくて **tabenakute**) is mainly used for expressing a cause/result relationship, and the one that ends in ないで **nai de** (e.g., 食べないで **tabenai de**) is used in other contexts, but there are some exceptional cases and you must learn which form should be used case-by-case.

Listing Actions and Properties Using the Te-Form

In this section, you will learn how to use multiple verbs and adjectives in a sentence.

LISTING ACTIONS

You can list multiple events and actions using the te-form. All the verbs should be in the te-form except for the last verb. For example, the following sentence means that you did your homework and watched TV.

昨日の晩は、宿題をして、テレビを見ました。
Kinō no ban wa, shukudai o shite, terebi o mimashita.

In this sentence, doing homework most likely took place before watching TV. On the other hand, in the following sentence, watching TV most likely took place before doing homework.

昨日の晩は、テレビを見て、宿題をしました。
Kinō no ban wa, terebi o mite, shukudai o shimashita.

If you prefer to have two separate sentences, you can relate them using the conjunction それから **sorekara** (*and then*) (see Chapter 7), as shown here:

昨日の晩はテレビを見ました。それから、宿題をしました。
Kinō no ban wa terebi o mimashita. Sorekara, shukudai o shimashita.
Last night, I watched TV. Then, I did my homework.

When a negative te-form is used in this construction, it means "*instead of doing . . .*" or "*without doing . . .*"

バスに乗らないで、タクシーに乗りました。
Basu ni noranai de, takushī ni norimashita.
Instead of taking a bus, I took a taxi.

朝ご飯を食べないで、学校に行きました。
Asa-gohan o tabenai de, gakkō ni ikimashita.
I went to school without eating breakfast.

辞書を使わないで、日本語で手紙を書きました。
Jisho o tsukawanai de, Nihon-go de tegami o kakimashita.
I wrote a letter in Japanese without using a dictionary.

お金を借りないで、家を買いました。
O-kane o karinai de, ie o kaimashita.
I bought a house without borrowing money.

Oral Practice

 TRACK 38

Practice saying the following sentences. As you say each one, think about whether they took place in the past or will take place in the future.

昨日は晩ご飯を食べて、ビールを飲んで、ねました。
Kinō wa bangohan o tabete, bīru o nonde, nemashita.
Yesterday, I ate supper, drank beer, and went to bed.

明日はそうじをして、洗濯をします。
Ashita wa sōji o shite, sentaku o shimasu.
Tomorrow, I'll clean and do laundry.

地下鉄に乗って、バスに乗って、5分歩きます。
Chikatetsu ni notte, basu ni notte, go-fun arukimasu.
I'll take a subway, take a bus, and walk for 5 minutes.

銀行に行って、お金をおろして、洋服を買いました。
Ginkō ni itte, okane o oroshite, yōfuku o kaimashita.
I went to the bank, withdrew some money, and bought clothes.

LISTING PROPERTIES

You can list properties of a person or a thing using the adjectives in the te-form. The last adjective should not be in the te-form, but should be in the regular form that represents the actual tense.

山田さんはきれいで、やさしいです。
Yamada-san wa kirei de, yasashii desu.
Ms. Yamada is pretty and kind.

あのレストランはまずくて、きたないです。
Ano resutoran wa mazukute, kitanai desu.
That restaurant is not delicious and dirty.

EXPRESSING A CAUSE-AND-EFFECT RELATIONSHIP USING THE TE-FORM

Depending on the context, a phrase with a te-form can express the cause of the event or state, as in the following examples.

ねぼうして、クラスに遅れました。
Nebō shite, kurasu ni okuremashita.
I overslept, and (as a result) I was late for the class.

働いて、つかれました。
Hataraite, tsukaremashita.
I worked, and (as a result) I got tired.

仕事がきらいで、会社をやめました。
Shigoto ga kirai de, kaisha o yamemashita.
I hated the work, and (as a result) I quit the company.

昨日のテストは難しくて、わかりませんでした。
Kinō no tesuto wa muzukashikute, wakarimasendeshita.
Yesterday's test was hard, and I didn't understand it.

このクラスはテストが多くなくて、いいです。
Kono kurasu wa tesuto ga ōkunakute, ii desu.
This class doesn't have many tests, and so, it is great.

風邪をひいて、クラスを休みました。
Kaze o hiite, kurasu o yasumimashita.
I caught a cold and missed the class.

日本語の先生は大学院の学生で、あまりきびしくありません。
Nihon-go no sensei wa daigakuin no gakusei de, amari kibishiku arimasen.
The Japanese teacher is a graduate student and is not very strict.

EXPRESSING THE PROCESS USING THE TE-FORM

You can express the process or means for an action using the te-form:

歩いて大学に行きます。
Aruite daigaku ni ikimasu.
I walk to school.

CDを聞いて 練習しましょう。
CD o kiite renshū shimashō.
Let's practice by listening to the CD.

Written Practice 1

Connect the sentences to form one sentence.

1. 新聞を読みました。テレビを見ました。

   Shinbun o yomimashita. Terebi o mimashita.

   _____

2. 地下鉄に乗ります。友達のうちに行きます。

   Chikatetsu ni norimasu. Tomodachi no uchi ni ikimasu.

   _____

3. 優しいです。きれいです。頭がいいです。

   Yasashii desu. Kirei desu. Atama ga ii desu.

   _____

4. 風邪をひきました。クラスを休みました。

   Kaze o hikimashita. Kurasu o yasumimashita.

   _____

5. 難しかったです。わかりませんでした。

   Muzukashikatta desu. Wakarimasendeshita.

   _____

Requesting with the Te-Form + ください kudasai

To request someone to do something, use the verb in the te-form and ください **kudasai**. The latter is a derived form of the verb くださる **kudasaru**, which means *to give me/us*. For example, the idea behind the following sentence is *Stand up, and give it to me as a service or favor,* or something like that, and it actually means *Please stand up.*

立ってください。
Tatte kudasai.

If you are requesting someone not to do something, use the negative te-form that ends in ないで **nai de**.

立たないでください。
Tatanai de kudasai.

If you want to make your request sound more polite, add ませんか **masen ka** at the end.

立ってくださいませんか。
Tatte kudasai masen ka.

立たないでくださいませんか。
Tatanai de kudasai masen ka.

Oral Practice

 TRACK 39

Practice saying the following requests.

すみません。名前を言ってください。
Sumimasen. Namae o itte kudasai.
Excuse me. Could you say your name?

鉛筆で書かないでください。ペンで書いてください。
Enpitsu de kakanai de kudasai. Pen de kaite kudasai.
Please do not write with pencil. Please write with pen.

お金をかしてくださいませんか。
O-kane o kashite kudasai masen ka.
Excuse me. Could you lend me some money?

ここでタバコをすわないでくださいませんか。
Koko de tabako o suwanai de kudasai masen ka.
Could you please not smoke here?

Giving Directions

In this section, you will learn how to give directions using appropriate words and phrases in Japanese.

USEFUL VOCABULARY FOR GIVING DIRECTIONS

For giving directions, the following verbs and nouns are useful:

行く	iku	*to go*
曲がる	magaru	*to make a turn*
わたる	wataru	*to cross*
すぎる	sugiru	*to pass*
歩く	aruku	*to walk*
交差点	kōsaten	*intersection*
角	kado	*corner*
つきあたり	tsukiatari	*end of the street*
橋	hashi	*bridge*
道	michi	*street, road*
3番通り	sanban-dōri	*Third Street*
信号	shingō	*traffic light*

EXPRESSING LOCATIONS AFFECTED BY MOVEMENT WITH THE PARTICLE を O

The location over which a movement action takes place is marked by the particle
を **o**:

橋をわたる
hashi o wataru
to cross a bridge

あの銀行をすぎる
ano ginkō o sugiru
to pass that bank

この道をまっすぐ行く
kono michi o massugu iku
to go straight on this street

三つ目の交差点を曲がる
mit-tsu-me no kōsaten o magaru
to make a turn at the third intersection

For ordinal numbers such as 三つ目 **mit-tsu-me** (*third*) in the last example, see
Chapter 7.

EXPRESSING DIRECTION WITH THE PARTICLE に NI

The direction of a movement such as turning can be marked by the particle に **ni**,
as in:

あの交差点を右に曲がる
ano kōsaten o migi ni magaru
to make a right turn at that intersection

この道を北に行く
kono michi o kita ni iku
to go north on this street

For terms of relative location such as 右 **migi** and 北 **kita** in the above examples,
see Chapter 3.

Oral Practice

 TRACK 40

Practice giving directions by reading the following sentences out loud.

3番通りを南に行ってください。
Sanban-dōri o minami ni itte kudasai.
Please go south on Third Street.

三つ目の交差点を左に曲がってください。
Mit-tsu-me no kōsaten o hidari ni magatte kudasai.
Please make a left turn at the third intersection.

あの橋をわたってください。
Ano hashi o watatte kudasai.
Please cross that bridge.

郵便局をすぎてください。
Yūbinkyoku o sugite kudasai.
Please pass the post office.

つきあたりまで歩いてください。
Tsukiatari made aruite kudasai.
Please walk to the end of the street.

For the particle まで **made** in the last sentence, see Chapter 3.

Written Practice 2

Fill in the blanks with one of the following particles: を **o**, に **ni**, まで **made**, or の **no**. You may use the same particle more than once.

1. この道＿＿＿＿まっすぐ行ってください。

   Kono michi ＿＿＿＿ massugu itte kudasai.　　*Go straight on this street.*

2. 三つ目＿＿＿＿交差点をすぎてください。

   Mit-tsu-me ＿＿＿＿ kōsaten o sugite kudasai.　　*Please pass the third
   intersection.*

3. 3番通りを南＿＿＿＿行ってください。

   Sanban-dōri o minami＿＿＿＿itte kudasai.　　*Go south on Third Street.*

4. つきあたり ＿＿＿＿ 歩いてください。

   Tsukiatari ＿＿＿＿ aruite kudasai.　　　*Walk up to the end of the street.*

5. あの角を右 ＿＿＿＿ 曲がってください。

   Ano kado o migi ＿＿＿＿ magatte kudasai.　　*Please make a right turn at that corner.*

INDICATING THE RESULT WITH THE CONJUNCTION そうすると SŌSURUTO

For stating the result after some action, use the conjunction そうすると **sōsuruto**:

2つ目の交差点を右に曲がってください。そうすると、左に本屋があります。
Futa-tsu-me no kōsaten o migi ni magatte kudasai. Sōsuruto, hidari ni hon'ya ga arimasu.
Please make a right turn at the second intersection. Then, you'll see a bookstore on your left.

Do not mix up そうすると **sōsuruto** with それから **sorekara,** discussed in Chapter 7. Both of them translate as *then,* but そうすると **sōsuruto** shows what happens after the first action, whereas それから **sorekara** shows what action takes place after the first action. The following passage contains both そうすると **sōsuruto** and それから **sorekara.**

この道をまっすぐ行ってください。それから、2つ目の交差点を右に曲がってください。そうすると、左に本屋があります。
Kono michi o massugu itte kudasai. Sorekara, futa-tsu-me no kōsaten o migi ni magatte kudasai. Sōsuruto, hidari ni hon'ya ga arimasu.
Go straight on this street. Then, make a right turn at the second intersection. Then, you'll see a bookstore on your left.

Written Practice 3

Translate the following directions into English. *Hint:* The demonstrative adjective その **sono** discussed in Chapter 2 can be used to mean *that* when you are giving directions even though the item is invisible.

この道をまっすぐ行ってください。 それから、三つ目の交差点を右に曲がってください。そうすると、右に本屋があります。 その本屋をすぎてください。 それから、橋をわたってください。 そうすると、病院が左にあります。 私のうちはその病院の隣です。

Kono michi o massugu itte kudasai. Sorekara, mit-tsu-me no kōsaten o migi ni magatte kudasai. Sōsuruto, migi ni hon'ya ga arimasu. Sono hon'ya o sugite kudasai. Sorekara, hashi o watatte kudasai. Sōsuruto, byōin ga hidari ni arimasu. Watashi no uchi wa sono byōin no tonari desu.

_____

_____

_____

_____

Te-Form + いる iru

The complex verb phrase composed of a verb in the te-form and いる **iru** (*to exist*) expresses a state, which can be a progressive state, habitual state, or resulting state.

PROGRESSIVE STATE

The on-going activity can be expressed by the te-form plus いる **iru**. For example:

母は今、料理をしています。
Haha wa ima ryōri o shite imasu.
My mother is cooking right now.

You can use いらっしゃる **irassharu** instead of いる **iru** to show politeness.

山田さんのお母さんは今、料理をしていらっしゃいます。
Yamada-san no okāsan wa ima, ryōri o shite irasshaimasu.
Ms. Yamada's mother is cooking right now.

For additional information on いらっしゃる **irassharu** or いらっしゃいます **irasshaimasu**, see Chapter 5.

If いる **iru** is in the past tense, the sentence expresses the prolonging activity in the past.

昨日の午後は宿題をしていました。
Kinō no gogo wa shukudai o shite imashita.
I was doing my homework in the afternoon yesterday.

Oral Practice

 TRACK 41

Practice asking and answering the questions by reading the following sentences out loud.

今、何をしていますか。
Ima, nani o shite imasu ka.
What are you doing right now?

手紙を書いています。
Tegami o kaite imasu.
I'm writing a letter.

お父さんは今、何をしていらっしゃいますか。
Otōsan wa ima, nani o shite irasshai masu ka.
What is your father doing right now?

父は今、ビールを飲んで、テレビを見ています。
Chichi wa ima, bīru o nonde, terebi o mite imasu.
My father is drinking beer and watching TV now.

昨日の3時に何をしていましたか。
Kinō no san-ji ni nani o shite imashita ka.
What were you doing at 3 P.M. yesterday?

妹とテレビを見ていました。
Imōto to terebi o mite imashita.
I was watching TV with my younger sister.

HABITUAL STATE

When the te-form + いる **iru** is used with adverbs such as 毎日 **mainichi** (*every day*), いつも **itsumo** (*always*), and 時々 **tokidoki** (*sometimes*), the sentence expresses a habitual activity.

父は毎日オレンジジュースを飲んでいます。
Chichi wa mainichi orenji-jūsu o nonde imasu.
My father drinks orange juice every day.

母はいつも働いています。
Haha wa itsumo hataraite imasu.
My mother is always working.

私は時々運動をしています。
Watashi wa tokidoki undō o shiteimasu.
I sometimes do exercise.

EXPRESSING AN EXTREME HABIT WITH ばかり BAKARI

You can add ばかり **bakari** at the end of the verb in the te-form to express an extreme habit. For example:

弟は遊んでばかりいます。
Otōto wa asonde bakari imasu.
My younger brother does nothing but play.

妹は食べてばかりいます。
Imōto wa tabete bakari imasu.
My younger sister does nothing but eat.

ばかり **bakari** can also be added after a noun. The following two sentences are almost synonymous:

姉はテレビを見てばかりいます。
Ane wa terebi o mite bakari imasu.
My older sister does nothing but watch TV.

姉はテレビばかり見ています。
Ane wa terebi bakari mite imasu.
My older sister watches nothing but TV.

Just like the particle は **wa** and も **mo**, ばかり **bakari** cannot be used with the particle が **ga** or を **o**, although it can co-occur with other particles such as に **ni**. (See Chapter 5 about particle cluster.) For example, ばかり **bakari** co-occurs with に **ni** in the following sentence.

兄は居酒屋にばかり行っています。
Ani wa izakaya ni bakari itte imasu.
My brother doesn't go anywhere but izakaya bars.

RESULTING STATE

Some actions can cause a certain resulting state. For example, a drinking action will cause the state of being drunk. To describe the current state that results from a past action, use the te-form + いる **iru**. For example, the following sentence can mean he is drunk:

お酒を飲んでいます。
O-sake o nonde imasu.

Verbs that express change-of-state actions such as 結婚する **kekkon suru** can only yield the resulting state interpretation when they are used in the te-form + いる **iru** construction. For example, the following sentence means *Mike is married*, or more literally, *he got married in the past, and as a result, he is married.*

マイクさんは結婚しています。
Maiku-san wa kekkon shite imasu.

Written Practice 4

Write the meaning of the following sentences. Pay attention to the context because the sentences with te-form + いる **iru** can mean progressive, habitual, or resulting state depending on the context.

1. 兄は毎朝テニスをしています。

   Ani wa maiasa tenisu o shite imasu. (毎朝 maiasa: *every morning*)

   _____

2. 猫は今どこにいますか。—今、ソファーの上でねています。

   Neko wa ima doko ni imasu ka. —Ima, sofā no ue de nete imasu.

3. 山田さんはいますか。—いいえ。山田さんは今、東京に行っています。

   Yamada-san wa imasu ka. — Īe. Yamada-san wa ima, Tōkyō ni itte imasu.

4. 兄は35歳です。銀行で働いています。

   Ani wa sanjūgo-sai desu. Ginkō de hataraite imasu.

5. 今、何をしていますか。—今、新聞を読んでいます。

   Ima, nani o shite imasu ka. —Ima, shinbun o yonde imasu.

6. 山田さんはまだ来ていません。

   Yamada-san wa mada kite imasen.

STATIVE VERBS IN ENGLISH

English verbs such as *to know* and *to live* express a state rather than an action. These states are often expressed by the te-form + いる **iru** construction in Japanese, as in the following examples:

田中さんを知っていますか。
Tanaka-san o shitte imasu ka.
Do you know Mr. Tanaka?

姉はパリに住んでいます。
Ane wa Pari ni sunde imasu.
My older sister lives in Paris.

この漢字を覚えていますか。
Kono kanji o oboete imasu ka.
Do you remember this kanji?

QUIZ

Circle the letter of the word or phrase that best completes each sentence.

1. 昨日は本を_____、映画を_____ 。

   Kinō wa hon o _____ , eiga o _____ .

   (a) 読みました yomimashita, 見ました mimashita

   (b) 読む yomu, 見ました mimashita

   (c) 読んで yonde, 見ました mimashita

   (d) 読んで yonde, 見て mite

2. あのレストランは_____、おいしかったです。

   Ano resutoran wa _____ , oishikatta desu.

   (a) 安くて yasukute   (c) 安いです yasui desu

   (b) 安いで yasui de   (d) 安かった yasukatta

3. すみません。名前を_____ください。

   Sumimasen. Namae o _____ kudasai.

   (a) 言う iu   (c) 言った itta

   (b) 言って itte   (d) 言います iimasu

4. この道_____まっすぐ行ってください。

   Kono michi _____ massugu itte kudasai.

   (a) に ni   (c) を o

   (b) で de   (d) の no

5. あの交差点を右_____曲がってください。

   Ano kōsaten o migi _____ magatte kudasai.

   (a) に ni   (c) を o

   (b) で de   (d) の no

6. 三つ目の交差点を左に曲がってください。_____、本屋があります。

   Mit-tsu-me no kōsaten o hidari ni magatte kudasai. _____ , hon'ya ga
   arimasu.

   (a) それに soreni   (c) そうすると sōsuruto

   (b) ですから desukara   (d) それから sorekara

7. 三つ目の交差点を左に曲がってください。_____、つきあたりまで歩いてください。

Mit-tsu-me no kōsaten o hidari ni magatte kudasai. _____ , tsukiatari made aruite kudasai.

(a) それに soreni　　(c) そうすると sōsuruto

(b) ですから desukara　　(d) それから sorekara

8. 母は今、料理を_____。

Haha wa ima ryōri o_____ .

(a) するいます suru imasu　　(c) しいます shi imasu

(b) したいます shita imasu　　(d) しています shite imasu

9. 弟は_____。

Otōto wa _____ .

(a) 遊ぶばかりいます asobu bakari imasu

(b) 遊んでいますばかり asonde imasu bakari

(c) ばかり遊んでいます bakari asonde imasu

(d) 遊んでばかりいます asonde bakari imasu

10. この漢字を_____。

Kono kanji o _____ .

(a) 知っていますか shitte imasu ka

(b) 知りますか shirimasu ka

(c) 知るですか shiru desu ka

(d) 知ってありますか shitte arimasu ka

CHAPTER 10

Asking for Permission

In this chapter you'll learn:

Permission and Prohibition
Obligation and Discretion
Permissibility and Minimal Requirements
Potential and Ability
Sports and Hobbies

Permission and Prohibition

In this section, you will learn how to express permission and prohibition in Japanese.

GIVING PERMISSION WITH てもいいです TE MO II DESU

Japanese doesn't have a convenient simple word like *may* in English. To give permission to someone to do something, use the verb in the te-form, the particle も **mo** (*also*), and the adjective いいです **ii desu** (*It is good*). For example:

食べてもいいです。
Tabete mo ii desu.
It is okay to eat./You may eat.

The permission sentences are often followed by the particle よ **yo**, which was discussed in Chapter 4. For example, the following sentence literally means *It is okay to eat*, but it sounds like a friendly reminder, offer, or encouragement in this context because よ **yo** conveys the speaker's enthusiasm.

食べてもいいですよ。
Tabete mo ii desu yo.
It is okay to eat! (Go ahead.)

Oral Practice

 TRACK 42

Practice asking for permission and answering it by reading the following sentences out loud.

うちに帰ってもいいですか。
Uchi ni kaette mo ii desu ka.
Can I go home?

ええ、いいですよ。
Ē, ii desu yo.
Sure.

ここでタバコをすってもいいですか。
Koko de tabako o sutte mo ii desu ka.
Is it okay to smoke here?

ちょっと、困ります。外でお願いします。
Chotto komarimasu. Soto de onegai shimasu.
It's not good. Please smoke outside.

この部屋を使ってもいいですか。
Kono heya o tsukatte mo ii desu ka.
Is it okay to use this room?

ええ、いいですよ。あの部屋も使ってもいいですよ。
Ē, ii desu yo. Ano heya mo tsukatte mo ii desu yo.
Sure. You can use that room also.

EXPRESSING PROHIBITION WITH てはいけません TE WA IKEMASEN

To express prohibition, take the sentence construction used for giving permission discussed above, and replace the particle も **mo** and いいです **ii desu** (*It is fine*), with the particle は **wa** and いけません **ikemasen** (*It is not good*), respectively. For example, compare the following two sentences: the first one expresses permission whereas the second one expresses prohibition.

食べてもいいです。
Tabete mo ii desu.
It is okay to eat. / You may eat. (permission)

食べてはいけません。
Tabete wa ikemasen.
It is not okay to eat. / You may not eat. (prohibition)

REJECTING INDIRECTLY

Unless one is talking about specific rules, instructions, and disciplines, the Japanese prefer not to give a direct negative reply or rejection to others. For rejecting other people's ideas, suggestions, or requests, it is often enough to say:

それはちょっと困ります。
Sore wa chotto komarimasu.
It is a bit problem.

or just say ちょっと **chotto** (*a little bit*) with a hesitant intonation.

Oral Practice

 TRACK 43

Practice asking for permission and answering it by reading the following sentences out loud.

ここに座ってもいいですか。
Koko ni suwatte mo ii desu ka.
Is it okay to sit here?

すみません。ここはちょっと。
Sumimasen. Koko wa chotto.
Sorry. It is a little bit . . .

この本を借りてもいいですか。
Kono hon o karite mo ii desu ka.
Is it okay to borrow this book?

ええ、いいですよ。
Ē, ii desu yo.
Yes, sure.

運動をしてもいいですか。
Undō o shite mo ii desu ka.
Is it okay to do exercise?

はい、軽い運動はしてもいいです。
Hai, karui undō wa shite mo ii desu.
Yes, light exercise is fine.

でも、テニスや、サッカーはしてはいけません。
Demo, tenisu ya, soccer wa shite wa ikemasen.
But you may not play tennis, soccer, etc.

THE CONJUNCTION ですから DESUKARA

You can start a sentence with the conjunction ですから **desukara**, if it expresses the conclusion from the previous statement. A slightly informal counterpart of ですから **desukara** is だから **dakara**. For example:

これはテストです。ですから、辞書を使ってはいけません。
Kore wa tesuto desu. Desukara, jisho o tsukatte wa ikemasen.
This is a test. So, you may not use a dictionary.

これはテストじゃありません。ですから、辞書を使ってもいいですよ。
Kore wa tesuto ja arimasen. Desukara, jisho o tsukatte mo iidesu yo.
This is not a test. So, you may use the dictionary.

今日は宿題がたくさんあります。だから、テレビは見ません。
Kyō wa shukudai ga takusan arimasu. Dakara, terebi wa mimasen.
I have a lot of homework today. So, I will not watch TV.

Written Practice 1

Translate the following English sentences to Japanese.

1. You must not play tennis. _____

2. You may go home. _____

3. This is a test. So, you cannot use the dictionary. _____

_____

4. May I sit here? _____

5. May I borrow this book? _____

Obligation and Discretion

In this section, you will learn how to express obligations and discretions in Japanese.

EXPRESSING OBLIGATION WITH なくてはいけません NAKUTE WA IKEMASEN

Obligation can be expressed by converting a prohibition sentence. Just make the verb in the te-form negative, creating the negative te-form that ends in なくて

nakute. (See Chapter 9 for the formation of the negative te-form.) Compare the following sentences, where the first one expresses prohibition while the second one expresses obligation:

食べてはいけません。
Tabete wa ikemasen.
It is not okay if you eat./ You must not eat.

食べなくてはいけません。
Tabenakute wa ikemasen.
It is not okay if you don't eat./ You must eat.

If you can think that prohibition and obligation are both something unfavorable, then the fact that both end in いけません ikemasen (*It is not okay*) becomes intuitively clear to you. Note that なくてはいけません **nakute wa ikemasen** can also be replaced by なければいけません **nakereba ikemasen** or なければなりません **nakereba narimasen**, which gives the impression that the obligation is something inevitable rather than something imposed by the speaker. For example, the above sentence can also be:

食べなければいけません。
Tabenakere ba ikemasen.

食べなければなりません。
Tabenakere ba narimasen.

EXPRESSING DISCRETION WITH なくてもいいです NAKUTE MO IIDESU

When something is not obligatory, it is optional or under discretion. Discretion is expressed by converting a permission sentence. Compare the following sentences, where the first one expresses permission while the second one expresses discretion:

食べてもいいです。
Tabete mo ii desu.
You may eat.

食べなくてもいいです。
Tabenakute mo ii desu.
You don't have to eat.

ANSWERING A NEGATIVE QUESTION WITH はい HAI AND いいえ ĪE

As mentioned in Chapter 3, はい **hai** shows agreement and いいえ **ie** shows dis-agreement. When the question is affirmative, はい **hai** and いいえ **ie** correspond to *Yes* and *No* in English, but when the question is negative, *Yes* and *No* switch. For example, the sentences that express prohibition and obligation end in いけません **ikemasen**, which is in the negative form. Thus, you must be careful when answer-ing the question with a prohibition or obligation sentence. Don't be misled by English translations. Use はい **hai** and いいえ **ie** to express "agreement" and "dis-agreement". For example:

パーティーに行ってはいけませんか。
Pātī ni itte wa ikemasen ka.
Is it not okay to go to the party?

はい、行ってはいけません。
Hai, itte wa ikemasen.
Right, it is not okay to go there. (No, you cannot go.)

クラスに行かなくてはいけませんか。
Kurasu ni ikanakute wa ikemasen ka.
Is it not okay not to go to the class?

はい、行かなくてはいけません。
Hai, ikanakute wa ikemasen.
Right, it is not okay not to go there. (No, it is not okay not to go there.)

テレビを見てはいけませんか。
Terebi o mite wa ikemasen ka.
Is it not okay to watch TV?

いいえ、見てもいいですよ。
Īe, mite mo ii desu yo.
It is fine to watch it. (Yes, it is fine to watch it.)

この漢字は覚えなくてはいけませんか。
Kono kanji wa oboenakute wa ikemasen ka.
Is it not okay not to memorize this kanji?

いいえ、覚えなくてもいいですよ。
Īe, oboenakute mo ii desu yo.
It is fine not to memorize it. (Yes, it is fine not to memorize it.)

Written Practice 2

Translate the following English sentences to Japanese.

1. You may not watch TV. _____
2. You must memorize kanji. _____
3. You are not allowed to drink beer. _____
4. I have to work from 9 to 5. _____
5. Do I have to go to Ms. Yamada's house? _____

Acceptability and Minimal Requirements

The construction used for expressing permission, prohibition, obligation and discretion discussed in the above sections in this chapter can be applied to nouns and adjectives to express acceptable, nonacceptable, required, or nonrequired properties and situations.

EXPRESSING WHAT IS ACCEPTABLE WITH でもいいです DE MO II DESU AND ではいけません DE WA IKEMASEN

Using adjectives and the copular verb in the te-form, you can express what is acceptable and what is not acceptable. The following are examples:

中古車でもいいです。
Chūkosha de mo ii desu.
A used car is acceptable.

中古車ではいけません。
Chūkosha de wa ikemasen.
A used car is not okay.

高くてもいいです。
Takakute mo ii desu.
It's all right if it's expensive.

高くてはいけません。
Takakute wa ikemasen.
If it is expensive, it is not okay.

不便でもいいです。
Fuben de mo ii desu.
It's okay to be inconvenient.

不便ではいけません。
Fuben de wa ikemasen.
It's not okay if it's inconvenient.

EXPRESSING WHAT IS REQUIRED WITH なくてはいけません NAKUTE WA IKEMASEN/なくてもいいです NAKUTE MO II DESU

Using adjectives and the copular verb in the negative te-form (see Chapter 9), you can also express what is a required condition and what is not. The following are examples:

新車じゃなくてはいけません。
Shinsha ja nakute wa ikemasen.
It has to be a brand new car.

新車じゃなくてもいいです。
Shinsha ja nakute mo ii desu.
It is okay even if it is not a brand new car.

安くなくてはいけません。
Yasuku nakute wa ikemasen.
It has to be cheap.

安くなくてもいいです。
Yasuku nakute mo ii desu.
It doesn't have to be cheap.

静かじゃなくてはいけません。
Shizuka ja nakute wa ikemasen.
It has to be quiet.

静かじゃなくてもいいです。
Shizuka ja nakute mo ii desu.
It doesn't have to be quiet.

Written Practice 3

Pretend that you must look for an apartment. What kind of apartment is good for you? Answer the following questions in Japanese.

1. ちょっとせまくてもいいですか。 Chotto semakute mo ii desu ka.
   Is it okay if it is a little small? _____

2. 家賃は高くてもいいですか。 Yachin wa takakute mo ii desu ka.
   Is it okay if the rent is high? _____

3. 静かじゃなくてもいいですか。 Shizuka ja nakute mo ii desu ka.
   Is it okay if it is not quiet? _____

4. ルームメートがいてもいいですか。 Rūmumēto ga ite mo ii desu ka.
   Is it okay if you get a roommate? _____

Potential and Ability

You can express one's ability and potential using the verbs in the potential form, or using the verb できる **dekiru** (*can do*).

THE POTENTIAL FORMS OF VERBS

The potential form of a ru-verb is created by dropping the final syllable **ru** from the dictionary form and adding **rareru**. (Note that more and more Japanese add **reru** instead of **rareru** nowadays.) The potential form of a u-verb is created by dropping the final **u** from the dictionary form and adding **eru**. The potential form of the verb くる **kuru** (come) is こられる **korareru** (can come). The potential form of the verb する **suru** (do) is substituted by the verb できる **dekiru** (can do).

The following table lists the potential form of some ru-verbs and u-verbs as well as irregular verbs:

Dictionary Form	Potential Form
ru-verbs	
食べる taberu (*eat*)	食べられる taberareru (*can eat*)
見る miru (*watch*)	見られる mirareru (*can watch*)

u-verbs

帰る kaeru (*return*)   帰れる kaereru (*can return*)
書く kaku (*write*)   書ける kakeru (*can write*)
泳ぐ oyogu (*swim*)   泳げる oyogeru (*can swim*)
買う kau (*buy*)   買える kaeru (*can buy*)
待つ matsu (*wait*)   待てる materu (*can wait*)
話す hanasu (*speak*)   話せる hanaseru (*can speak*)
飲む nomu (*drink*)   飲める nomeru (*can drink*)
死ぬ shinu (*die*)   死ねる shineru (*can die*)
飛ぶ tobu (*fly*)   飛べる toberu (*can fly*)

Irregular Verbs

来る kuru (*come*)   来られる korareru (*can come*)
する suru (*do*)   できる dekiru (*can do*)

These potential verbs can be conjugated as a ru-verb.

The direct object particle を **o** is usually replaced by the particle が **ga** when the verb is in the potential form. For example:

私はカタカナで名前が書けます。
Watashi wa katakana de namae ga kakemasu.
I can write my name in katakana.

If the verb is できる **dekiru** (*can do*), を **o** must be replaced by が **ga**.

Oral Practice

 **TRACK 44**

Practice asking and answering questions about what one can do by reading the following sentences out loud.

スミスさんはカタカナで名前が書けますか。
Sumisu-san wa katakana de namae ga kakemasu ka.
Can you write your name in katakana, Mr. Smith?

はい、書けます。いつもカタカナで名前を書いています。
Hai, kakemasu. Itsumo katakana de namae o kaite imasu.
Yes, I can. I always write my name in katakana.

弟さんは自転車に乗れますか。
Otōtosan wa jitensha ni noremasu ka.
Can your little brother ride a bicycle?

いいえ、まだ乗れません。
Īe, mada noremasen.
No, not yet.

明日のパーティーには行きますか。
Ashita no pātī ni wa ikimasu ka.
Will you attend tomorrow's party?

明日は仕事があります。ですから、行けません。
Ashita wa shigoto ga arimasu. Desukara, ikemasen.
I have to work tomorrow. So, I can't go.

武さんは料理ができますか。
Takeshi-san wa ryōri ga dekimasu ka.
Can you cook, Takeshi?

いいえ、できません。
Īe, dekimasen.
No, I can't.

Written Practice 4

Following the example, convert the sentences by conjugating the verbs into their potential forms.

本を読みます。 Hon o yomimasu. *(I) read a book.*

本が読めます。 Hon ga yomemasu. _____

1. はしで食べます。 Hashi de tabemasu. *(I) eat with chopsticks.*

   _____

2. 自転車に乗ります。 Jitensha ni norimasu. *(I) ride a bicycle.*

   _____

3. テニスをします。 Tenisu o shimasu. *(I) play tennis.*

   _____

4. 漢字を書きます。 Kanji o kakimasu. *(I) write kanji.*

5. 日本語を話します。 Nihon-go o hanashimasu. *(I) speak Japanese.*

EXPRESSING POTENTIAL WITH ことができる KOTO GA DEKIRU

One's potential can be expressed using the construction ことができる **koto ga dekiru** *(can do . . .)* instead of using the potential forms discussed above. こと **koto** in this construction is a nominalizer (Chapter 8). For example, if you want to say that you can write your name in katakana, create a phrase in the plain form, カタカナで名前を書く **katakana de namae o kaku**, and just add ことができる **koto ga dekiru**.

カタカナで名前を書くことができます。
Katakana de namae o kaku koto ga dekimasu.
I can write my name in katakana.

Note that こと **koto** cannot be replaced by the nominalizer の **no** in this construction.

Written Practice 5

Convert the sentences by following the example.

私は本を読みます。
Watashi wa hon o yomimasu.
I read a book.

私は本を読むことができます。Watashi wa hon o yomu koto ga dekimasu.

1. ジョアナさんは折り紙でバラを作ります。

   Joana-san wa origami de bara o tsukurimasu.
   Joanna makes a (paper) rose with origami.

2. スコットさんは日本のうたをうたいます。

   Sukotto-san wa Nihon no uta o utaimasu.
   Scott sings a Japanese song.

   _____

3. トムさんは大きいトラックを運転します。

   Tomu-san wa ōkii torakku o unten-shimasu.
   Tom drives a large truck.

   _____

4. マリアさんは一人で着物を着ます。

   Maria-san wa hitori de kimono o kimasu.
   Maria puts on kimono by herself.

   _____

VERBS WITH INHERENT POTENTIAL MEANINGS

The verbs 聞こえる **kikoeru**, 見える **mieru**, and わかる **wakaru** already have potential meanings and cannot be conjugated into the potential form discussed above. Their expected direct objects are marked by the particle が **ga** rather than the particle を **o**. For example:

今日は天気がいいですね。富士山が見えますね。
Kyō wa tenki ga ii desu ne. Fujisan ga miemasu ne.
Today, the sky is clear, isn't it? We can see Mt. Fuji, right?

この電話は変です。ぜんぜん聞こえません。
Kono denwa wa hen desu. Zenzen kikoemasen.
This phone is strange. I cannot hear at all.

ニコラスさんは日本語が少し分かりますか。
Nikorasu-san wa Nihon-go ga sukoshi wakarimasu ka.
Nicolas, can you understand Japanese a little?

Sports and Hobbies

In this section, you will learn some vocabulary words that denote sports and hobbies.

SPORTS

The following words represent Japanese martial arts.

相撲	sumō	*sumo wrestling*
空手	karate	*karate*
剣道	kendō	*kendo*
柔道	jūdō	*judo*
合気道	aikidō	*aikido*

The following are popular sports in Japanese.

サッカー	sakkā	*soccer*
野球	yakyū	*baseball*
ゴルフ	gorufu	*golf*
テニス	tenisu	*tennis*
バスケットボール	basuketto-bōru	*basketball*
バレーボール	barē-bōru	*volleyball*
スキー	sukī	*skiing*
スケート	sukēto	*skating*
水泳	suiei	*swimming*

To say you play these sports, use the verb する **suru** (*to do*). For example:

兄はゴルフをします。
Ani wa gorufu o shimasu.
My older brother plays golf.

HOBBIES

The following phrases show a variety of popular pastime activities.

絵を描く	e o kaku	*to draw, to paint*
つりをする	tsuri o suru	*to fish*
料理をする	ryōri o suru	*to cook*
写真を撮る	shashin o toru	*to take pictures*
生け花をする	ikebana o suru	*to do flower arranging*
ゲームをする	gēmu o suru	*to play games*
アニメを見る	anime o miru	*to watch anime*
マンガを読む	manga o yomu	*to read comic books*

QUIZ

Circle the letter of the word or phrase that best completes each sentence.

1. うちに ＿＿＿＿＿ いいですか。

   Uchi ni ＿＿＿＿＿ ii desu ka.

   (a) 帰っては kaette wa   (c) 帰りも kaeri mo

   (b) 帰っても kaette mo   (d) 帰るも kaeru mo

2. ここに座っては ＿＿＿＿＿ 。

   Koko ni suwatte wa ＿＿＿＿＿ .

   (a) いいです ii desu   (c) いいですか ii desu ka

   (b) いけません ikemasen   (d) いきます ikimasu

3. クラスに ＿＿＿＿＿ いけませんか。

   Kurasu ni ＿＿＿＿＿ ikemasen ka.

   (a) 行かなくても ikanakute mo

   (b) 行かないでは ikanai de wa

   (c) 行っても itte mo

   (d) 行かなくては ikanakute wa

4. クラスに＿＿＿＿いいです。

Kurasu ni ＿＿＿＿ ii desu.

(a) 行かなくても ikanakute mo

(b) 行かないでは ikanai de wa

(c) 行っては itte wa

(d) 行かなくては ikanakute wa

5. 今日は宿題がたくさんあります。＿＿＿＿, テレビは見ません。

Kyō wa shukudai ga takusan arimasu. ＿＿＿＿, terebi wa mimasen.

(a) でも demo   (c) ですから desukara

(b) それから sorekara   (d) そうすると sōsuruto

6. 不便＿＿＿＿いいですか。

Fuben＿＿＿＿ii desu ka.

(a) では de wa   (c) じゃないも ja nai mo

(b) でも de mo   (d) じゃなくては ja nakute wa

7. ＿＿＿＿いいです。

＿＿＿＿ ii desu.

(a) 静かじゃなくても shizuka ja nakute mo

(b) 静かじゃないでも shizuka ja nai de mo

(c) 高くては takakute wa

(d) 高くなくては takakunakute wa

8. 漢字が＿＿＿＿。

Kanji ga ＿＿＿＿ .

(a) 読みます yomimasu   (c) 読めません yomemasen

(b) 読んでいます yonde imasu (d) 読む yomu

9. 一人で着物を＿＿＿＿できます。

Hitori de kimono o ＿＿＿＿ dekimasu.

(a) 着るが kiru ga   (c) 着るのが kiru no ga

(b) 着てが kite ga   (d) 着ることが kiru koto ga

10. ＿＿＿＿が好きです。毎日泳ぎます。

＿＿＿＿ ga suki desu. Mainichi oyogimasu.

(a) サッカー sakkā   (c) 水泳 suiei

(b) 野球 yakyū   (d) 相撲 sumō

PART TWO TEST

Circle the letter of the word or phrase that corresponds to the English or that best completes each sentence.

1. 昨日は病院に＿＿＿＿。明日は銀行に＿＿＿＿。

   Kinō wa byōin ni ＿＿＿＿ . Ashita wa ginkō ni ＿＿＿＿ .

   (a) 来ました kimashita, 行きました ikimashita

   (b) 来ます kimasu, 行きます ikimasu

   (c) 行きます ikimasu, 行きました ikimashita

   (d) 行きました ikimashita, 行きます ikimasu

2. さしみはよく＿＿＿＿。でも、すしはあまり＿＿＿＿。

   Sashimi wa yoku ＿＿＿＿ . Demo, sushi wa amari ＿＿＿＿ .

   (a) 食べます tabemasu, 食べます tabemasu

   (b) 食べません tabemasen, 食べません tabemasen

   (c) 食べます tabemasu, 食べません tabemasen

   (d) 食べません tabemasen, 食べます tabemasu

3. 明日は ＿＿＿＿ へ行きますか。

   Ashita wa ＿＿＿＿ e ikimasu ka.

   (a) だれ dare   (c) どこ doko

   (b) いくら ikura   (d) いつ itsu

4. 私＿＿＿＿車＿＿＿＿京都＿＿＿＿行きませんか。

   Watashi ＿＿＿＿ kuruma ＿＿＿＿ Kyōto ＿＿＿＿ ikimasen ka.

   (a) を o, で de, に ni   (c) と to, に ni, で de

   (b) と to, で de, に ni   (d) と to, が ga, で de

5. A: この着物は＿＿＿＿ですか。B: 35,900 ＿＿＿＿です。

   A: Kono kimono wa ＿＿＿＿ desu ka. B: Sanman-gosen-kyūhyaku ＿＿＿＿ desu.

   (a) いくら ikura, 円 en   (c) だれ dare, 枚 mai

   (b) どこ doko, 本 hon   (d) いくら ikura, 匹 hiki

6. 兄＿＿＿＿車 ＿＿＿＿買います。

   Ani ＿＿＿＿ kuruma ＿＿＿＿ kaimasu.

   (a) が ga, が ga   (c) を o, が ga

   (b) が ga, を o   (d) を o, を o

7. カフェテリア_____新聞_____読みます。

Kafeteria _____ shinbun _____ yomimasu.

(a) に ni, を o   (c) で de, が ga

(b) が ga, を o   (d) で de, を o

8. レストランに行きます。それから、_____。

Resutoran ni ikimasu. Sorekara, _____ .

(a) よう子さんは学生です Yōko-san wa gakusei desu

(b) 映画を見ます Eiga o mimasu

(c) 妹が3人います Imōto ga san-nin imasu

(d) 犬はあそこにいます Inu wa asoko ni imasu

9. 母には時計を_____。社長にはワインを_____。

Haha ni wa tokei o _____ . Shachō ni wa wain o _____ .

(a) くれます kuremasu, あげます agemasu

(b) 下さいます kudasaimasu, 差し上げますsashiagemasu

(c) くれます kuremasu, 下さいます kudasaimasu

(d) あげます agemasu, 差し上げますsashiagemasu

10. _____交差点まで歩きます。

_____ kōsaten made arukimasu.

(a) 2つ目の Futa-tsu me no

(b) 2つずつ Futa-tsu zutsu

(c) 2つ Futa-tsu

(d) 2つの Futa-tsu no

11. 今日は_____。昨日も_____。

Kyō wa _____ . Kinō mo _____ .

(a) 暑いです atsui desu, 暑かったです atsukatta desu

(b) 暑いです atsui desu, 涼しかったです suzushikatta desu

(c) 暑かったです atsukatta desu, 涼しかったです suzushikatta desu

(d) 暑かったです atsukatta desu, 暑いです atsui desu

12. A: 昨日は＿＿＿＿行きましたか。B: いいえ、＿＿＿＿行きませんでした。

    A: Kinō wa ＿＿＿＿ ikimashita ka. B: Īe, ＿＿＿＿ ikimasendeshita.

    (a) どこか dokoka, どこに doko ni

    (b) どこにか doko ni ka, どこにも doko ni mo

    (c) どこかに dokoka ni, どこもに doko mo ni

    (d) どこかに dokoka ni, どこにも doko ni mo

13. うなぎを＿＿＿＿ありますか。

    Unagi o ＿＿＿＿ arimasu ka.

    (a) 食べるが taberu ga

    (b) 食べたことが tabeta koto ga

    (c) 食べたが tabeta ga

    (d) 食べるのが taberu no ga

14. 私は車＿＿＿＿好きです。新しい車＿＿＿＿ほしいです。

    Watashi wa kuruma ＿＿＿＿ suki desu.

    Atarashii kuruma ＿＿＿＿ hoshii desu.

    (a) が ga, が ga　　　　　　(c) を o, が ga

    (b) が ga, を o　　　　　　(d) を o, を o

15. 洋服を＿＿＿＿が好きです。ブラウスやスカートを＿＿＿＿たいです。

    Yōfuku o ＿＿＿＿ ga suki desu. Burausu ya sukāto o ＿＿＿＿ tai desu.

    (a) 買うの kau no, 買う kau　　(c) 買う kau, 買う kau

    (b) 買うの kau no, 買い kai　　(d) 買う kau, 買い kai

16. 昨日は宿題を＿＿＿＿、テレビを見ました。

    Kinō wa shukudai o ＿＿＿＿ , terebi o mimashita.

    (a) します shimasu　　　　　(c) して shite

    (b) する suru　　　　　　　(d) した shita

17. 山田さんは＿＿＿＿、＿＿＿＿、頭がいいです。

    Yamada-san wa ＿＿＿＿ , ＿＿＿＿ , atama ga ii desu.

    (a) きれいて kireite, やさして yasashite

    (b) きれいて kireite, やさしくて yasashikute

    (c) きれいで kirei de, やさしいて yasashiite

    (d) きれいで kirei de, やさしくて yasashikute

18. 漢字で＿＿＿＿＿くださいい。カタカナで＿＿＿＿＿＿くださいい。

Kanji de ＿＿＿＿＿ kudasai. Katakana de ＿＿＿＿＿＿ kudasai.

(a) 書かなくて kakanakute, 書き kaki

(b) 書かなくて kakanakute, 書いて kaite

(c) 書かないで kakanai de, 書き kaki

(d) 書かないで kakanai de, 書いて kaite

19. あの交差点＿＿＿＿＿右＿＿＿＿＿曲がってください。＿＿＿＿＿、左に銀行があります。

Ano kōsaten ＿＿＿＿＿ migi ＿＿＿＿＿ magatte kudasai. ＿＿＿＿＿, hidari ni ginkō ga arimasu.

(a) を o, に ni, それから sorekara

(b) を o, に ni, そうすると sōsuruto

(c) に ni, を o, それから sorekara

(d) に ni, を o, そうすると sōsuruto

20. A: 山田さんは＿＿＿＿＿か。B: いいえ、山田さんは東京に＿＿＿＿＿＿。

A: Yamada-san wa ＿＿＿＿＿ ka. B: Īe, Yamada-san wa Tōkyō ni ＿＿＿＿＿ .

(a) 来ています kite imasu, 行きます ikimasu

(b) 来ています kite imasu, 行っています itte imasu

(c) 来ます kimasu, 行っていました itte imashita,

(d) 来ます kimasu, 行きませんでした ikimasendeshita

21. A: ビールを＿＿＿＿＿いいですか。B: いいえ、＿＿＿＿＿いけません。

A: Bīru o ＿＿＿＿＿ ii desu ka. B: Īe, ＿＿＿＿＿ ikemasen.

(a) 飲んでは nonde wa, 飲んでは nonde wa

(b) 飲んでも nonde mo, 飲んでも nonde mo

(c) 飲んでは nonde wa, 飲んでも nonde mo

(d) 飲んでも nonde mo, 飲んでは nonde wa

22. A: 車を＿＿＿＿＿いけませんか。B: いいえ、＿＿＿＿＿いいです。

A: Kuruma o ＿＿＿＿＿ ikemasen ka. B: Īe, ＿＿＿＿＿ ii desu.

(a) 買わなくては kawanakute wa, 買わなくても kawanakute mo

(b) 買わなくては kawanakute wa, 買わなくては kawanakute wa

(c) 買わなくても kawanakute mo, 買わなくても kawanakute mo

(d) 買わなくても kawanakute mo, 買わなくては kawanakute wa

23. 家賃は_____いいです。でも、静か_____いけません。

Yachin wa _____ ii desu. Demo, shizuka _____ ikemasen.

(a) 高くても takakute mo, でも de mo

(b) 高くても takakute mo, じゃなくては ja nakute wa

(c) 高くては takakute wa, じゃなくては ja nakute wa

(d) 高くては takakute wa, では de wa

24. スミスさんは漢字が_____。_____、日本語の本が読めません。

Sumisu-san wa kanji ga _____ . _____ , Nihon-go no hon ga yomemasen.

(a) 読めません yomemasen, ですから desukara

(b) 読めます yomemasu, ですから desukara

(c) 読みません yomimasen, ですから desukara

(d) 読めません yomemasen, でも demo

25. マイクさんは日本語_____分かりません。ですから、田中さんと話す_____できません。

Maiku-san wa Nihon-go _____ wakarimasen. Desukara, Tanaka-san to hanasu _____ dekimasen.

(a) を o, ことが koto ga   (c) が ga, のが no ga

(b) が ga, ことが koto ga   (d) を o, のが no ga

PART THREE

STATING FACTS

CHAPTER 11

Stating Your Opinions

In this chapter you'll learn:

The Plain Forms of Verbs and Adjectives
Embedded Sentences
Embedded Questions
Expressing Or
Some Useful Modals
Asking Why?

The Plain Forms of Verbs and Adjectives

As discussed in Chapter 6, the plain form is not just the form used for an informal conversation but also the form required in certain grammatical constructions such as an embedded sentence regardless of the formality of the conversational context. The following table summarizes the plain forms of verbs and adjectives.

The Plain Forms		Present	Past
Verb	Affirmative	食べる taberu	食べた tabeta
	Negative	食べない tabenai	食べなかった tabenakatta
(Noun +) Copula	Affirmative	学生だ gakusei da	学生だった gakusei datta
	Negative	学生じゃない gakusei ja nai	学生じゃなかった gakusei ja nakatta
Na-type Adjective	Affirmative	便利だ benri da	便利だった benri datta
	Negative	便利じゃない benri ja nai	便利じゃなかった benri ja nakatta
I-type Adjective	Affirmative	高い takai	高かった takakatta
	Negative	高くない takaku nai	高くなかった takaku nakatta

じゃ **ja** that appears in the negative forms of copular verb and na-type adjectives in the above table can be では **dewa**.

Take a look at the verb forms, first. The plain present forms, for example, 食べる **taberu** and 食べない **tabenai**, are discussed in Chapter 7, and the plain past affirmative forms, for example, 食べた **tabeta**, are discussed in Chapter 8. The plain past negative forms can be created just by replacing ない **nai** in the plain present negative form with なかった **nakatta**, as in 食べなかった **tabenakatta**.

Oral Practice

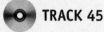 **TRACK 45**

Practice converting verbs from the polite form into the plain form.

食べます tabemasu (*will eat*)	→	食べる taberu
飲みます nomimasu (*will drink*)	→	飲む nomu

行きました ikimashita (*went*)   →   行った itta

来ました kimashita (*came*)   →   来た kita

買いません kaimasen (*will not buy*)   →   買わない kawanai

読みません yomimasen (*will not read*) →   読まない yomanai

書きませんでした kakimasendeshita   →   書かなかった
(*didn't write*)   kakanakatta

見ませんでした mimasendeshita   →   見なかった minakatta
(*didn't see*)

Next, take a look at the copular verb and na-type adjective in the table. They actually pattern similarly. The plain counterpart of です **desu** and でした **deshita** are だ **da** and だった **datta**, respectively. The plain negative forms are created by replacing ありません **arimasen** and ありませんでした **arimasendeshita** in the polite negative forms with ない **nai** and なかった **nakatta**, respectively.

Oral Practice

 TRACK 46

Practice converting the copular verb and na-type adjectives in the polite form into their plain form.

学生です gakusei desu (*is student*)   →   学生だ gakusei da

便利です benri desu (*is convenient*)   →   便利だ benri da

静かでした shizuka deshita (*was*   →   静かだった shizuka datta
quiet*)

アメリカ人じゃありません Amerika-   →   アメリカ人じゃない Amerika-jin
jin ja arimasen (*is not an American*)   ja nai

上手じゃありません jōzu ja arimasen   →   上手じゃない jōzu ja nai
(*is not good at . . .*)

好きじゃありませんでした suki ja   →   好きじゃなかった suki ja nakatta
arimasendeshita (*didn't like . . .*)

きれいじゃありませんでした kirei ja   →   きれいじゃなかった kirei ja
arimasendeshita (*was not pretty*)   nakatta

辞書じゃありませんでした jisho ja   →   辞書じゃなかった jisho ja nakatta
arimasendeshita (*was not a
dictionary*)

Finally, take a look at i-type adjectives in the above table. Their plain affirmative forms can be created just by dropping です **desu** found in their polite affirmative forms. Plain negative forms can be created just by replacing ありません **arimasen** and ありませんでした **arimasendeshita** in the polite negative forms with ない **nai** and なかった **nakatta**, respectively.

Oral Practice

 TRACK 47

Practice converting the i-type adjectives in the polite form into their plain form.

高いです takai desu (*is expensive*)   →   高い takai

大きいです ōkii desu (*is big*)   →   大きい ōkii

安かったです yasukatta desu
(*was cheap*)   →   安かった yasukatta

よかったです yokatta desu
(*was good*)   →   よかった yokatta

難しくありません muzukashiku
arimasen (*is not difficult*)   →   難しくない muzukashikunai

おいしくありません oishiku
arimasen (*is not delicious*)   →   おいしくない oishiku nai

高くありませんでした takaku
arimasendeshita (*was not
expensive*)   →   高くなかった takaku nakatta

おもしろくありませんでした
omoshiroku arimasendeshita
(*was not fun*)   →   おもしろくなかった omoshiroku
nakatta

Embedded Sentences

Different verbs require different kinds of items to complete their meanings. For example, the verb *to eat* will require a noun that expresses what is eaten, for example, *pizza*, and the verb *to go* needs a preposition and a noun that show the destination, for example, *to Boston*. What kind of item does the verb *to think* require? It needs a sentence that shows the content of what one thinks, for example, *I think that Santa Claus will come*. The sentence *that Santa Claus will come* is contained in another sentence, so it is called an embedded sentence.

INDICATING AN EMBEDDED SENTENCE AND A QUOTATION WITH THE PARTICLE と TO

In Japanese, the verb 思う **omou** (*to think*) takes an embedded sentence, which must be in the plain form and is marked by the particle と **to**.

私はサンタクロースは来ると思います。
Watashi wa Santa Kurōsu wa kuru to omoimasu.
I think that Santa Claus will come.

Note that if the thinker is the third person, 思う **omou** must be in a progressive form, 思っています **omotte imasu** (*to be thinking*). For example:

弟はサンタクロースは来ると思っています。
Otōto wa Santa Kurōsu wa kuru to omotte imasu.
My little brother thinks that Santa Claus will come.

Just like 思う **omou**, the verb 言う **iu** (*to say*) also takes an embedded sentence. The following sentence takes the form of an indirect quotation:

山田さんは英語は難しいと言いました。
Yamada-san wa eigo wa muzukashii to iimashita.
Ms. Yamada said that English is hard.

If you prefer a direct quotation, you can use a pair of quotation marks, 「 and 」, but you still need to use the particle と **to**:

山田さんは「英語は難しいですよ。」と言いました。
Yamada-san wa "Eigo wa muzukashī desu yo." to iimashita.
Ms. Yamada said, "English is hard."

Oral Practice

 TRACK 48

Practice exchanging opinions by reading the following sentences out loud.

あなたは学歴は大切だと思いますか。
Anata wa gakureki wa taisetsu da to omoimasu ka.
Do you think an academic background is important?

はい、私は学歴は大切だと思います。
Hai, watashi wa gakureki wa taisetsu da to omoimasu.
Yes, I think an academic background is important.

いいえ、私は学歴は大切じゃないと思います。
Īe, watashi wa gakureki wa taisetsu ja nai to omoimasu.
No, I think an academic background isn't important.

いいえ、私は学歴は大切だと思いません。
Īe, waatashi wa gakureki wa taisetsu da to omoimasen.
No, I do not think an academic background is important.

弟も学歴は大切じゃないと思っています。
Otōto mo gakureki wa taisetsu ja nai to omotte imasu.
My brother also thinks that an academic background is not important.

田中先生の日本語のクラスはどう思いますか。
Tanaka sensei no Nihon-go no kurasu wa dō omoimasu ka.
What do you think about Prof. Tanaka's Japanese class?

とてもいいと思います。
Totemo ii to omoimasu.
I think it is very good.

良子さんは独身ですか。
Yoshiko-san wa dokushin desu ka.
Is Yoshiko single?

結婚していると思います。
Kekkon shite iru to omoimasu.
I think she is married.

Written Practice 1

Rephrase the following sentences using 思います.

明日は雨が降ります。
Ashita wa ame ga furimasu.
It will rain tomorrow.

明日は雨が降ると思います。Ashita wa ame ga furu to omoimasu.

1. 田中さんは社長になります。

   Tanaka-san wa shachō ni narimasu.
   Mr. Tanaka will become a company president.

2. マイクさんはやさしいです。

   Maiku-san wa yasashii desu.
   Mike is kind.

3. 日本の映画はおもしろいです。

   Nihon no eiga wa omoshiroi desu.
   Japanese films are interesting.

4. 漢字は難しくありません。

   Kanji wa muzukashiku arimasen.
   Kanji is not difficult.

5. トムさんは毎日イタリア語を勉強しています。

   Tomu-san wa mainichi Itaria-go o benkyō shite imasu.
   Tom is studying Italian every day.

Embedded Questions

Some verbs such as *to know* require an embedded question, for example, *I know whether he will come, I know if he will come,* or *I don't know what to do.*

MARKING AN EMBEDDED QUESTION WITH THE PARTICLE か KA

A Japanese verb such as 知る **shiru** (*to know*) needs an embedded question. Embedded questions in Japanese are marked by the particle か **ka**. For example:

父は私が何を勉強しているか知りません。
Chichi wa watashi ga nani o benkyō shite iru ka shirimasen.
My father doesn't know what I am studying.

卒業できるか分かりません。
Sotsugyō dekiru ka wakarimasen.
I don't know whether I can graduate.

The predicate in the embedded question is in the plain form in general, but だ that appears in the plain present affirmative form of a copula or a na-type adjective is usually deleted in this context, as in the following sentences:

スミスさんの専攻は何か知っていますか。
Sumisu-san no senkō wa nani ka shitte imasu ka.
Do you know what Mr. Smith's major is?

あの人は本当に弁護士か調べてください。
Ano hito wa hontō ni bengoshi ka shirabete kudasai.
Please check whether he is really a lawyer.

田中さんは本当にまじめか分かりません。
Tanaka-san wa hontō ni majime ka wakarimasen.
I don't know whether Mr. Tanaka is truly serious.

MARKING AN EMBEDDED QUESTION WITH かどうか KA DŌKA

When an embedded question is a Yes-No question and doesn't contain a question word such as だれ **dare** (*who*) and 何 **nani** (*what*), かどうか **ka dō ka** can be used instead of か **ka** at the end of the embedded question. So, both of the following sentences are grammatical:

トムさんは来るか分かりません。
Tomu-san wa kuru ka wakarimasen.
I don't know whether Tom will come.

トムさんは来るかどうか分かりません。
Tomu-san wa kuru ka dō ka wakarimasen.
I don't know whether Tom will come.

Oral Practice

 TRACK 49

Practice saying the sentences with an embedded question by reading the following
sentences out loud.

何をするか決めましょう。
Nani o suru ka kimemashō.
Let's decide on what to do.

だれが来るか教えてください。
Dare ga kuru ka oshiete kudasai.
Please let me know who will come.

昨日、何を食べたか言ってください。
Kinō, nani o tabeta ka itte kudasai.
Please tell me what you ate yesterday.

銀行はどこにあるか知っていますか。
Ginkō wa doko ni aru ka shitte imasu ka.
Do you know where the bank is?

それは何か分かりますか。
Sore wa nani ka wakarimasu ka.
Do you know what it is?

中古車でもいいか教えてください。
Chūkosha de mo ii ka oshiete kudasai.
Please let me know whether a used car is acceptable.

あそこは静かかどうか分かりません。
Asoko wa shizuka ka dō ka wakarimasen.
I don't know whether that place is quiet.

Written Practice 2

At the end of the sentence marked as **a**, add the sentence marked as **b**, following the example.

    a. 明日は雨が降りますか。　Ashita wa ame ga furimasu ka.
    b. 分かりません。　Wakarimasen.

明日は雨が降るか分かりません。　Ashita wa ame ga furu ka wakarimasen.

1. a. どのレストランがいいですか。Dono resutoran ga ii desu ka.
   b. 分かりますか。　Wakarimasu ka.

_____

2. a. 郵便局はどこにありますか。　Yūbinkyoku wa doko ni arimasu ka.
   b. 教えてください。　Oshiete kudasai.

_____

3. a. あの人の名前は何ですか。　Ano hito no namae wa nan desu ka.
   b. 教えてください。　Oshiete kudasai.

_____

4. a. どの映画がおもしろいですか。　Dono eiga ga omoshiroi desu ka.
   b. 知っていますか。　Shitte imasu ka.

_____

5. a. プレゼントは何がいいですか。　Purezento wa nani ga ii desu ka.
   b. 考えてください。　Kangaete kudasai.

_____

Expressing *Or*

The concept of "or" is expressed by the particle か **ka**, the conjunction それか **soreka**, or the conjunction それとも **soretomo**, depending on the context.

LISTING NOUNS TO SHOW OPTIONS WITH THE PARTICLE か KA

For presenting multiple options, use the particle か **ka**. か **ka** should be added after each noun except for the last one, just like the particle と **to** (Chapter 5) and the particle や **ya** (Chapter 8). For example:

すしかさしみを食べます。
Sushi ka sashimi o tabemasu.
I will eat sushi or sashimi.

父か母がここに来ます。
Chichi ka haha ga koko ni kimasu.
Either my father or my mother will come here.

東京か名古屋か大阪に行きましょう。
Tōkyō ka Nagoya ka Ōsaka ni ikimashō.
Let's go to Tokyo, Nagoya, or Osaka.

来学期は日本語か中国語か韓国語をとります。
Raigakki wa Nihon-go ka Chūgoku-go ka Kankoku-go o torimasu.
I'll take Japanese, Chinese, or Korean next school term.

THE CONJUNCTION それか SOREKA

For conjoining two non-question sentences that express alternative ideas to each other, begin the second one with それか **soreka**. For example:

今晩はすしを食べます。それか、さしみを食べます。
Konban wa sushi o tabemasu. Soreka, sashimi o tabemasu.
I'll eat sushi tonight. Or, I'll eat sashimi.

料理をしてください。それか、掃除をしてください。
Ryōri o shite kudasai. Soreka, sōji o shite kudasai.
Please cook. Or, please clean.

日曜日はテニスをしましょう。それか、ゴルフをしましょう。
Nichiyōbi wa tenisu o shimashō. Soreka, gorufu o shimashō.
Let's play tennis on Sunday. Or, let's play golf.

THE CONJUNCTION それとも SORETOMO

For conjoining two question sentences that express alternative ideas to each other, begin the second question with それとも **soretomo**. For example:

今晩はすしを食べますか。それとも、さしみを食べますか。
Konban wa sushi o tabemasu ka. Soretomo, sashimi o tabemasu ka.
Will you eat sushi tonight? Or, will you eat sashimi?

手で書きますか。それとも、タイプしますか。
Te de kakimasu ka. Soretomo, taipu shimasu ka.
Will you write it by hand? Or, will you type it?

Oral Practice

TRACK 50

Practice asking or answering questions using the notion of *or*, by reading the following sentences out loud.

どこで働きたいですか。
Doko de hataraki-tai desu ka.
Where would you like to work?

東京か大阪で働きたいです。
Tōkyō ka Ōsaka de hataraki-tai desu.
I want to work in Tokyo or Osaka.

夏休みは何をしますか。
Natsu-yasumi wa nani o shimasu ka.
What would you do during the summer vacation?

アルバイトをします。それか、旅行をします。
Arubaito o shimasu. Soreka, ryokō o shimasu.
I'll work part-time. Or, I'll travel.

今晩は何が食べたいですか。
Konban wa nani ga tabetai desu ka.
What would you like to eat tonight?

すしか、さしみか、てんぷらが食べたいです。
Sushi ka, sashimi ka, tenpura ga tabetai desu.
I want to eat sushi, sashimi, or tempura.

レストランで食べますか。それとも、うちで食べますか。
Resutoran de tabemasu ka. Soretomo, uchi de tabemasu ka.
Will you eat at the restaurant? Or, will you eat at home?

レストランで食べます。
Resutoran de tabemasu.
I'll eat at the restaurant.

Some Useful Modals

There are many modals that express the speaker's sureness or attitude toward his/her statement. They can be added at the end of the sentence, and most of them are composed of abstract nouns, particles, the copula, and other items. The sentence predicate preceding such modals are usually in the plain form, but you must be careful because there are some exceptions.

EXPRESSING POSSIBILITY WITH かもしれない KAMOSHIRENAI

When there is any chance for some situation to hold, regardless of whether it is only for 1 percent or 99 percent, you can make a statement with かもしれない **kamoshirenai**, to say *It is possible that . . .* or *It may be the case that . . .* Its polite version is かもしれません **kamoshiremasen**. The predicate that precedes it must be in the plain form except that だ **da** found in the copular verb or in a na-type adjective in the plain present affirmative form must be deleted. The following are some examples:

山田さんは来ないかもしれません。
Yamada-san wa konai kamoshiremasen.
Ms. Yamada may not come.

明日、雪が降るかもしれません。
Ashita, yuki ga furu kamoshiremasen.
It may snow tomorrow.

田中さんはもう帰ったかもしれません。
Tanaka-san wa mō kaetta kamoshiremasen.
Mr. Tanaka may have left for home.

あのレストランはちょっと高いかもしれませんよ。
Ano resutoran wa chotto takai kamoshiremasen yo.
That restaurant may be a bit expensive.

肺がんかもしれません。
Haigan kamoshiremasen.
It may be lung cancer.

EXPRESSING PROBABILITY WITH だろう DARŌ/ でしょう DESHŌ

When some situation is very likely to hold, you can make a statement with だろう **darō** to mean *It is probably the case that . . .* or *I guess that . . .* Its polite counterpart is でしょう **deshō**. The predicate that precedes it must be in the plain form except that だ **da** found in the copular verb or a na-type adjective in the plain present affirmative form must be deleted. The following are some examples:

明日は雨が降るでしょう。
Ashita wa ame ga furu deshō.
It will probably rain tomorrow.

日曜日は晴れるでしょう。
Nichiyōbi wa hareru deshō.
It will be clear (sky) on Sunday.

スミスさんはもう成田空港に着いたでしょう。
Sumisu-san wa mō Narita Kūkō ni tsuita deshō.
I guess Mr. Smith has already arrived at Narita Airport.

あのレストランは高いでしょう。
Ano resutoran wa takai deshō.
I guess that restaurant is expensive.

たぶん風邪でしょう。ゆっくり休んでください。
Tabun kaze deshō. Yukkuri yasunde kudasai.
It is probably a cold. Please take a good rest.

EXPRESSING PLANS WITH つもりだ TSUMORI DA

You can make a statement about what you are planning to do by using つもりだ **tsumori da**, to mean *I plan to . . .* Its polite counterpart is つもりです **tsumori desu**. The verb that precedes it must be in the plain form. For example:

来年スペインに行くつもりです。
Rainen Supein ni iku tsumori desu.
I plan to go to Spain next year.

明日はクラスに行かないつもりです。
Ashita wa kurasu ni ikanai tsumori desu.
I plan not to go to class tomorrow.

FACILITATING CONVERSATIONAL INTERACTION WITH んだ NDA

In conversational contexts, many statements end in んだ **nda**, or its polite counterpart, んです **ndesu** in Japanese. ん **n** is the contracted form of の **no**, which is an abstract nominal in this case, and it is followed by the copula. Thus, their uncontracted counterparts are のだ and のです, respectively. んだ **nda** is hard to translate into English. Its function is to implicitly show that the statement is related to the previous conversation or that the speaker is inviting a response or comments from his conversation partner. Therefore, it is vital for smooth interactive conversation in Japanese.

Suppose someone asked you whether you will come to his house tomorrow, and you said you cannot. And suppose you want to add that the reason why you cannot come is because you have a lot of homework. Then, it is better to say:

宿題がたくさんあるんです。
Shukudai ga takusan aru ndesu.
I have a lot of homework.

If you just say 宿題がたくさんあります **Shukudai ga takusan arimasu** instead, it would sound detached from the on-going conversation and the listener would not be able to make a connection easily. Of course, there is an explicit way of saying *because* in Japanese, which will be discussed later in this chapter, but indicating a reason briefly with んです **ndesu** is very common in Japanese daily-life conversations.

Consider another example. Suppose that you are going to break the news of your getting married next month to your colleague. In this context, it is better to say:

来月、結婚するんです。
Raigetsu, kekkon suru ndesu.

If you just say 来月、結婚します **Raigetsu, kekkon shimasu** instead, it sounds too blunt and gives the impression that you are not interested in hearing any comments or response from your conversation partner. It is not natural in a conversational context although it is perfectly fine in a public speech, recording, or writing, in which the information is one-directionally given from you to the audience and any immediate response is not expected from them.

んです **ndesu** follows a predicate in the plain form, but だ **da** in the copula or a na-type adjective in the plain present affirmative form changes to な **na**. For example:

私の母はフランス人なんです。
Watashi no haha wa Furansu-jin na ndesu.
My mother is French.

弟は勉強が嫌いなんです。
Otōto wa benkyō ga kirai na ndesu.
My little brother hates studying.

Oral Practice

 TRACK 51

Practice showing your certainty and attitude with modals by reading the following sentences out loud.

明日は雨が降りますか。
Ashita wa ame ga furimasu ka.
Will it rain tomorrow?

いいえ、降らないでしょう。
Īe, furanai deshō.
No, it won't, I guess.

ちょっとのどが痛いんです。
Chotto nodo ga itai ndesu.
My throat hurts a little.

たぶん風邪でしょう。
Tabun kaze deshō.
It is probably a cold.

卒業できますか。
Sotsugyō dekimasu ka.
Can you graduate?

できないかもしれません。
Dekinai kamoshiremasen.
I may not be able to.

明日トムさんのうちに行きますか。
Ashita Tomu-san no uchi ni ikimasu ka.
Will you go to Tom's house tomorrow?

いいえ、行かないつもりです。友達が来るんです。
Īe, ikanai tsumori desu. Tomodachi ga kuru ndesu.
No, I plan not to. My friend is coming.

Written Practice 3

Rewrite the following sentences by using the given items.

田中さんは来ません。 Tanaka san wa kimasen.
でしょう deshō
田中さんは来ないでしょう。 Tanaka san wa konai deshō.

1. 日本の大学に行きます。Nihon no daigaku ni ikimasu.
   つもりです tsumori desu

2. あの人は韓国人です。 Ano hito wa Kankoku-jin desu.
   かもしれません kamoshiremasen.

3. 明日は晴れます。 Ashita wa haremasu.
   でしょう deshō

4. 今、数学を勉強しています。　Ima sūgaku o benkyō shite imasu.
   んです ndesu

5. この辞書は便利です。　Kono jisho wa benri desu.
   んです ndesu

Asking *Why*?

In this section, you will learn how to ask reasons as well as how to provide them.

THE QUESTION WORD どうして DŌSHITE

For asking reasons, use the question word どうして **dōshite** or なぜ **naze**. They both mean *why*, but the former is used more frequently than the latter in conversations. It is important to end your question with んですか **ndesu ka**. (For んです **ndesu**, see the above section in this chapter.) For example:

どうして日本語を勉強しているんですか。
Dōshite Nihon-go o benkyō shite iru ndesu ka.
Why are you studying Japanese?

どうして納豆が嫌いなんですか。
Dōshite nattō ga kirai na ndesu ka.
Why do you hate Japanese fermented soybeans?

ANSWERING QUESTIONS WITH からです KARA DESU

To answer the question with *why*, make a statement sentence that indicates the reason and add からです **kara desu** at the end. Make sure to use the predicate in the plain form before からです **kara desu**. For example:

どうして日本に行きたいんですか。—日本の文化が好きだからです。
Dōshite Nihon ni iki-tai ndesu ka. — Nihon no bunka ga suki da kara desu.
Why do you want to go to Japan? —Because I like Japanese culture.

どうして昼ご飯を食べなかったんですか。—ダイエットをしているからです。
Dōshite hiru-gohan o tabenakatta ndesu ka. — Daietto o shite iru kara desu.
Why didn't you eat lunch? —Because I'm on diet.

Oral Practice

 TRACK 52

Practice asking and answering questions with *why* in Japanese by reading the following sentences out loud.

どうしてマイクさんのうちに行ったんですか。
Dōshite Maiku-san no uchi ni itta ndesu ka.
Why did you go to Mike's house?

辞書を借りたかったからです。
Jisho o kari-takatta kara desu.
Because I wanted to borrow his dictionary.

どうしてこの車は高いんですか。
Dōshite kono kuruma wa takai ndesu ka.
Why is this car expensive?

エンジンがいいからです。
Enjin ga ii kara desu.
Because its engine is good.

どうして勉強しているんですか。
Dōshite benkyō shite iru ndesu ka.
Why are you studying?

明日テストがあるからです。
Ashita tesuto ga aru kara desu.
Because I have a test tomorrow.

どうしてドレスを買わなかったんですか。
Dōshite doresu o kawanakatta ndesu ka.
Why didn't you buy the dress?

お金がないからです。
O-kane ga nai kara desu.*
Because I don't have money.

---

*Note that ない **nai** is the negative form of the verb ある **aru** (*to exist*). ある **aru** is a u-verb, but its plain negative form is not あらない **aranai** but ない **nai**.

Written Practice 4

Following the example, create a question that asks the reason for the given fact.

バナナをたくさん食べています。

Banana o takusan tabete imasu.

どうしてバナナをたくさん食べているんですか。

Dōshite banana o takusn tabete iru ndesu ka.

_____

1. 日本語を勉強しています。

   Nihon-go o benkyō shite imasu.

   _____

2. 漢字が嫌いです。

   Kanji ga kirai desu.

   _____

3. 納豆が好きです。

   Nattō ga suki desu.

   _____

4. パーティーに行きませんでした。

   Pātī ni ikimasendeshita.

   _____

5. 看護師になりたいです。

   Kangoshi ni nari-tai desu.

   _____

QUIZ

Circle the letter of the word or phrase that best completes each sentence.

1. 良子さんは＿＿＿＿思います。

   Yoshiko-san wa ＿＿＿＿ omoimasu.

   (a) 結婚しています kekkon shite imasu

   (b) 結婚している kekkon shite iru

   (c) 結婚していると kekkon shite iru to

   (d) 結婚していない kekkon shite inai

2. 卒業＿＿＿＿分かりません。

   Sotsugyō ＿＿＿＿ wakarimasen.

   (a) できると dekiru to   (c) できるかどうか dekiru ka dō ka

   (b) できる dekiru   (d) できないと dekinai to

3. すし ＿＿＿＿ さしみを食べます。

   Sushi ＿＿＿＿ sashimi o tabemasu.

   (a) が ga   (c) で de

   (b) か ka   (d) を o

4. 料理をしてください。＿＿＿＿、掃除をしてください。

   Ryōri o shite kudasai. ＿＿＿＿ , sōji o shite kudasai.

   (a) ですから desukara   (c) そうすると sōsuruto

   (b) それか soreka   (d) それとも soretomo

5. バスに乗りますか。＿＿＿＿、タクシーに乗りますか。

   Basu ni norimasu ka. ＿＿＿＿ , takushī ni norimasu ka.

   (a) ですから desukara   (c) そうすると sōsuruto

   (b) それか soreka   (d) それとも soretomo

6. 雪が＿＿＿＿かもしれません。

   Yuki ga ＿＿＿＿ kamoshiremasen.

   (a) 降る furu   (c) 降ります furimasu

   (b) 降っています futte imasu   (d) 降ると furu to

7. たぶん風邪＿＿＿でしょう。

Tabun kaze ＿＿＿ deshō.

(a) だ da   (c) だと da to

(b) です desu   (d) nothing

8. 来年スペインに＿＿＿つもりです。

Rainen Supein ni ＿＿＿ tsumori desu.

(a) 行って itte   (c) 行く iku

(b) 行きます ikimasu   (d) 行き iki

9. 勉強が嫌い＿＿＿んです。

Benkyō ga kirai ＿＿＿ ndesu.

(a) です desu   (c) だ da

(b) な na   (d) nothing

10. A: どうして昼ご飯を＿＿＿んですか。B: ＿＿＿からです。

A: Dōshite hiru-gohan o ＿＿＿ ndesu ka. B: ＿＿＿ kara desu.

(a) 食べない tabenai, いそがしい isogashii

(b) 食べない tabenai, いそがしくて isogashikute

(c) 食べません tabemasen, いそがしい isogashii

(d) 食べません tabemasen, いそがしくて isogashikute

CHAPTER 12

Creating Adverbs and Adverbial Clauses

In this chapter you'll learn:

Adverbs Derived from Adjectives

Adverbs describe how an action takes place or how a state holds. In English, many adverbs are created by adding -ly to adjectives, for example, *quickly*, *fortunately*, and *certainly*. It is also possible to create adverbs from adjectives in Japanese.

FORMING ADVERBS WITH く KU

To create an adverb from an i-type adjective, change the inflection い **i** to く **ku**, as in:

速い hayai (*fast*)	→	速く hayaku
早い hayai (*early*)	→	早く hayaku
遅い osoi (*late*)	→	遅く osoku
大きい ōkii (*big*)	→	大きく ōkiku

The adjective いい **ii** is irregular:

いい ii (*good*)	→	よく yoku

FORMING ADVERBS WITH に NI

For creating an adverb from a na-type adjective, change the inflection な **na** to に **ni**.

きれいな kirei na (*pretty*)	→	きれいに kirei ni
静かな shizuka na (*quiet*)	→	静かに shizuka ni
上手な jōzu na (*skillful*)	→	上手に jōzu ni
まじめな majime na (*serious*)	→	まじめに majime ni

Oral Practice

 TRACK 53

Practice using adverbs to request something by reading the following sentences out loud.

速く歩いてください。
Hayaku aruite kudasai.
Please walk faster.

早く来てください。
Hayaku kite kudasai.
Please come early.

もう少し大きく書いてください。
Mō sukoshi ōkiku kaite kudasai.
Please write it a bit bigger.

よく勉強してください。
Yoku benkyō shite kudasai.
Please study well.

きれいに書いてください。
Kirei ni kaite kudasai.
Please write (it) neatly.

静かに本を読んでください。
Shizuka ni hon o yonde kudasai.
Please read the book quietly.

USING AN ADVERB WITH THE VERB する SURU

You can express some intentional change using an adverb along with the verb する **suru** (*to do*). For example, 髪を長くする **kami o nagaku suru** means to *make one's hair long* or *to grow one's hair*. If there is no direct object, it usually means to change the person in some way. For example, 静かにする **shizuka ni suru** means *to make oneself quiet* or *to be quiet.*

Oral Practice

 TRACK 54

Practice using adverbs to request something by reading the following sentences out loud.

部屋をきれいにしてください。
Heya o kirei ni shite kudasai.
Please tidy up your room.

安くしてください。
Yasuku shite kudasai.
Please make it cheaper.

ラジオの音を小さくしてください。
Rajio no oto o chīsaku shite kudasai.
Please turn down the volume of the radio.

静かにしてください。
Shizuka ni shite kudasai.
Please be quiet.

まじめにしてください。
Majime ni shite kudasai.
Please be serious.

Written Practice 1

Use the following adjectives to fill in the blanks. Conjugate them appropriately, if necessary.

1. 大きい ōkii:
   この家は＿＿＿＿＿ですね。Kono ie wa ＿＿＿＿＿ desu ne.
2. 大きい ōkii:
   ＿＿＿＿＿書いてください。＿＿＿＿＿ kaite kudasai.
3. 高い takai:
   これは＿＿＿＿＿ありません。Kore wa ＿＿＿＿＿ arimasen.

4. 静かな shizuka na:

ここは＿＿＿＿＿＿＿ですね。Koko wa ＿＿＿＿＿＿＿ desu ne.

5. 静かな shizuka na:

＿＿＿＿＿＿＿してください。＿＿＿＿＿＿＿ shite kudasai.

6. まじめな majime na:

とても＿＿＿＿＿＿＿人です。Totemo ＿＿＿＿＿＿＿ hito desu.

7. まじめな majime na:

弟は＿＿＿＿＿＿＿ありません。Otōto wa ＿＿＿＿＿＿＿ arimasen.

Sound Symbolism

Japanese has a large inventory of sound symbolic words that describe items by imitating or sound-symbolically representing their sound, action, movement, appearance, and inner state. They are categorized into phonomimes, phenomimes, and psychomimes. Most of them consist of the repetition of one or two syllables, and are often written in katakana.

PHONOMIMES (ONOMATOPOEIA)

Phonomimes, more commonly known as onomatopoeia, imitate the actual sounds associated with the action and movement of people, animals, and things. For example, ゲラゲラ **geragera** represents the sound a person makes when laughing loudly. The following are examples of sentences with phonomimes:

兄がゲラゲラ笑いました。
Ani ga geragera waraimashita.
My brother laughed loudly.

犬がワンワンほえています。
Inu ga wanwan hoete imasu.
The dog is barking, "wanwan."

雨がザーザー降っています。
Ame ga zāzā futte imasu.
It is raining very heavily.

PHENOMIMES

Phenomimes describe the manner, action, appearance, and condition of people and things. For example, ネバネバ **nebaneba** represents a sticky or gluey texture. The following are some example sentences with phenomimes.

このご飯はネバネバしていますね。
Kono gohan wa nebaneba shite imasu ne.
This (cooked) rice is sticky, isn't it?

この紙はザラザラですよ。
Kono kami wa zarazara desu yo.
This paper has a rough surface.

PSYCHOMIME

Psychomimes represent psychological states. For example:

姉は今日プンプンしています。
Ane wa kyō punpun shite imasu.
My older sister is in a bad mood (fuming) today.

マイクさんは今日ソワソワしています。
Maiku-san wa kyō sowasowa shite imasu.
Mike is restless today.

Oral Practice

 TRACK 55

Pronounce the following animal sounds.

犬	inu	*dog*	ワンワン	wanwan
猫	neko	*cat*	ニャーニャー	nyānyā
豚	buta	*pig*	ブーブー	būbū
蜂	hachi	*bee*	ブンブン	bunbun
鼠	nezumi	*mouse*	チューチュー	chūchū
牛	ushi	*cow*	モーモー	mōmō

Adverbials for Time

As discussed in Chapter 8, the time of an action can be specified by time phrases such as 月曜日に **Getsuyōbi ni** (*on Monday*) and 7時に **shichi-ji ni** (*at 7 o'clock*).

月曜日に病院に行きます。
Getsuyōbi ni byōin ni ikimasu.
I'll go to the hospital on Monday.

7時に起きました。
Shichi-ji ni okimashita.
I woke up at 7 o'clock.

It is also possible to specify the time of an action in relation with another action using a variety of time adverbial clauses/phrases.

EXPRESSING "BEFORE" WITH 前に MAE NI

前に **mae ni** can be used after a verb in the plain present form to mean *before doing something*. For example:

食べる前に、手を洗います。
Taberu mae ni, te o araimasu.
I wash my hands before eating.

Remember that the verb before 前に **mae ni** must be in the present form regardless of the time of the action. The following are additional examples:

日本に行く前に、日本語を勉強します。
Nihon ni iku mae ni, Nihon-go o benkyō shimasu.
Before I go to Japan, I will study Japanese.

寝る前に、歯をみがきます。
Neru mae ni, ha o migakimasu.
Before going to bed, I brush my teeth.

父がうちに帰る前に、母は料理をしました。
Chichi ga uchi ni kaeru mae ni, haha wa ryōri o shimashita.
Before my father came home, my mother cooked.

EXPRESSING "AFTER" WITH 後に ATO NI

後に **ato ni** means *after* and can be used after a verb in the plain past form to mean *after doing something*. For example:

食べた後に、歯をみがきます。
Tabeta ato ni, ha o migakimasu.
I brush my teeth after eating.

Remember that the verb before 後に **ato ni** must be in the past form regardless of the time of the action. The following are additional examples:

卒業した後に、仕事を探します。
Sotsugyō shita ato ni, shigoto o sagashimasu.
I'll look for a job after graduating.

子供が寝た後に、映画を見ました。
Kodomo ga neta ato ni, eiga o mimashita.
I watched a movie after my child went to bed.

Note that に **ni** is sometimes dropped in this context.

EXPRESSING "DURING" WITH 間に AIDA NI

間に **aida ni** can be used after a verb in the progressive form (see Chapter 9) and means *during the time of doing something*. For example:

食べている間に、テレビは見ません。
Tabete iru aida ni, terebi wa mimasen.
I won't watch TV during my meal time.

先生が話している間に、しゃべってはいけません。
Sensei ga hanashite iru aida ni, shabette wa ikemasen.
It is not good to chat while the teacher is talking.

Written Practice 2

Choose the correct item in the parentheses.

1. 日本に（行く、行った）前に、日本語を勉強しました。

   Nihon ni (iku, itta) mae ni, nihongo o benkyō shimashita.

2. (食べる, 食べている) 間に、テレビを見ません。

   (Taberu, Tabete iru) aida ni, terebi o mimasen.

3. 映画を見る (前, 後) に、本を読みます。

   Eiga o miru (mae, ato) ni, hon o yomimasu.

4. (食べる, 食べた) 後に、テレビを見ます。

   (Taberu, Tabeta) ato ni, terebi o mimasu.

EXPRESSING "AT THE TIME WHEN" WITH ときに TOKI NI

とき **toki** is a noun that means *time*. You can use it with a verb, adjective, or another noun to make a time adverbial phrase that means *at the time when . . .* It is often followed by the particle に **ni**.

When using a verb before とき **toki**, the form of the verb must be correctly chosen: use the simple present tense form for referring to the time right before the action; use the progressive form for referring to the time in the middle of the action; use the simple past tense form for referring to the time right after the action. These apply regardless of the actual time of the actions. For example:

バスに乗るときに、お金を払いました。
Basu ni noru toki ni, o-kane o haraimashita.
I paid right before getting on the bus.

食べているときに、テレビは見ません。
Tabete iru toki ni, terebi wa mimasen.
I do not watch TV when I am eating.

空港に着いたときに、電話します。
Kūkō ni tsuita toki ni, denwa shimasu.
I will call you right after I arrive at the airport.

Recall that ...前に **mae ni** and ...後に **ato ni** also refer to the time *before* and *after*, but they don't just refer to *right before* and *right after*, but *any time before* and *any time after*. By contrast, ... ときに **toki ni** can be used only for the time very close to the time of the action or during the time of the action.

You can also use a noun or an adjective before とき **toki**, but they need to be in the prenominal form because とき **toki** itself is a noun. For example:

高校生のときに、ピアノを習いました。
Kōkōsei no toki ni, piano o naraimashita.
I took piano lessons when I was a high school student.

暇なときに、来てください。
Hima na toki ni, kite kudasai.
Please come over when you are free.

寂しいときに、母に電話をします。
Sabishii toki ni, haha ni denwa o shimasu.
I call my mother when I feel lonely.

Written Practice 3

Fill in the blanks using the items provided in the parentheses. You need to conjugate them appropriately.

1. _____ ときに、本を読みます。(静かな shizuka na *quiet*)

   _____ toki ni, hon o yomimasu. *When it's quiet, I read.*

2. _____ ときに、テレビは見ません。 (食事 shokuji *meal time*)

   _____ toki ni, terebi wa mimasen. *I don't watch TV during the meal time.*

3. 新聞を_____ ときに、めがねをかけます。 (読む yomu *to read*)

   Shinbun o_____ toki ni, megane o kakemasu. *I put on my glasses when I read the newspaper.*

4. 朝、_____ ときに、シャワーをあびます。 (起きる okiru *to get up*)

   Asa, _____ toki ni, shawā o abimasu. *I take a shower when I get up.*

5. 宿題を_____ ときに、田中さんが来ました。 (する suru *to do*)

   Shukudai o _____ toki ni, Tanaka-san ga kimashita.
   Mr. Tanaka came when I was doing my homework.

EXPRESSING TWO SIMULTANEOUS ACTIONS WITH ながら NAGARA

ながら **nagara** follows a verb in the stem form and shows that two activities take place simultaneously.

宿題をしながら、ピザを食べました。
Shukudai o shi-nagara, piza o tabemashita.
I ate pizza while doing my homework.

This sentence is slightly different from the following sentence in that the following sentence is true as long as pizza-eating time is included in the homework-doing time and they do not have to be taking place simultaneously throughout, whereas these activities must go on together throughout in the previous sentence.

宿題をしている間に、ピザを食べました。
Shukudai o shite iru aida ni, piza o tabemashita.
I ate pizza during the time I was doing my homework.

EXPRESSING A TIME WITH SPECIAL BENEFIT WITH うちに UCHI NI

うちに **uchi ni** is very similar to 間に **aida ni**, but unlike the latter, うちに **uchi ni** implies that there is a special benefit in doing the action during the specified time, and failing to do so will result in some negative consequence. It is understood as *while* if the preceding verb is in the progressive form or expresses a state, but is understood as *before* if the preceding verb is in the negative form. For example:

赤ちゃんが寝ているうちに、新聞を読みます。
Akachan ga nete iru uchi ni, shinbun o yomimasu.
I will read the newspaper while the baby is sleeping.

ピザがあついうちに、食べましょう。
Piza ga atsui uchi ni, tabemashō.
Let's eat pizza while it is hot.

警察が来ないうちに、逃げましょう。
Keisatsu ga konai uchi ni, nigemashō.
Let's run away before the police come.

Written Practice 4

Fill in the blanks using the verbs provided in the parentheses as well as either ながら **nagara** or うちに **uchi ni.** You need to conjugate the verb or the adjective appropriately.

1. 音楽を＿＿＿＿、勉強します。(聞く kiku *to listen*)

   Ongaku o ＿＿＿＿＿＿＿＿＿, benkyō shimasu. *I study while listening to the music.*

2. 警察が＿＿＿＿、逃げましょう。(来る kuru *to come*)

   Keisatsu ga ＿＿＿＿＿＿＿＿＿, nigemashō. *Let's leave before the police come.*

3. ＿＿＿＿、帰りましょう。(明るい akarui *bright*)

   ＿＿＿＿＿＿＿＿＿, kaerimashō. *Let's go home while it is still bright.*

4. コーヒを＿＿＿＿、話しましょう。(飲む nomu *to drink*)

   Kōhī o ＿＿＿＿＿＿＿＿＿, hanashimashō. *Let's talk over coffee.*

EXPRESSING A TIME OR A CONDITION WITH と TO

と **to** follows a verb or an adjective in the plain present form, and creates a time adverbial clause or a conditional clause (see Chapter 18) depending on the tense of the main verb.

If the main verb is in the past tense, the clause with と **to** functions as a time adverbial clause, and the entire sentence expresses what happened after some event. For example:

ドアをあけると、犬がいました。
Doa o akeru to, inu ga imashita.
When I opened the door, there was a dog.

図書館に行くと、高橋さんがいました。
Toshokan ni iku to, Takahashi-san ga imashita.
When I went to the library, I saw Ms. Takahashi.

In this construction, the speaker should not have a control over the event described in the main clause. For expressing two sequentially ordered actions that the speaker has a control over, use the te-form (Chapter 9), as in the following examples:

ドアをあけて犬を出しました。
Doa o akete inu o dashimashita.
I opened the door and let the dog go out.

図書館に行って高橋さんと話しました。
Toshokan ni itte Takahashi-san to hanashimashita.
I went to the library and talked with Ms. Takahashi.

If the main verb is in the present tense, the clause with と **to** expresses some situation that necessarily holds after a certain event. For example:

春になると、花が咲きます。
Haru ni naru to, hana ga sakimasu.
When it is spring, flowers blossom.

3に1をたすと、4になります。
3 ni 1 o tasu to, 4 ni narimasu.
When we add 1 to 3, we get 4.

会費が高いと、だれも来ません。
Kaihi ga takai to, dare mo kimasen.
If the admission fee is expensive, no one will come.

女性だと、25%のディスカウントがもらえます。
Josei da to, 25% no disukaunto ga moraemasu.
If you are a woman, you can get 25 percent discount.

Again, the speaker should not have a control over the event expressed in the main clause.

Written Practice 5

Complete the sentences appropriately.

1. _____と、100点がとれますよ。

   _____ to, hyaku-ten ga toremasu yo. *If you study well, you can get 100.*

2. _____と、100点がとれませんよ。

   _____ to, hyaku-ten ga toremasen yo. *If you do not study well, you cannot get 100.*

3. _____ と、太りますよ。

_____ to, futorimasu yo. *If you eat a lot, you will gain weight.*

4. 冬になると、_____。

Fuyu ni naru to, _____. *When the winter comes, it snows.*

Adverbials for Reasons and Causes

In this section, you will learn some adverbial clauses that express reasons and causes.

INDICATING A REASON WITH から KARA

You can create an adverbial clause using から **kara** to specify the reason for the fact stated in the main sentence. The predicate before から **kara** is in the plain form if the main clause is in the plain form, and it is usually in the polite form if the main clause is in the polite form. The following two sentences have the same meaning.

家内は日本人だから、うちでは日本語で話す。
Kanai wa Nihon-jin da kara, uchi de wa Nihon-go de hanasu.
家内は日本人ですから、うちでは日本語で話します。
Kanai wa Nihon-jin desu kara, uchi de wa Nihon-go de hanashimasu.
Because my wife is Japanese, I speak in Japanese at home.

The following are additional examples:

今日は忙しいですから、明日来てください。
Kyō wa isogashii desu kara, ashita kite kudasai.
Because I'm busy today, please come tomorrow.

電車は不便ですから、車で行きませんか。
Densha wa fuben desu kara, kuruma de ikimasen ka.
Because the train is inconvenient, how about going there by car?

お金がありませんから、旅行に行けません。
O-kane ga arimasen kara, ryokō ni ikemasen.
As I don't have money, I cannot go on a trip.

Recall that Chapter 10 discusses the conjunction ですから **desukara** (*therefore*), and Chapter 11 shows how to answer the question with *why* using からです **kara desu**. These are all related to から **kara** discussed here.

INDICATING A REASON WITH ので NODE

You can create an adverbial clause using ので **node** to express reasons. The predicate before ので **node** is usually in the plain form.

高かったので、買いませんでした。
Takakatta node, kaimasendeshita.
Because it was expensive, I didn't buy it.

今日は忙しいので、早く帰れません。
Kyō wa isogashii node, hayaku kaeremasen.
Because I am busy today, I cannot go home early.

お金がないので、レストランに行けません。
O-kane ga nai node, resutoran ni ikemasen.
Because I don't have money, I cannot go to a restaurant.

だ **da** in the copula and in a na-type adjective in the plain present affirmative form must be changed to な **na**, when preceding ので **node**.

まだ子供なので、字が書けません。
Mada kodomo na node, ji ga kakemasen.
(He) is still a child, so he cannot write.

Unlike から **kara**, ので **node** cannot be used when the cause-result relationship is not self-evident.

Adverbials for Contrast or Contradiction

In this section, you will learn how to relate contrasting or contradicting facts in the same sentence using adverbial clauses. In addition, you will learn how to contrast items using the particle は **wa**.

INDICATING CONTRAST OR CONTRADICTION WITH が GA

が **ga** can create an adverbial clause that shows conflict, contrast, or contradiction. For example:

旅行をしたいですが、お金がありません。
Ryokō o shitai desu ga, o-kane ga arimasen.
I want to travel, but I don't have money.

私は犬が好きですが、兄は犬が嫌いです。
Watashi wa inu ga suki desu ga, ani wa inu ga kirai desu.
I like dogs, but my older brother hates dogs.

甘いものは嫌いですが、アイスクリームはよく食べます。
Amai mono wa kirai desu ga, aisukurīmu wa yoku tabemasu.
I hate sweet things, but I often eat ice cream.

The predicate that precedes が **ga** should be in the polite form if the predicate in the main clause is in the polite form, as in the above sentences, but it should be in the plain form if the predicate in the main clause is in the plain form:

甘いものは嫌いだが、アイスクリームは大好きだ。
Amai mono wa kirai da ga, aisukurīmu wa daisuki da.
I hate sweet things, but I love ice cream.

The interesting fact about が **ga** is that it can also be used when there is no obvious conflict or contrast and/or when the main sentence expresses a suggestion or a request. For example, in the following sentence, が **ga** just shows a logical transition:

明日パーティーをしますが、美香さんも来ませんか。
Ashita pātī o shimasu ga, Mika-san mo kimasen ka.
I'm throwing a party tomorrow; would you like to come, too, Mika?

私はABCビジネスの渡辺と申しますが、社長さんはいらっしゃいますか。
Watashi wa ABC Bizinesu no Watanabe to mōshimasu ga, shachō-san wa irasshaimasu ka.
I'm Mr. Watanabe from ABC Business; is your company president available?

リチャードさんはうちにもよく来ますが、とてもいい人ですよ。
Richādo-san wa uchi ni mo yoku kimasu ga, totemo ii hito desu yo.
Richard also often comes to my house; he is a very nice person.

失礼ですが、お名前を教えてくださいませんか。

Shitsurei desu ga, o-namae o oshiete kudasaimasen ka.

I may be rude, but could you let me know your name?

INDICATING CONTRAST OR THE SCOPE OF NEGATION WITH THE PARTICLE は WA

The particle は **wa** functions as a topic marker (see Chapter 2), but it can also show contrast by highlighting the items that are in contrast, which is similar to stressing in English. For example, in the following sentence, 犬 **inu** and 猫 **neko** are in contrast, and they are highlighted by the particle は **wa**:

私は犬は好きですが、猫はきらいです。

Watashi wa inu wa suki desu ga, neko wa kirai desu.

*I like **dogs**, but I hate **cats**.*

Sometimes, only one item in a sentence is highlighted by は **wa** if it is clear what is being contrasted within the context. For example, the following sentence makes sense if the conversation participants have some idea about who the speaker doesn't like:

私は田中さんは好きです。

Watashi wa Tanaka-san wa suki desu.

*I like **Mr. Tanaka**.*

は **wa** is often used in a negative sentence. It can be understood as giving a highlighting effect, clarifying the scope of negation, even though there is nothing specific to be contrasted.

私はワインは飲みません。

Watashi wa wain wa nomimasen.

I don't drink wine.

大阪には行きませんでした。

Ōsaka ni wa ikimasendeshita.

I didn't go to Osaka.

As for the particle cluster には **ni wa** in the above sentence, see Chapter 5.

INDICATING CONTRADICTION WITH のに NONI

のに **noni** can create an adverbial clause that shows an obvious contradiction or conflict, expressing surprise, dissatisfaction, dissappointment, or regret. The predicate that precedes のに **noni** is usually in the plain form. だ **da** in the copula and in a na-type adjective in the plain present affirmative form must be changed to な **na** when preceding のに **noni**.

> この車は高かったのに、エンジンがもうこわれました。
> Kono kuruma wa takakatta noni, enjin ga mō kowaremashita.
> *Although this car was expensive, its engine already broke down.*

> この辞書は便利なのに、だれも使いません。
> Kono jisho wa benri na noni, dare mo tsukaimasen.
> *This dictionary is convenient, but no one uses it.*

> 兄は明日テストがあるのに、ぜんぜん勉強していません。
> Ani wa ashita tesuto ga aru noni, zenzen benkyō shite imasen.
> *Although my brother has a test tomorrow, he hasn't studied at all.*

のに **noni** cannot be used if a main sentence expresses the speaker's controllable act, intention, suggestion, or request, although が **ga** can.

Written Practice 6

Choose the correct options in the parentheses.

1. 高かった（ので、のに）、買いませんでした。

   Takakatta (node, noni), kaimasendeshita.

2. 高かった（ので、のに）、よくありませんでした。

   Takakatta (node, noni), yoku arimasendeshita.

3. 兄はお金がない（ので、のに）、よくレストランに行きます。

   Ani wa okane ga nai (node, noni), yoku resutoran ni ikimasu.

4. 明日は日本語のテストがある（ので、のに）、今晩は勉強します。

   Ashita wa Nihon-go no tesuto ga aru (node, noni), konban wa benkyō shimasu.

5. 私は猫が好きです（が、から）、妹は猫が嫌いです。

   Watashi wa neko ga suki desu (ga, kara), imōto wa neko ga kirai desu.

6. 電車は便利です（が、から）、電車で行きませんか。

   Densha wa benri desu (ga, kara), densha de ikimasen ka.

7. 今日は忙しいです (が, から) 、明日来てください。

Kyō wa isogashii desu (ga, kara), ashita kite kudasai.

8. 私はABCビジネスの田中と (申しますが, 申すのに) 、社長さんはいらっしゃいますか。

Watashi wa ABC Bizinesu no Tanaka to (mōshimasu ga, mōsu noni), shachō-san wa irasshaimasu ka.

Adverbials for Purpose

In this section, you will learn how to express the purpose of the action using adverbial phrases in Japanese.

INDICATING PURPOSE OF COMING AND GOING WITH に NI

For specifying the purpose of coming and going, you can use the phrase that consists of a verb in the stem form and the particle に **ni**. For example:

映画を見に行きましょう。
Eiga o mi ni ikimashō.
Let's go see a movie.

祖母に会いに中国に行きます。
Sobo ni ai ni Chūgoku ni ikimasu.
I'll go to China to see my grandmother.

財布をとりにうちに帰ります。
Saifu o tori ni uchi ni kaerimasu.
I'll go home to pick up my wallet.

郵便局に切手を買いに行きます。
Yūbinkyoku ni kitte o kai ni ikimasu.
I'll go to the post office to buy stamps.

うちに晩ご飯を食べに来ませんか。
Uchi ni bangohan o tabe ni kimasen ka.
Would you like to come to my home for dinner?

This purpose phrase is very short and convenient but can only be used for specifying the purpose of coming and going. To express the purpose of other actions, use ためにtame ni, which will be discussed in the following subsection.

Written Practice 7

Translate the following English sentences into Japanese.

1. Let's go see a movie.

   _____

2. I will go to the post office to buy stamps.

   _____

3. I'll go to Japan to see my grandmother.

   _____

4. I went home to have lunch.

   _____

INDICATING PURPOSE WITH ために TAME NI

For specifying the purpose of a variety of actions, use the phrase that consists of a verb in the plain form and ために **tame ni**. For example:

日本語を勉強するために辞書を買います。
Nihon-go o benkyō suru tame ni jisho o kaimasu.
I'll buy a dictionary to study Japanese.

日本語を勉強するために日本に行きます。
Nihon-go o benkyō suru tame ni Nihon ni ikimasu.
I'll go to Japan to study Japanese.

家を買うために、お金を借ります。
Ie o kau tame ni, o-kane o karimasu.
I'll borrow money in order to buy a house.

Adverbials for Manner

In this section, you will learn how to express the manner of some action using adverbial phrases in Japanese.

INDICATING MANNER WITH ように YŌ NI

To show the manner needed to obtain some result, use the adverbial phrase with a verb in the plain form and ように **yō ni**. For example:

聞こえません。聞こえるように言ってください。
Kikoemasen. Kikoeru yō ni itte kudasai.
I can't hear you. Please say it so I can hear you.

分かるように話してください。
Wakaru yō ni hanashite kudasai.
Please speak in a way that I can understand it.

こわさないように運んでください。
Kowasanai yō ni hakonde kudasai.
Please carry it without breaking it.

こぼさないように食べてください。
Kobosanai yō ni tabete kudasai.
Please eat without spilling.

私が言ったように作ってください。
Watashiga itta yō ni tsukutte kudasai.
Please make it in the way that I told you.

ここから見えるようにテレビを置いてください。
Koko kara mieru yō ni terebi o oite kudasai.
Please place the TV so we can see it from here.

車が買えるようにお金をためます。
Kuruma ga kaeru yō ni okane o tamemasu.
I'll save money so I can buy a car.

忘れないように書いてください。
Wasurenai yō ni kaite kudasai.
Please write it down so you won't forget.

For additional uses of ように **yō ni**, see Chapter 15.

Written Practice 8

Fill in the blanks using some of the given words. You may have to conjugate the verbs into their negative or potential forms. *Hint*: Remember that some verbs originally include the meaning of potential and cannot be conjugated into potential forms (Chapter 10).

(分かる wakaru, 見える mieru, 読む yomu, こわす kowasu, こぼす kobosu)

1. ちょっと見えません。_____ように置いて下さい。

   Chotto miemasen. _____ yō ni oite kudasai.

2. 小さくて読めません。 _____ように書いて下さい。

   Chīsakute yomemasen. _____ yō ni kaite kudasai.

3. よく分かりません。 _____ように言って下さい。

   Yoku wakarimasen. _____ yō ni itte kudasai.

4. これは高いんです。 _____ように運んで下さい。

   Kore wa takai ndesu. _____ yō ni hakonde kudasai.

5. また、こぼしましたね。 _____ように食べて下さい。

   Mata, koboshimashita ne. _____ yō ni tabete kudasai.

QUIZ

Circle the letter of the word or phrase that best completes each sentence.

1. _____ 書いてください。

   _____ kaite kudasai.

   (a) 大きい ōkii   (c) 大きく ōkiku

   (b) 大きな ōki na   (d) 大きいに ōkii ni

2. まじめ_____してください。

   Majime _____ shite kudasai.

   (a) く ku   (c) で de

   (b) な na   (d) に ni

3. 日本に行く ＿＿＿＿＿ 日本語を勉強します。

   Nihon ni iku ＿＿＿＿＿ Nihon-go o benkyō shimasu.

   (a) 前に mae ni   (c) 間に aida ni

   (b) 後に ato ni   (d) ながら nagara

4. 日本に行った ＿＿＿＿＿ 日本語を勉強します。

   Nihon ni itta ＿＿＿＿＿ Nihon-go o benkyō shimasu.

   (a) 前に mae ni   (c) 間に aida ni

   (b) 後に ato ni   (d) ながら nagara

5. 音楽を聞き ＿＿＿＿＿勉強します。

   Ongaku o kiki ＿＿＿＿＿ benkyō shimasu.

   (a) 前に mae ni   (c) 間に aida ni

   (b) 後に ato ni   (d) ながら nagara

6. 赤ちゃんが ＿＿＿＿＿うちに新聞を読みます。

   Akachan ga ＿＿＿＿＿ uchi ni shinbun o yomimasu.

   (a) 寝る neru   (c) 寝た neta

   (b) 寝ている nete iru   (d) 寝て nete

7. 3に1をたす ＿＿＿＿＿ 、4になります。

   San ni ichi o tasu ＿＿＿＿＿ , yon ni narimasu.

   (a) のに noni   (c) と to

   (b) が ga   (d) に ni

8. まだ子ども ＿＿＿＿＿ 、字が書けません。

   Mada kodomo ＿＿＿＿＿ , ji ga kakemasen.

   (a) だので da node   (c) から kara

   (b) ですが desu ga   (d) なので na node

9. 明日テストがあります ＿＿＿＿＿ 、ぜんぜん勉強していません。

   Ashita tesuto ga arimasu ＿＿＿＿＿ , zenzen benkyō shite imasen.

   (a) から kara   (c) が ga

   (b) と to   (d) ので node

10. 日本語を勉強＿＿＿＿＿ 、辞書を買います。

   Nihon-go o benkyō ＿＿＿＿＿ , jisho o kaimasu.

   (a) するに suru ni   (c) しに shi ni

   (b) するために suru tame ni   (d) しないように shinai yō ni

CHAPTER 13

Comparing People and Things

In this chapter, you'll learn:

Comparing Two Items
Making Superlative Comparisons

Comparing Two Items

In this section, you will learn how to make a statement or ask a question comparing two items in Japanese.

MAKING COMPARISONS WITH THE PARTICLE より YORI

Suppose Ms. Watanabe is kind. Then, you'll say:

渡辺さんはやさしいです。
Watanabe-san wa yasashii desu.
Ms. Watanabe is kind.

Suppose Ms. Watanabe is kinder than Ms. Takahashi. You do not need to create a special comparative form like *kinder* in Japanese. You can continue to use the adjective in the same form, やさしいです **yasashii desu**. All you need to do is to add the item you are comparing to with the particle より **yori** (*than*):

渡辺さんは高橋さんよりやさしいです。
Watanabe-san wa Takahashi-san yori yasashii desu.
Ms. Watanabe is kinder than Ms. Takahashi.

The same applies to adverbs such as よく **yoku** (*well, a lot*), 早く **hayaku** (*early*), and ゆっくり **yukkuri** (*slowly*).

兄は私よりよく勉強します。
Ani wa watashi yori yoku benkyō shimasu.
My older brother studies harder than I.

妹は私よりよく食べます。
Imōto wa watashi yori yoku tabemasu.
My younger sister eats more than I do.

弟は私より早く起きます。
Otōto wa watashi yori hayaku okimasu.
My younger brother wakes up earlier than I.

祖父は父よりゆっくり話します。
Sofu wa chichi yori yukkuri hanashimasu.
My grandfather speaks more slowly than my father.

DEGREE ADVERBS USED FOR COMPARISON

You can use degree adverbs such as ずっと **zutto** (*by far, much*), ちょっと **chotto** (*a little, slightly*), and 少し **sukoshi** (*a little, slightly*) to specify the extent of the difference between the two items.

漢字はひらがなよりずっと難しいです。
Kanji wa hiragana yori zutto muzukashii desu.
Kanji are much harder than hiragana.

父は母よりちょっと厳しいです。
Chichi wa haha yori chotto kibishii desu.
My father is a little stricter than my mother.

この車はあの車より少し高いです。
Kono kuruma wa ano kuruma yori sukoshi takai desu.
This car is slightly more expensive than that car.

Note that ちょっと **chotto** and 少し **sukoshi** both mean *a little* or *slightly*, but the latter is slightly more formal than the former. Also note that ちょっと **chotto** has more functions than 少し **sukoshi**. For example, you can say ちょっと **chotto**, but not 少し **sukoshi**, to get attention from someone.

EXPRESSING "NOT AS . . . AS . . . " USING THE PARTICLE ほど HODO

To express "not as . . . as . . . ", use the particle ほど **hodo** and an adjective in the negative form. For example, the following sentence means *Ms. Takahashi is not as kind as Ms. Watanabe*:

高橋さんは渡辺さんほどやさしくありません。
Takahashi-san wa Watanabe-san hodo yasashiku arimasen.

Oral Practice

 TRACK 56

Practice reading the following sentences that compare two items.

父は母より厳しいです。
Chichi wa haha yori kibishii desu.
My father is stricter than my mother.

母は父ほど厳しくありません。
Haha wa chichi hodo kibishiku arimasen.
My mother is not as strict as my father.

兄は私よりよく勉強します。
Ani wa watashi yori yoku benkyō shimasu.
My older brother studies harder than I.

私は兄ほどよく勉強しません。
Watashi wa ani hodo yoku benkyō shimasen.
I do not study as hard as my older brother.

COMPARING TWO SIMILAR ITEMS WITH 同じぐらい ONAJI GURAI

For saying *as . . . as . . .*, expressing a similar degree of some property, use 同じぐらい **onaji gurai** right before the predicate. You can say either:

AはBと同じぐらい...
A wa B to onaji gurai ...
A is as . . . as B . . .

AとBは同じぐらい...
A to B wa onaji gurai ...
A and B are equally . . .

The difference between the two is whether just A is the topic or both A and B are the topic of the sentence. The following are some examples:

カタカナはひらがなと同じぐらい簡単です。
Katakana wa hiragana to onaji gurai kantan desu.
Katakana is as easy as hiragana.

カタカナとひらがなは同じぐらい簡単です。
Katakana to hiragana wa onaji gurai kantan desu.
Katakana and hiragana are equally easy.

母は父と同じぐらいよく働きます。
Haha wa chichi to onaji gurai yoku hatarakimasu.
My mother works as hard as my father.

母と父は同じぐらいよく働きます。
Haha to chichi wa onaji gurai yoku hatarakimasu.
My mother and my father work equally hard.

Written Practice 1

Fill in the blanks based on the actual facts about you and about the people around you. You may use terms like 母 **haha** *(my mother)* or proper names like スティーブ **Stību** *(Steve)*.

1. 私は_____より背が高いです。

   Watashi wa _____ yori se ga takai desu.

2. 私は_____ほど背が高くありません。

   Watashi wa _____ hodo se ga takaku arimasen.

3. 私は_____よりよく食べます。

   Watashi wa _____ yori yoku tabemasu.

4. 私は_____ほどたくさん食べません。(たくさん *a lot*)

   Watashi wa _____ hodo takusan tabemasen.

ASKING QUESTIONS OF COMPARISON WITH どちら DOCHIRA

To ask a question that compares two items, use the question word どちら **dochira** *(which one)*. First, list the two items you are comparing, adding the particle と **to** after each, as in 渡辺さんと、高橋さんと **Watanabe-san to, Takahahsi-san to**. Then, add どちらが **dochira ga** and the relevant predicate in the question format, for example, 若いですか **wakai desu ka**. The entire sentence will look like:

渡辺さんと、高橋さんと、どちらが若いですか。
Watanabe-san to Takahashi-san to dochira ga wakai desu ka.
(Between) Ms. Watanabe and Ms. Takahashi, which one is younger?

Many people say どちらの方 **dochira no hō** *(which side)* instead of just どちら **dochira**.

渡辺さんと、高橋さんと、どちらの方が若いですか。
Watanabe-san to Takahashi-san to dochira no hō ga wakai desu ka.

In addition, many people place では **de wa** after the items that are compared.

渡辺さんと、高橋さんとでは、どちらの方が若いですか。
Watanabe-san to, Takahashi-san to de wa dochira no hō ga wakai desu ka.

A typical answer to a comparison question also has 方 hō (*side*):

高橋さんの方が若いです。
Takahashi-san no hō ga wakai desu.
Ms. Takahashi is younger.

Oral Practice

TRACK 57

Practice asking and answering questions that compare two items.

猫と、犬と、どちらの方が好きですか。
Neko to, inu to, dochira no hō ga suki desu ka.
(Between) cats and dogs, which do you like better?

犬の方が好きです。
Inu no hō ga suki desu.
I like dogs better.

コカ・コーラと、ペプシとでは、どちらが好きですか。
Koka Kōra to, Pepushi to de wa, dochira ga suki desu ka.
Which one do you like better, Coca Cola or Pepsi?

私はペプシの方が好きです。でも、兄はコカ・コーラの方が好きです。
Watashi wa Pepushi no hō ga suki desu. Demo, ani wa Koka Kōra no hō ga suki desu.
I like Pepsi better. But my older brother likes Coca Cola better.

パンと、ご飯とでは、どちらの方をよく食べますか。
Pan to, gohan to de wa, dochira no hō o yoku tabemasu ka.
Between bread and rice, which do you eat more often?

もちろん、ご飯です。
Mochiron, gohan desu.
Of course, rice.

中国語と、日本語と、どちらの方が難しいですか。
Chūgoku-go to, Nihon-go to, dochira no hō ga muzukashii desu ka.
(Between) Chinese and Japanese, which is harder?

中国語の方がちょっと難しいです。漢字がたくさんありますから。
Chūgoku-go no hō ga chotto muzukashii desu. Kanji ga takusan arimasu kara.
Chinese is a little harder. That's because there are many Chinese characters.

マイクさんと、ジョンさんと、どちらの方が背が高いですか。
Maiku-san to, Jon-san to, dochira no hō ga se ga takai desu ka.
(Between) Mike and John, which is taller?

マイクさんです。ジョンさんはマイクさんほど背が高くありません。
Maiku-san desu. Jon-san wa Maiku-san hodo se ga takaku arimasen.
Mike. John is not as tall as Mike.

飛行機と、車とでは、どちらの方が安全ですか。
Hikōki to, kuruma to de wa, dochira no hō ga anzen desu ka.
(Between) airplanes and cars, which are safer?

飛行機の方が安全だと思います。
Hikōki no hō ga anzen da to omoimasu.
I think airplanes are safer.

日本の高校生と、韓国の高校生とでは、どちらの方がよく勉強しますか。
Nihon no kōkōsei to, Kankoku no kōkōsei to de wa, dochira no hō ga yoku benkyō shimasu ka.
(Between) Japanese high school students and Korean high school students, which study more?

さあ、よくわかりません。同じぐらいでしょう。
Sā, yoku wakarimasen. Onaji gurai deshō.
Well, I'm not sure. About the same, I guess.

COMPARING ACTIVITIES

For comparing two activities using verbs, add the particle の **no** right after the verb in the dictionary form to make it like a noun. の **no** functions as a nominalizer. Once you nominalize a verb, particles such as は **wa**, で **de**, and と **to** can follow it without causing ungrammaticality. However, the particle より **yori** and ほど **hodo** can directly follow a verb in the dictionary form without being intervened by の **no**. In fact, の **no** is not allowed before ほど **hodo**. These are shown in the following examples:

読むのと、書くのとでは、どちらの方が好きですか。
Yomu no to, kaku no to de wa, dochira no hō ga suki desu ka.
(Between) reading and writing, which do you like better?

読む方が書くより好きです。
Yomu hō ga kaku yori suki desu.
I like reading better than writing.

読むのは書くほど難しくありません。
Yomu no wa kaku hodo muzukashiku arimasen.
Reading is not as hard as writing.

カタカナを書くのは、ひらがなを書くのと同じぐらい簡単です。
Katakana o kaku no wa, hiragana o kaku no to onaji gurai kantan desu.
Writing katakana is as easy as writing hiragana.

Written Practice 2

Following the example, make a question using the given items.

みかん mikan (*oranges*), りんご ringo (*apples*), 好きだ suki da (*like*)

みかんと、りんごとでは、どちらの方が好きですか。 Mikan to, ringo to

de wa, dochira no hō ga suki desu ka.

1. お父さん otōsan (*father*), お母さん okāsan (*mother*), 厳しい kibishii (*strict*)

2. コーヒー kōhī (*coffee*), 紅茶 kōcha (*black tea*), よく飲む yoku nomu (*often drink*)

3. 寝る neru (*sleep*), 食べる taberu (*eat*), 好きだ suki da (*like*)

4. 日本語を話す Nihon-go o hanasu (*speak Japanese*), 日本語を聞く Nihon-go o kiku (*listen to Japanese*), 難しい muzukashii (*difficult*)

RECOMMENDING ACTIONS WITH 方がいい HŌ GA II

A typical way of recommending someone to do something is to use 方 **hō** (*side*) discussed in the above section along with the subject particle が **ga** and the adjective いい **ii** (*good*). The recommended action is expressed by the verb in the past tense even though the action did not take place in the past. If you are using a negative verb to say *It is better not to . . .* , then the verb must be in the present tense. In conversation, such a statement is often followed by the particle よ **yo** discussed in Chapter 4. The following are some examples:

野菜をもっと食べた方がいいですよ。
Yasai o motto tabeta hō ga ii desu yo.
It is better to eat more vegetables.

卵は食べない方がいいですよ。
Tamago wa tabenai hō ga ii desu yo.
It is better not to eat eggs.

早く寝た方がいいですよ。
Hayaku neta hō ga ii desu yo.
It is better to go to bed early.

タバコは吸わない方がいいですよ。
Tabako wa suwanai hō ga ii desu yo.
It is better not to smoke.

Making Superlative Comparisons

In this section, you will learn how to make superlative comparisons in Japanese.

INDICATING THE SUPERLATIVE WITH 一番 ICHI-BAN

Suppose Ms. Watanabe is kind. Then, you'll say:

渡辺さんはやさしいです。
Watanabe-san wa yasashii desu.
Ms. Watanabe is kind.

Suppose Ms. Watanabe is the kindest person at the company you work for. You do not need to create a special superlative form like *kindest* in Japanese. You can continue to use the adjective in the same form, やさしいです **yasashii desu**. All you need to do is to add the adverb 一番 **ichi-ban**, which literally means *number 1* or

Japanese Demystified

first, but actually means *the best* or *the most* in this context, and specify the setting with the particle で **de**. For example:

渡辺さんは会社で一番やさしいです。
Watanabe-san wa kaisha de ichi-ban yasashii desu.
Ms. Watanabe is the kindest in the company.

You can specify the group or the list at the beginning of the sentence, by marking it with the particle で **de** and the topic marker は **wa**, as in:

会社では渡辺さんが一番やさしいです。
Kaisha de wa Watanabe-san ga ichi-ban yasashii desu.
Ms. Watanabe is the kindest in the company.

高橋さんと、山田さんと、渡辺さんとでは、渡辺さんが一番やさしいです。
Takahashi-san to, Yamada-san to, Watanabe-san to de wa, Watanabe-san ga ichi-ban yasashii desu.
Among Ms. Takahashi, Ms. Yamada, and Ms. Watanabe, Ms. Watanabe is the kindest.

The group or the list can be followed by の中 **no naka** (*in*, *within*, *among*), as in:

会社の中では渡辺さんが一番やさしいです。
Kaisha no naka de wa Watanabe-san ga ichi-ban yasashii desu.

高橋さんと、山田さんと、渡辺さんの中では、渡辺さんが一番やさしいです。
Takahashi-san to, Yamada-san to, Watanabe-san no naka de wa, Watanabe-san ga ichi-ban yasashii desu.

Once you add の中 **no naka**, the last item in the list may not be followed by と **to**, as you can see in the previous example.

Oral Practice

 TRACK 58

Practice saying superlative sentences by reading the following sentences out loud.

アイスクリームの中では、ストロベリーが一番好きです。
Aisukurīmu no naka de wa, sutoroberī ga ichi-ban suki desu.
Among ice cream (flavors), I like strawberry the best.

魚の中では、鮭が一番おいしいです。
Sakana no naka de wa, sake ga ichi-ban oishii desu.
Among fish, salmon is most delicious.

サッカーと、野球と、テニスの中では、サッカーが一番人気があります。
Sakkā to, yakyū to, tenisu no naka de wa, sakkā ga ichi-ban ninki ga arimasu.
Among soccer, baseball, and tennis, soccer is most popular.

ロシア語と、フランス語と、スペイン語の中では、ロシア語が一番難しいです。
Roshia-go to, Furansu-go to, Supein-go no naka de wa, Roshia-go ga ichi-ban muzukashii desu.
Among Russian, French, and Spanish, Russian is most difficult.

歌うのと、踊るのと、ピアノを弾くのとでは、歌うのが一番好きです。
Utau no to, odoru no to, piano o hiku no to de wa, utau no ga ichi-ban suki desu.
Among singing, dancing, and playing the piano, I like singing the best.

ASKING SUPERLATIVE QUESTIONS

For asking a superlative question about non-human non-location items, use 何 **nani** (*what*) or どれ **dore** (*which one*): if the basis of comparison is a group, use 何 **nani**; if the basis of comparison is a list, use どれ **dore**. For example:

スポーツでは、何が一番好きですか。
Supōtsu de wa, nani ga ichi-ban suki desu ka.
Among sports, which one do you like the best?

野球と、サッカーと、バスケットボールの中では、どれが一番人気がありますか。
Yakyū to, sakkā to, basukettobōru no naka de wa, dore ga ichi-ban ninki ga arimasu ka.
Among baseball, soccer, and basketball, which one is most popular?

動物の中では何が一番好きですか。
Dōbutsu no naka de wa nani ga ichi-ban suki desu ka.
Among animals, what do you like the most?

犬と、猫と、うさぎの中では、どれが一番好きですか。
Inu to, neko to, usagi no naka de wa, dore ga ichi-ban suki desu ka.
Among dogs, cats, and rabbits, which do you like the best?

歌うのと、踊るのと、ピアノを弾くのとでは、どれが一番好きですか。

Utau no to, odoru no to, piano o hiku no to de wa, dore ga ichi-ban suki desu ka.

Among singing, dancing, and playing the piano, which one do you like the best?

By contrast, for asking a superlative question about people, just use だれ **dare** (*who*) regardless of whether the basis of comparison is a group or a list. Similarly, for locations, just use どこ **doko** (*where*).

お兄さんと、お姉さんと、弟さんの中では、だれが一番よくテレビを見ますか。

Onīsan to, onēsan to, otōtosan no naka de wa, dare ga ichi-ban yoku terebi o mimasu ka.

Among your older brother, older sister, and younger brother, who watches TV the most?

日本の歌手ではだれが一番人気がありますか。

Nihon no kashu de wa dare ga ichi-ban ninki ga arimasu ka.

Among Japanese singers, who is most popular?

日本ではどこが一番寒いですか。

Nihon de wa doko ga ichi-ban samui desu ka.

Which place is the coldest in Japan?

ニューヨークと、サンフランシスコと、ボストンの中では、どこが一番物価が高いですか。

Nyūyōku to, San Furanshisuko to, Bosuton no naka de wa, doko ga ichi-ban bukka ga takai desu ka.

Among New York, San Francisco, and Boston, which place has the highest cost of living?

Written Practice 3

Fill in the blanks with どちら **dochira**, だれ **dare**, どこ **doko**, 何 **nani**, or どれ **dore**.

1. スポーツでは＿＿＿＿＿が一番好きですか。

   Supōtsu de wa ＿＿＿＿＿＿＿＿＿ ga ichi-ban suki desu ka.
   Among sports, which one do you like the best?

2. 日本では＿＿＿＿＿が一番物価が高いですか。

   Nihon de wa ＿＿＿＿＿＿＿＿＿ ga ichi-ban bukka ga takai desu ka.
   In Japan, which place is most expensive to live? (物価 bukka [*cost of living*])

3. 映画を見るのと、本を読むのとでは、＿＿＿＿＿が好きですか。

   Eiga o miru no to, hon o yomu no to de wa, ＿＿＿＿＿＿＿＿＿ ga suki desu ka.
   Which do you like better, watching a film or reading a book?

4. クラスでは＿＿＿＿が一番背が高いですか。

   Kurasu de wa ＿＿＿＿＿＿＿＿＿＿ ga ichi-ban se ga takai desu ka.
   Who is the tallest in the class?

5. 作家では＿＿＿＿が一番好きですか。

   Sakka de wa ＿＿＿＿＿＿＿＿＿＿ ga ichi-ban suki desu ka.
   Which writer do you like the best?

6. 赤と、青と、白とでは＿＿＿＿が一番好きですか。

   Aka to, ao to, shiro to de wa ＿＿＿＿＿＿＿＿＿＿ ga ichi-ban suki desu ka.
   Among red, blue, and white, which do you like the best?

QUIZ

Circle the letter of the word or phrase that best completes each sentence.

1. 弟は私＿＿＿＿早く起きます。

   Otōto wa watashi ＿＿＿＿＿ hayaku okimasu.

   (a) より yori   (c) ほど hodo

   (b) と to   (d) で de

2. 母は父＿＿＿＿厳しくありません。

   Haha wa chichi ＿＿＿＿＿ kibishiku arimasen.

   (a) より yori   (c) ほど hodo

   (b) と to   (d) で de

3. 母は父＿＿＿＿同じぐらいよく働きます。

   Haha wa chichi ＿＿＿＿＿ onaji gurai yoku hatarakimasu.

   (a) より yori   (c) ほど hodo

   (b) と to   (d) で de

4. 猫と、犬と、＿＿＿＿が好きですか。

   Neko to, inu to, ＿＿＿＿＿ ga suki desu ka.

   (a) どちら dochira   (c) 何 nani

   (b) どれ dore   (d) だれ dare

5. 猫と、犬と、うさぎの中では、＿＿＿＿が一番好きですか。

Neko to, inu to, usagi no naka de wa, ＿＿＿＿ ga ichi-ban suki desu ka.

(a) どちら dochira   (c) 何 nani

(b) どれ dore   (d) だれ dare

6. 動物の中では＿＿＿＿が一番好きですか。

Dōbutsu no naka de wa ＿＿＿＿ ga ichi-ban suki desu ka.

(a) どちら dochira   (c) 何 nani

(b) どれ dore   (d) だれ dare

7. ＿＿＿＿と、＿＿＿＿とでは、どちらが好きですか。

＿＿＿＿ to, ＿＿＿＿ to de wa, dochira ga suki desu ka.

(a) 書き, 読み kaki, yomi

(b) 書くの kaku no, 読むの yomu no

(c) 書いて kaite, 読んで yonde

(d) 書く kaku, 読む yomu

8. 早く＿＿＿＿方がいいですよ。タバコは＿＿＿＿方がいいですよ。

Hayaku ＿＿＿＿ hō ga ii desu yo. Tabako wa ＿＿＿＿ hō ga ii desu yo.

(a) 寝る neru, すう suu

(b) 寝る neru, すわなかった suwanakatta

(c) 寝た neta, すわなかった suwanakatta

(d) 寝た neta, すわない suwanai

9. ニューヨークと、サンフランシスコと、ボストンの中では、＿＿＿＿が一番物価が高いですか。

Nyūyōku to, San Furanshisuko to, Bosuton no naka de wa, ＿＿＿＿ ga ichi-ban bukka ga takai desu ka.

(a) どこ doko   (c) 何 nani

(b) どれ dore   (d) だれ dare

10. 日本の歌手では ＿＿＿＿ が一番人気がありますか。

Nihon no kashu de wa ＿＿＿＿ ga ichi-ban ninki ga arimasu ka.

(a) どこ doko   (c) 何 nani

(b) どれ dore   (d) だれ dare

CHAPTER 14

Creating Complex Phrases and Clauses

In this chapter, you'll learn:

Compound Verbs and Adjectives
Creating Complex Modifiers
Creating Sentence-Like Noun Modifiers

Compound Verbs and Adjectives

Certain verbs and adjectives can directly follow another verb or adjective in the stem form (see Chapter 4 and 6 for stem forms), creating a compound verb or a compound adjective. In this section, you will see many useful verbs and adjectives that can create compound verbs and adjectives.

COMPOUND VERBS THAT SHOW TIMING

はじめる **hajimeru** is a verb that means *to begin* or *to start*, as in 仕事をはじめる **shigoto o hajimeru** (*to start one's work*), but it can follow another verb in the stem form, creating a compound verb that means *to start ...ing*. For example:

昨日、レポートを書きはじめました。
Kinō, repōto o kaki-hajimemashita.
I started writing the report yesterday.

来学期から、日本語を勉強しはじめます。
Raigakki kara, Nihon-go o benkyō shi-hajimemasu.
I'll start studying Japanese from next semester.

Additional verbs that can create compound verbs to show the timing of an action include おわる **owaru** (*to finish ...ing*), だす **dasu** (*to start ...ing with dynamism*), かける **kakeru** (*to start ... ing*), つづける **tsuzukeru** (*to continue ...ing*), and やむ **yamu** (*to stop ...ing*). The following are their example sentences:

ローンを払いおわりました。
Rōn o harai-owarimashita.
I finished paying off the loan.

由美子ちゃんが泣きだしました。
Yumiko-chan ga naki-dashimashita.
Yumiko broke into tears.

ワインを飲みかけました。
Wain o nomi-kakemashita.
I started drinking wine.

日本語を勉強しつづけてください。
Nihon-go o benkyō shi-tsuzukete kudasai.
Please continue studying Japanese.

雨が降りやみました。
Ame ga furi-yamimashita.
The rain stopped.

COMPOUND VERBS THAT SHOW THE EXTENT OF AN ACTION

Some verbs create compound verbs to show the extent of an action. They include すぎる **sugiru** (*to do/be ... too much*), なれる **nareru** (*to get used to ...ing*), つくす **tsukusu** (*to do ...exhaustively*), きる **kiru** (*to do ... completely*), and まくる **makuru** (*to do... without a break*). Note that すぎる **sugiru** can follow not only verbs but also adjectives:

お酒を飲みすぎました。頭が痛いです。
O-sake o nomi-sugimashita. Atama ga itai desu.
I drank too much sake. I have a headache.

このグラスは小さすぎます。大きいのを下さい。
Kono gurasu wa chīsa-sugimasu. Ōkii no o kudasai.
This glass is too small. Please give me a bigger one.

食べすぎないでくださいね。
Tabe-suginai de kudasai ne.
Please do not overeat.

父は働きすぎます。よく残業をします。
Chichi wa hataraki-sugimasu. Yoku zangyō o shimasu.
My father works too much. He often works overtime.

スミスさんは頭がよすぎます。
Sumisu-san wa atama ga yo-sugimasu.
Mr. Smith is too smart.

この町は住みなれました。
Kono machi wa sumi-naremashita.
I got used to living in this town.

日本の古い映画は見つくしました。
Nihon no furui eiga wa mi-tsukushimashita.
I watched all the old Japanese movies.

100メートルを泳ぎきりました。
100-mētoru o oyogi-kirimashita.
(He) swam a full 100 meters.

高校生の時は、マンガを読みまくりました。
Kōkōsei no toki wa, manga o yomi-makurimashita.
When I was a high school student, I read comic books all the time.

COMPOUND ADJECTIVES THAT SHOW DIFFICULTY

The adjectives やすい **yasui** (*easy to . . .*) and にくい **nikui** (*difficult to . . .*) create compound adjectives to express whether some action is easy or difficult to carry out. For example:

このサンドイッチは小さくて、食べやすいですね。
Kono sandoitchi wa chīsakute, tabe-yasui desu ne.
This sandwich is small and easy to eat, isn't it?

このかばんは大きくて、持ちにくいです。
Kono kaban wa ōkikute, mochi-nikui desu.
This bag is big and hard to carry.

山田先生はやさしくて、話しやすいです。
Yamada sensei wa yasashikute, hanashi-yasui desu.
Professor Yamada is kind and easy to talk to.

このペンはとても書きやすいです。
Kono pen wa totemo kaki-yasui desu.
This pen is very easy to write with.

COMPOUND VERBS THAT SHOW A FAILURE

Some verbs create compound verbs that show a failure. They include 忘れる **wasureru** (*to forget ...ing*), そこなう **sokonau** (*to miss the opportunity of doing ...ing*), まちがえる **machigaeru** (*to make a mistake in ...ing*), のこす **nokosu** (*to leave something without doing...*).

テレビを消し忘れました。
Terebi o keshi-wasuremashita.
I forgot to turn off the TV.

豆腐を買い忘れました。
Tōfu o kai-wasuremashita.
I forgot to buy tofu.

すしを食べそこないました。
Sushi o tabe-sokonaimashita.
I missed eating sushi.

お金をもらいそこないました。
O-kane o morai-sokonaimashita.
I missed the chance to receive money.

名前を書き間違えました。
Namae o kaki-machigaemashita.
I made a mistake in writing (his) name.

この仕事はやりのこしたんです。
Kono shigoto wa yari-nikoshita ndesu.
I left this work undone.

COMPOUND VERBS THAT SHOW A RECIPROCAL ACTION

The verb あう **au** (*to do . . . with each other*) creates a compound verb that shows the idea of two people doing something with each other. For example:

ロミオとジュリエットは愛しあっていました。
Romio to Jurietto wa aishi-atte imashita.
Romeo and Juliet loved each other.

父と母は文句を言いあっています。
Chichi to haha wa monku o ii-atte imasu.
My father and mother complain to each other.

Written Practice 1

Choose the appropriate option in the parentheses.

1. この本は難しくて、読み(やすいです, にくいです)。

    Kono hon wa muzukashikute, yomi-(yasui desu, nikui desu).

2. この宿題は昨日し(まくりました, はじめました)。

    Kono shukudai wa kinō shi-(makurimashita, hajimemashita).

3. このかばんは(高, 安)すぎます。買えません。

    Kono kaban wa (taka, yasu)-sugimasu. Kaemasen.

4. 村上春樹の小説は大好きで、読み (わすれました, つくしました)。

Murakami Haruki no shōsetsu wa daisuki de, yomi-(wasuremashita, tsukushimashita).

5. 日本語が好きですから、勉強し(おわります, つづけます)。

Nihon-go ga suki desu kara, benkyō shi-(owarimasu, tsuzukemasu).

Creating Complex Modifiers

In this section, you will learn some complex modifiers that can be created using a variety of words.

EXPRESSING CONJECTURE WITH そうな SŌ NA

The suffix そうな **sō na** follows an adjective or a verb in the stem form. The resulting complex adjective is a na-type adjective and can be conjugated just like a regular na-type adjective.

When そうな **sō na** is used with an adjective, it expresses the speaker's intuitive subjective guess about the property or quality of the item. For example, やさしそうな 人 **yasashi-sō na hito** means *a person who looks kind*. Since そうな **sō na** expresses the speaker's conjecture, it cannot be used for properties that are already known or visually obvious. The following are some examples of adjectives used with そうな **sō na**:

あの人は新しいマネージャーですよ。こわそうな人ですね。
Ano hito wa atarashii manējā desu yo. Kowa-sō na hito desu ne.
That person is a new manager. He is a scary-looking guy, isn't he?

あの人はまじめそうですね。
Ano hito wa majime-sō desu ne.
That person looks serious, isn't he?

おいしそうなステーキですね。
Oishi-sō na sutēki desu ne.
The steak looks delicious, doesn't it?

The adjective いい **ii** (*good*) becomes よさそうな **yosa-sō na** when followed by そうな **sō na**. For a negative adjective, さそうな **sa sōna** is added after dropping the final い **i**. For example, やさしくない **yasashiku nai** (*not kind*) becomes やさしくなさそうな **yasashiku nasa-sō na**.

この子供は頭がよさそうですね。
Kono kodomo wa atama ga yosa-sō desu ne.
This child looks smart.

この映画は面白くなさそうです。他の映画を見ましょう。
Kono eiga wa omoshiroku nasa-sō desu. Hoka no eiga o mimashō.
This movie doesn't look interesting. Let's watch another movie.

When そうな **sō na** is used with a verb, it expresses the speaker's intuitive conjecture about what will happen or what has happened.

雨が降りそうですね。
Ame ga furi-sō desu ne.
It looks like it's going to rain.

このカメラはこわれそうです。
Kono kamera wa koware-sō desu.
This camera is about to break.

このカメラはこわれていそうです。
Kono kamera wa kowarete i-sō desu.
This camera looks broken.

Written Practice 2

Choose the appropriate item in the parentheses.

1. これは何ですか。(おいしい, おいし)そうですね。

   Kore wa nan desu ka. (Oishii, oishi) -sō desu ne.

2. あの人は新しいマネージャーですよ。(まじめ, こわい) そうですね。

   Ano hito wa atarashii manējā desu yo. (Majime, Kowai) -sō desu ne.

3. あの女の人は (背が高, やさし) そうですね。

   Ano onna no hito wa (se ga taka, yasashi) -sō desu ne.

4. このテレビはつきません。(こわれ, こわれてい) そうですね。

   Kono terebi wa tsukimasen. (Koware, Kowarete i) -sō desu ne.

5. この子供は頭が (いさ, よさ) そうです。

   Kono kodomo wa atama ga (isa, yosa) -sō desu.

6. このかばんはあまり高く (な, なさ) そうです。

   Kono kaban wa amari takaku (na, nasa) -sō desu.

EXPRESSING A SIMILE WITH のような NO YŌ NA AND みたいな MITAI NA

By combining a noun and のような **no yō na**, you can describe things and people in terms of similarities and resemblances, as a simile. For example, 天使のような **tenshi no yō na** means *like an angel*. The resulting complex adjective is a na-type adjective that can be conjugated like a regular na-type adjective. The adverb まるで **marude** (*just like*) is often used with this construction.

サンディーさんはまるで天使のような人です。
Sandī-san wa marude tenshi no yō na hito desu.
Sandy is just like an angel.

父は子どものような人です。何も自分でできません。
Chichi wa kodomo no yō na hito desu. Nani mo jibun de dekimasen.
My father is like a child. He cannot do anything by himself.

母は男のようです。
Haha wa otoko no yō desu.
My mother is like a man.

スミスさんは日本人のように日本語を話します。
Sumisu-san wa Nihon-jin no yō ni Nihon-go o hanashimasu.
Mr. Smith speaks Japanese just like a Japanese person.

おこのみやきはパンケーキのような食べ物です。
Okonomiyaki wa pankēki no yō na tabemono desu.
Okonomiyaki is a food like pancake.

みたいな **mitai na** also follows a noun and can be used just like のような **no yō na** discussed above, but the former is slightly more casual than the latter.

兄は侍みたいな人です。
Ani wa samurai mitai na hito desu.
My big brother is just like a samurai.

子供みたいなしゃべり方をしないでください。
Kodomi mitai na shaberi-kata o shinaide kudasai.
Don't talk like a child.

Note that しゃべり方 **shaberi-kata** in the sentence 子供みたいなしゃべり方をしないでください/Kodomi mitai na shaberi-kata o shinaide kudasai means *the way one talks*. 方 **kata** can follow a verb in the stem form and create a noun that means "the way one does such and such" or "how to do such and such."

この辞書の使い方を教えてください。
Kono jisho no tsukai-kata o oshiete kudasai.
Please teach me how to use this dictionary.

EXPRESSING TYPICALITY WITH らしい RASHII

らしい **rashii** follows a noun and creates an adjective that means *like a typical model of . . .* or *like an ideal model of . . . .* The resulting complex adjective is an i-type adjective that can be conjugated just like a regular i-type adjective. For example:

母はとても母親らしい人ですが、父はあまり父親らしくありません。
Haha wa totemo hahaoya rashii hito desu ga, chichi wa amari chichioya rashiku arimasen.
My mother is an ideal model of mother, but my father is not very much like an ideal model of father.

もう少し大人らしくしてください。
Mō sukoshi otona rashiku shite kudasai.
Please act as an adult (because you are).

今日の田中さんはいつもの田中さんらしくありませんね。
Kyō no Tanaka-san wa itsumo no Tanaka-san rashiku arimasen ne.
Mr. Tanaka is not himself today, is he?

山田さんはとても女らしい人です。
Yamada-san wa totemo onna rashii hito desu.
Ms. Yamada is a very feminine person.

Written Practice 3

Choose the appropriate item in the parentheses.

1. 母はとても(女, 男)らしい人です。

   Haha wa totemo (onna, otoko) rashii hito desu.

2. 父は (女, 男) のような人です。

   Chichi wa (onna, otoko) no yō na hito desu.

3. あの子供は頭がよすぎて、(子供, 大人) らしくありません。

   Ano kodomo wa atama ga yo-sugite, (kodomo, otona) rashiku arimasen.

4. この猫は犬 (みたい, らしい) ですね。

   Kono neko wa inu (mitai, rashii) desu ne.

Creating Sentence-Like Noun Modifiers

In this section, you will learn how to create a noun modifier in the form of a sentence, placed right before a noun. Some of them are called relative clauses and their function is to qualify the noun, while others are called noun complement clauses and their function is to complement the meaning of the noun.

MODIFYING A NOUN WITH A RELATIVE CLAUSE

You can use a sentence to qualify a noun. Such a sentence is called a relative clause and it is placed right before the noun it modifies. For example:

私が昨日買った本
watashi ga kinō katta hon
the book I bought yesterday

As you can see, the predicate in a relative clause must be in the plain form and a phrase that corresponds to the modified noun should be missing in the relative clause. For example, it is wrong to say:

私が昨日本を買った本
watashi ga kinō hon o katta hon

The following sentences all include a relative clause:

私が昨日買った本は高かったです。
Watashi ga kinō katta hon wa takakatta desu.
The book I bought yesterday was expensive.

あそこに立っている人は田中さんです。
Asoko ni tatte iru hito wa Tanaka-san desu.
The person who is standing over there is Mr. Tanaka.

和子さんはあそこに座っている人です。
Kazuko-san wa asoko ni suwatte iru hito desu.
Kazuko is the person who is sitting over there.

昨日見た映画はあまりよくありませんでした。
Kinō mita eiga wa amari yoku arimasendeshita.
The movie I watched yesterday was not very good.

私が買いたい車はトヨタのカムリです。
Watashi ga kai-tai kuruma wa Toyota no Kamuri desu.
The car that I want to buy is Toyota's Camry.

MODIFYING A NOUN WITH A NOUN COMPLEMENT CLAUSE

You can use a sentence just to complement the meaning of a noun, rather than qualifying it or limiting it. Such a sentence is called a noun complement clause. Just like a relative clause, a noun complement clause is placed right before the noun it modifies. However, unlike a relative clause, there is no gap that corresponds to the noun. A noun complement clause is often followed by という **to iu**, which is the combination of the particle と **to** and the verb いう **iu** (*to say*). For example, the following noun phrase includes a noun that means "fact." To make it clear what fact, a noun complement clause meaning "Three students were injured" is added before it:

学生が3人怪我をした (という) 事実
gakusei ga san-nin kega o shita (to iu) jijitsu
the fact that three students were injured

The following are some example sentences that include a noun complement clause:

学生が3人怪我をした (という) 事実を知っていますか。
gakusei ga san-nin kega o shita (to iu) jijitsu o shitte imasu ka.
Do you know the fact that three students were injured?

他の人に答えを言わない (という) 約束をしました。
Hoka no hito ni kotae o iwanai (to iu) yakusoku o shimashita
I promised not to tell the answer to other people.

父の病気がよくなる (という) 望みはありません。
Chichi no byōki ga yoku naru (to iu) nozomi wa arimasen.
There is no hope of my sick father getting better.

Note that という **to iu** can also follow just a proper noun to modify a common noun that follows, as in:

エミリーという学生 。
Emirī to iu gakusei
A student called Emily

Such a construction is useful when you want to introduce some item that your conversation partner might not know—a person, a restaurant, a place, etc.

The following sentences all include this construction:

駅の前に紅花というレストランがあります。そこに7時に来てください。
Eki no mae ni Benihana to iu resutoran ga arimasu. Soko ni 7-ji ni kite kudasai.
There is a restaurant called Benihana in front of the train station. Please go there at 7 o'clock.

宇多田ヒカルという歌手を知っていますか。
Utada Hikaru to iu kashu o shitte imasu ka.
Do you know the singer named Hikaru Utada?

桃太郎という昔話を知っていますか。
Momotarō to iu mukashi-banashi o shitte imasu ka.
Do you know the old story called Momotaro (Peach Boy)?

Written Practice 4

By reordering the items in each set, form a grammatical sentence that yields in the intended meaning.

1. The sukiyaki I ate yesterday was good.

   (すきやき sukiyaki, 昨日 kinō, おいしかったです oishikatta desu, 食べた tabeta, は wa)

   _____

2. The person who came here yesterday was French.

   (昨日 kinō, フランス人でした Furansu-jin deshita, 来た kita, は wa, ここに koko ni, 人 hito)

   _____

3. The man who is eating pizza over there is my friend.

   (あそこで asoko de, は wa, ピザを piza o, 男の人 otoko no hito, 食べている tabete iru, です desu, 私の友達 watashi no tomodachi)

   _____

4. Do you know the violinist called Midori Goto?

   (知っていますか shitte imasu ka, バイオリニストを baiorinisuto o, という to iu, 五嶋みどり Gotō Midori)

   _____

QUIZ

Circle the letter of the word or phrase that best completes each sentence.

1. 日本語を勉強＿＿＿つづけてください。

   Nihon-go o benkyō ＿＿＿ -tsuzukete kudasai.

   (a) する suru　　　　　　(c) して shite

   (b) し shi　　　　　　　(d) した shita

2. お酒を飲み＿＿＿。頭が痛いです。

   O-sake o nomi- ＿＿＿ . Atama ga itai desu.

   (a) すぎました sugimashita

   (b) はじめました hajimemashita

   (c) すぎます sugimasu

   (d) はじめます hajimemasu

3. 山田先生はやさしくて、話し＿＿＿。

   Yamada sensei wa yasashikute, hanashi- ＿＿＿ .

   (a) すぎます sugimasu　　　(c) おわります owarimasu

   (b) やすいです yasui desu　　(d) にくいです nikui desu

4. すみません。テレビを消し＿＿＿。

   Sumimasen. Terebi o keshi- ＿＿＿ .

   (a) 忘れました wasuremashita

   (b) はじめました hajimemashita

   (c) おわりました owarimashita

   (d) やすいです yasui desu

5. ＿＿＿そうなステーキですね。食べましょう。

   ＿＿＿ -sō na sutēki desu ne. Tabemashō.

   (a) おいしい oishii　　　　(c) 高い takai

   (b) おいし oishi　　　　　(d) 高く takaku

6. この映画は＿＿＿そうです。他の映画を見ましょう。

   Kono eiga wa ＿＿＿ -sō desu. Hoka no eiga o mimashō.

   (a) 面白 omoshiro　　　　　(c) 面白い omoshiroi

   (b) 面白くな omoshiroku na　(d) 面白くなさ omoshiroku nasa

7. 父は＿＿＿＿ような人です。何も自分でできません。

Chichi wa ＿＿＿＿ yō na hito desu. Nani mo jibun de dekimasen.

(a) 男 otoko   (c) 子ども kodomo

(b) 子どもの kodomo no   (d) 大人の otona no

8. 父はとても＿＿＿＿らしいです。

Chichi wa totemo ＿＿＿＿ rashii desu.

(a) 男 otoko   (c) 子ども kodomo

(b) 子どもの kodomo no   (d) 女 onna

9. ＿＿＿＿は田中さんです。

＿＿＿＿ wa Tanaka-san desu.

(a) あそこに立っている人 Asoko ni tatte iru hito

(b) 人あそこに立っている Hito Asoko ni tatte iru

(c) 人があそこに立っている Hito ga Asoko ni tatte iru

(d) あそこに人が立っている Asoko ni hito ga tatte iru

10. ＿＿＿＿を知っていますか。

＿＿＿＿ o shitte imasu ka.

(a) 昔話という桃太郎 Mukashi-banashi to iu Momotarō

(b) 桃太郎という昔話 Momotarō to iu mukashi-banashi

(c) 桃太郎が昔話という Momotarō ga mukashi-banashi to iu

(d) 桃太郎と昔話いう Momotarō to mukashi-banashi iu

CHAPTER 15

Indicating Change

In this chapter, you'll learn:

Using the Verbs する **suru** *and* なる **naru** *to Indicate Change*
More Useful Particles
Things You Wear

Using the Verbs する suru and なる naru to Indicate Change

In this section, you will learn a variety of constructions that express changes with the verbs する **suru** (*to do*) and なる **naru** (*to become*).

USING する SURU AND なる NARU WITH AN ADVERB

The verb する **suru** (*to do*) and the verb なる **naru** (*to become*) contrast very sharply when used to express some change. When they are used with adverbs, する **suru** expresses a change of some property as something that someone makes whereas なる **naru** expresses it as something that happens. For example:

妹が部屋をきれいにしました。
Imōto ga heya o kirei ni shimashita.
My younger sister made the room neat.

部屋がきれいになりました。
Heya ga kirei ni narimashita.
The room became neat.

大家さんが家賃を高くしました。
Ōya-san ga yachin o takaku shimashita.
The landlord raised the rent.

家賃が高くなりました。
Yachin ga takaku narimashita.
The rent went up.

兄は最近やさしくなりました。
Ani wa saikin yasashiku narimashita.
My older brother became kind (kinder) lately.

ステレオの音を小さくしてください。
Sutereo no oto o chīsaku shite kudasai.
Please turn down the volume of the stereo.

宿題を少なくしてください。
Shukudai o sukunaku shite kudasai.
Please reduce the homework.

The item that changes can be the speaker or the listener:

もう少し弟にやさしくします。
Mō sukoshi otōto ni yasashiku shimasu.
I'll be a little nicer to my younger brother. (Literally: I'll make myself a little kinder to my younger brother.)

静かにしてください。
Shizuka ni shite kudasai.
Please be quiet. (Literally: Please make yourself quiet.)

まじめにしてください。
Majime ni shite kudasai.
Please be serious.

Written Practice 1

Fill in the blanks with adverbs creatively to make sensible requests.

1. 聞こえません。テレビの音を_____してください。

   Kikoemasen. Terebi no oto o _____ shite kudasai.

2. うるさいです。_____してさい。

   Urusai desu. _____ shite kudasai.

3. きたないですね。もう少し部屋を_____してください。

   Kitanai desu ne. Mō sukoshi heya o _____ shite kudasai.

4. 宿題が多すぎます。宿題を_____してください。

   Shukudai ga ō-sugimasu. Shukudai o _____ shite kudasai.

5. 高いですよ。もう少し_____してください。

   Takai desu yo. Mō sukoshi _____ shite kudasai.

USING する SURU AND なる NARU WITH ...ことに KOTO NI

Both ことにする **koto ni suru** and ことになる **koto ni naru** follow a verb in the plain form and express decision making. こと **koto** is a nominalizer introduced in Chapter 8. ことにする **koto ni suru** shows that the decision was made by the person denoted by the subject noun.

来年日本に行くことにしました。
Rainen Nihon ni iku koto ni shimashita.
I decided to go to Japan next year.

化学を勉強することにしました。
Kagaku o benkyō suru koto ni shimashita.
I decided to study chemistry.

アパートを借りないことにしました。

Apāto o karinai koto ni shimashita.

I decided not to rent an apartment.

私達は来年結婚することにしました。

Watashi-tachi wa rainen kekkon suru koto ni shimashita.

We decided to get married next year.

By contrast, ことになる **koto ni naru** doesn't explicitly show who made the decision.

私は来年日本に行くことになりました。

Watashi wa rainen Nihon ni iku koto ni narimashita.

It has been decided that I go to Japan next year.

ここに駐車できることになりました。

Koko ni chūsha dekiru koto ni narimashita.

It has been decided that we can park here.

Even a very personal decision is often expressed by ことになりました **koto ni narimashita**, especially in a polite-formal conversation context.

今日からここで働くことになりました。よろしくお願いします。

Kyō kara koko de hataraku koto ni narimashita. Yoroshiku o-negai shimasu.

It has been decided that I start working here starting today. I'm very pleased to meet you.

USING する SURU AND なる NARU WITH ...ように YŌ NI

Recall that ように **yō ni** creates an adverbial phrase that shows the manner needed to obtain some result (Chapter 12).

忘れないように書きます。

Wasurenai yō ni kakimasu.

I will write it down so I won't forget.

By adding the verb する **suru** (*to do*) after the phrase with ように **yō ni**, you can express your effort making. For example, see the difference between the previous sentence and the following sentence:

忘れないようにします。
Wasurenai yō ni shimasu.
I'll try not to forget.

The following are some example sentences for ようにする **yō ni suru**:

野菜をたくさん食べるようにしています。
Yasai o takusan taberu yō ni shite imasu.
I'm trying to eat a lot of vegetables.

肉や、たまごを食べないようにしています。
Niku ya, tamago o tabenai yō ni shite imasu.
I try not to eat meat, eggs, etc.

お酒を飲まないようにしています。
O-sake o nomanai yō ni shite imasu.
I'm trying not to drink.

This construction is useful for requesting others to make some effort:

たばこを吸わないようにしてください。
Tabako o suwanai yō ni shite kudasai.
Please refrain from smoking.

早くねるようにしてください。
Hayaku neru yō ni shite kudasai.
Please try to go to bed early.

毎日勉強するようにしてください。
Mainichi benkyō suru yō ni shite kudasai.
Please try to study every day.

Depending on what the subject is, the sentence may mean to make some arrangement to make a change.

目覚まし時計が7時になるようにします。
Mezamashi-dokei ga 7-ji ni naru yō ni shimasu.
I'll set my alarm so it will go off at 7 o'clock.

If you place the verb なる **naru** after the phrase with ように **yō ni**, you can express some change that happens or happened. Unlike ようにする **yō ni suru**,

ようになる **yō ni naru** doesn't express the speaker's conscious intention for making a change regardless of whether the action is intentionally done.

> 兄の子供は2歳です。最近よく話すようになりました。
> Ani no kodomo wa ni-sai desu. Saikin yoku hanasu yō ni narimashita.
> *My older brother's child is 2 years old. She recently started to talk a lot.*

> 私はカタカナが書けるようになりました。
> Watashi wa katakana ga kakeru yō ni narimashita.
> *I became able to write katakana.*

> 日本語で挨拶ができるようになりました。
> Nihon-go de aisatsu ga dekiru yō ni narimashita.
> *I became able to greet in Japanese.*

書ける **kakeru** and できる **dekiru** in the above two sentences are in the potential form (see Chapter 10). That's why the understood direct object is marked by the particle が **ga**.

ないように **nai yō ni** is often contracted to なく **naku** in this construction. So, the following two sentences are both grammatical and mean *My little brother stopped watching TV:*

> 弟はテレビを見ないようになりました。
> Otōto wa terebi o minai yō ni narimashita.

> 弟はテレビを見なくなりました。
> Otōto wa terebi o minaku narimashita.

Written Practice 2

Fill in the blanks with either よう **yō** or こと **koto**.

1. 今日からここで働く＿＿＿になりました。よろしくお願いします。

   Kyō kara koko de hataraku ＿＿＿ ni narimashita. Yoroshiku o-negai shimasu.

2. 弟は最近よく話す＿＿＿になりました。

   Otōto wa saikin yoku hanasu ＿＿＿ ni narimashita.

3. 来年、日本に行く＿＿＿にしました。

   Rainen Nihon ni iku ＿＿＿ ni shimashita.

4. もう少し野菜を食べる＿＿＿＿＿にしてください。

   Mō sukoshi yasai o taberu ＿＿＿＿＿ ni shite kudasai.

5. 漢字を勉強したので、日本の新聞が読める＿＿＿＿＿になりました。

   Kanji o benkyō shita node, Nihon no shinbun ga yomeru ＿＿＿＿＿ ni
   narimashita.

6. 肉や、たまごを食べすぎない＿＿＿＿＿にしてください。

   Niku ya, tamago o tabe-suginai ＿＿＿＿＿ ni shite kudasai.

More Useful Particles

In this section, you will learn two additional usages of the particle で **de**.

INDICATING THE TIME OF CHANGE WITH THE PARTICLE で DE

The particle で **de** specifies the time or the age at which some period or some state
ends or changes.

5歳でやっと話せるようになりました。
Go-sai de yatto hanaseru yō ni narimashita.
(He) finally became able to talk at the age of 5.

アメリカに来て、今年で10年になります。
Amerika ni kite, kotoshi de 10-nen ni narimasu.
As of this year, it's been ten years since I came to the U.S.

来週でこのプロジェクトは終わります。
Raishū de kono purojekuto wa owarimasu.
This project will end next week.

息子は27歳で社長になりました。
Musuko wa nijūnana-sai de shachō ni narimashita.
My son became a company president at the age of 27.

父は72歳で亡くなりました。
Chichi wa 72-sai de nakunarimashita.
My father passed away at the age of 72.

INDICATING THE LOCATION OF AN EVENT WITH THE PARTICLE で DE

When the verb ある **aru** (*to exist*) is used for talking about an event or incident, its location is marked by the particle で **de** rather than by the particle に **ni**.

明日、大学で文化祭があります。
Ashita, daigaku de bunkasai ga arimasu.
There will be a cultural festival at the university tomorrow.

昨日、北海道で地震がありました。
Kinō, Hokkaidō de jishin ga arimashita.
There was an earthquake in Hokkaido yesterday.

Written Practice 3

Translate the following sentences into English. Think about the meaning of the particle で **de** carefully.

1. 地下鉄で学校に行きます。Chikatetsu de gakkō ni ikimasu.

   _____

2. 明日、大学で文化祭があります。 Ashita, daigaku de bunkasai ga arimasu.

   _____

3. 陽子さんのうちで宿題をしました。 Yōko-san no uchi de shukudai o shimashita.

   _____

4. 1歳で歩けるようになりました。 Is-sai de arukeru yō ni narimashita.

   _____

5. 私ははしで食べます。 Watashi wa hashi de tabemasu.

   _____

6. 一人で日本に行きました。 Hito-ri de Nihon ni ikimashita.

   _____

7. 来週でこの仕事は終わります。 Raishū de kono shigoto wa owarimasu.

   _____

Things You Wear

The Japanese verb that means *to wear* or *to put on* varies depending on the item. For things that one puts on below the waist, such as skirts, pants, socks, and shoes, use the verb はく **haku**. For things that one puts over his/her head such as caps and hats, use the verb かぶる **kaburu**. For accessories such as watches, glasses, necklaces, earrings, and perfumes, use the verb する **suru**. For eyeglasses, the verb かける **kakeru** may also be used. Other items such as blouse, T-shirts, jacket, dress, suits, vest, sweaters, and coats, use the verb 着る **kiru**.

Verb	Item		
着る kiru	ジャケット	jaketto	*jacket*
	セーター	sētā	*sweater*
	ブラウス	burausu	*blouse*
	シャツ	shatsu	*shirt*
はく haku	ズボン	zubon	*pants*
	ジーンズ	zīnzu	*jeans*
	スカート	sukāto	*skirt*
	靴下	kutsushita	*socks*
	靴	kutsu	*shoes*
かぶる kaburu	帽子	bōshi	*hat, cap*
	キャップ	kyappu	*cap*
する suru	ネックレス	nekkuresu	*necklace*
	イヤリング	iyaringu	*earrings*
	時計	tokei	*watch*
	めがね	megane	*eyeglasses*
かける kakeru	めがね	megane	*eyeglasses*

Written Practice 4

Choose the correct item in the parentheses in the following passage.

姉はジーンズを (はいて、着て) います。それから、セーターを (はいて、着て) います。それから、ネックレスを (かぶって、して) います。

Ane wa jīnzu o (haite, kite) imasu. Sorekara, sētā o (haite, kite) imasu.
Sorekara, nekkuresu o (kabutte, shite) imasu.

QUIZ

Circle the letter of the word or phrase that best completes each sentence.

1. 妹が部屋を＿＿＿＿＿。

    Imōto ga heya o ＿＿＿＿＿ .

    (a) きれいにしました kirei ni shimashita

    (b) きれいになりました kirei ni narimashita

    (c) きれいくしました kireiku shimashita

    (d) きれいくなりました kireiku narimashita

2. 兄は最近＿＿＿＿＿。

    Ani wa saikin ＿＿＿＿＿ .

    (a) やさしいにしました yasashii ni shimashita

    (b) やさしいになりました yasashii ni narimashita

    (c) やさしいしました yasashii shimashita

    (d) やさしくなりました yasashiku narimashita

3. 弟は最近テレビを ＿＿＿＿＿。

    Otōto wa saikin terebi o ＿＿＿＿＿ .

    (a) 見なくしました minaku shimashita

    (b) 見ないようになりました minai yō ni narimashita

    (c) 見ないしました minai shimashita

    (d) 見ないなりました minai narimashita

4. お酒はあまり飲まない＿＿＿＿＿。

    O-sake wa amari nomanai ＿＿＿＿＿ .

    (a) ようにしてください yō ni shite kudasai

    (b) ようにください yō ni kudasai

    (c) ことにください koto ni kudasai

    (d) ことになってください koto ni natte kudasai

5. 来年から化学を勉強する ＿＿＿＿＿。

    Rainen kara kagaku o benkyō suru ＿＿＿＿＿ .

    (a) ことにしました koto ni shimashita

    (b) にしました ni shimashita

    (c) ことなりました koto narimashita

    (d) になりました ni narimashita

6. 今日からこの会社で働く＿＿＿＿。よろしくお願いします。

    Kyō kara koko kaisha de hataraku ＿＿＿＿ . Yoroshiku o-negai shimasu.

    (a) ことです koto desu

    (b) ことになりました koto ni narimashita

    (c) ようにしました yō ni shimashita

    (d) ようになりました yō ni narimashita

7. 田中さんは27歳＿＿＿＿社長になりました。

    Tanaka-san wa nijū-nana-sai ＿＿＿＿ shachō ni narimashita.

    (a) に ni   (c) を o

    (b) で de   (d) が ga

8. 昨日、陽子さんの大学＿＿＿＿コンサートがありました。

    Kinō Yōko-san no daigaku ＿＿＿＿ konsāto ga arimashita.

    (a) に ni   (c) を o

    (b) が ga   (d) で de

9. 妹はスニーカーを＿＿＿＿います。

    Imōto wa sunīkā o ＿＿＿＿ imasu.

    (a) きて kite   (c) かぶって kabutte

    (b) はいて haite   (d) して shite

10. 姉はブラウスを＿＿＿＿います。

    Ane wa burausu o ＿＿＿＿ imasu.

    (a) きて kite   (c) かぶって kabutte

    (b) はいて haite   (d) して shite

PART THREE TEST

Circle the letter of the word or phrase that best completes each sentence.

1. 日本語は_____思います。

   Nihongo wa _____ omoimasu.

   (a) 難しいです muzukashii desu

   (b) 難しくないと muzukashikunai to

   (c) 難しい muzukashii

   (d) 難しいですと muzukashii desu to

2. スミスさんはどこにいる_____分かりますか。

   Sumisu-san wa doko ni iru _____ wakarimasu ka.

   (a) かどうか ka dōka   (c) と to

   (b) か ka   (d) を o

3. フランスに行きます。_____、韓国に行きます。

   Furansu ni ikimasu. _____ , Kankoku ni ikimasu.

   (a) それか soreka   (c) ですから desukara

   (b) それとも soretomo   (d) でも demo

4. あの人は中国人_____かもしれません。

   Ano hito wa Chūgoku-jin _____ kamoshiremasen.

   (a) だ da   (c) です desu

   (b) な na   (d) nothing

5. A: どうして_____んですか。B: 明日テストが_____からです。

   A: Dōshite _____ ndesu ka. B: Ashita tesuto ga _____ kara desu.

   (a) 来ない konai, ある aru

   (b) 来ない konai, あります arimasu

   (c) 来ます kimasu, あると aru to

   (d) 来る kuru, あるの aru no

6. 映画を見る_____、本を読みます。

   Eiga o miru _____ , hon o yomimasu.

   (a) 間に aida ni   (c) ながら nagara

   (b) 後に ato ni   (d) 前に mae ni

7. 高校生＿＿＿＿＿ときに、ピアノを習いました。

   Kōkōsei ＿＿＿＿＿ toki ni, piano o naraimashita.

   (a) だ da   (c) な na

   (b) の no   (d) です desu

8. 宿題を＿＿＿＿＿間に、ピザを食べました。

   Shukudai o ＿＿＿＿＿ aida ni, piza o tabemashita.

   (a) する suru   (c) している shite iru

   (b) し shi   (d) して shite

9. ドアを＿＿＿＿＿と、犬がいました。

   Doa o ＿＿＿＿＿ to, inu ga imashita.

   (a) 開ける akeru   (c) 開けた aketa

   (b) 開けて akete   (d) 開けます akemasu

10. こぼさない＿＿＿＿＿に食べてください。

    Kobosanai ＿＿＿＿＿ ni tabete kudasai.

    (a) する suru   (c) よう yō

    (b) ながら nagara   (d) です desu

11. 私は兄＿＿＿＿＿よく食べます。

    Watashi wa ani ＿＿＿＿＿ yoku tabemasu.

    (a) より yori   (c) ほど hodo

    (b) 同じ onaji   (d) で de

12. 兄は私＿＿＿＿＿食べません。

    Ani wa watashi ＿＿＿＿＿ tabemasen.

    (a) より yori   (c) ほど hodo

    (b) 同じ onaji   (d) で de

13. コーヒーと、紅茶と、＿＿＿＿＿の方が好きですか。

    Kōhi to, kōcha to, ＿＿＿＿＿ no hō ga suki desu ka.

    (a) どちら dochira   (c) 何 nani

    (b) どれ dore   (d) だれ dare

14. アイスクリームの中では、＿＿＿＿＿が一番好きです。

    Aisukurīmu no naka de wa, ＿＿＿＿＿ ga ichi-ban suki desu.

    (a) どこ doko   (c) 何 nani

    (b) どれ dore   (d) だれ dare

15. 日本語を＿＿＿＿と、日本語を＿＿＿＿とでは、どちらが難しいですか。

Nihon-go o ＿＿＿＿ to, Nihon-go o ＿＿＿＿ to de wa, dochira ga muzukashii desu ka.

(a) 話す hanasu, 聞く kiku

(b) 話すが hanasu ga, 聞くが kiku ga

(c) 話すの hanasu no, 聞くの kiku no

(d) 話して hanashite, 聞いて kiite

16. このスニーカーは＿＿＿＿やすいです。

Kono sunīkā wa ＿＿＿＿ yasui desu.

(a) 歩く aruku   (c) 歩かない arukanai

(b) 歩いて aruite   (d) 歩き aruki

17. 父は働き＿＿＿＿。よく残業をします。

Chichi wa hataraki ＿＿＿＿ . Yoku zangyō o shimasu.

(a) おわります owarimasu   (c) すぎます sugimasu

(b) 忘れます wasuremasu   (d) にくいです nikui desu

18. あの人は＿＿＿＿そうですね。

Ano hito wa ＿＿＿＿ -sō desu ne.

(a) 静か shizuka   (c) 静かで shizuka de

(b) やさしく yasashiku   (d) 静かに shizuka ni

19. 母は＿＿＿＿のようです。父はとても＿＿＿＿らしいです。

Haha wa ＿＿＿＿ no yō desu. Chichi wa totemo ＿＿＿＿ rashii desu.

(a) 女 onna, 男 otoko   (c) 男 otoko, 女 onna

(b) 男 otoko, 男 otoko   (d) 女 onna, 女 onna

20. ＿＿＿＿は面白かったです。

＿＿＿＿ wa omoshirokatta desu.

(a) 昨日見た映画 kinō mita eiga

(b) 映画を昨日見た eiga o kinō mita

(c) 昨日映画を見た kinō eiga o mita

(d) 昨日映画を見て kinō eiga o mite

21. うるさいですよ。もう少し _____ ください。

Urusai desu yo. Mō sukoshi _____ kudasai.

(a) しずかにして shizuka ni shite

(b) しずか shizuka

(c) しずかな shizuka na

(d) しずかに shizuka ni

22. 日本語でアニメが _____ 。

Nihon-go de anime ga _____ .

(a) 見るようになりました miru yō ni narimashita

(b) 見られるようになりました mirareru yō ni narimashita

(c) 見るなりました miru narimashita

(d) 見ないになりました minai ni narimashita

23. 9月からニューヨークの大学で勉強する _____ 。

Ku-gatsu kara Nyūyōku no daigaku de benkyō suru _____ .

(a) ようにしました yō ni shimashita

(b) ことにしました koto ni shimashita

(c) ようなりました yō narimashita

(d) になりました ni narimashita

24. 2歳 _____ 話せるようになりました。

Ni-sai _____ hanaseru yō ni narimashita.

(a) に ni   (c) を o

(b) で de   (d) が ga

25. 兄は帽子を _____ います。姉はネックレスを _____ います。

Ani wa bōshi o _____ imasu. Ane wa nekkuresu o _____ imasu.

(a) きて kite, はいて haite

(b) はいて haite, して shite

(c) かぶって kabutte, かけて kakete

(d) かぶって kabutte, して shite

PART FOUR

Expressing Implication, Attitude, and Perspective

CHAPTER 16

Expressing Implication

In this chapter, you'll learn:

Transitive and Intransitive Verbs
Auxiliary Verbs That Follow the Te-Form
Expressing One's Desire
Listing Actions and Properties

Transitive and Intransitive Verbs

Any verbs take a subject. However, not all the verbs take a direct object. Transitive verbs are the verbs that take a direct object and intransitive verbs are those that do not. English has some transitive and intransitive verbs whose pronunciations and

meanings are similar, for example, the transitive verb *to raise* and its intransitive counterpart *to rise*. Although they both express the situation where something goes up, the item that goes up is the direct object of the verb *to raise*, as in *Someone raises something*, but it is the subject of the verb *to rise*, as in *Something rises*. Interestingly, Japanese has many such transitive/intransitive pairs. In such pair of sentences, the item that undergoes the action is marked by を **o** (direct object marker) if the verb is transitive, but by が **ga** (subject marker) if the verb is intransitive. The following table lists some of such pairs:

Transitive	**Intransitive**
あげる ageru *to raise*	あがる agaru *to rise*
(Someone raises something.)	*(Something rises.)*
父が旗をあげます。	旗があがります。
Chichi ga hata o agemasu.	Hata ga agarimasu.
My father raises the flag.	*The flag rises.*
こわす kowasu *to break*	こわれる kowareru *to break*
(Someone breaks something.)	*(Something breaks.)*
弟がカメラをこわしました。	カメラがこわれました。
Otōto ga kamera o kowashimashita.	Kamera ga kowaremashita.
My younger brother broke the camera.	*The camera broke.*
あける akeru *to open*	あく aku *to open*
(Someone opens something.)	*(Something opens.)*
ドアをあけました。	ドアがあきました。
Doa o akemashita.	Doa ga akimashita.
(I) opened the door.	*The door opened.*
しめる shimeru *to close*	しまる shimaru *to close*
(Someone closes something.)	*(Something closes.)*
ドアをしめました。	ドアがしまりました。
Doa o shimemashita.	Doa ga shimarimashita.
(I) closed the door.	*The door closed.*
つける tsukeru *to turn on*	つく tsuku *to turn on*
(Someone turns on something.)	*(Something turns on.)*
妹がテレビをつけました。	テレビがつきました。
Imōto ga terebi o tsukemashita.	Terebi ga tsukimashita.
My little sister turned on the TV.	*The TV came on.*
けす kesu *to turn off*	きえる kieru *to turn off*
(Someone turns off something.)	*(Something turns off.)*
妹が電気をけしました。	電気がきえました。
Imōto ga denki o keshimashita.	Denki ga kiemashita.
My little sister turned off the light.	*The light went off.*

Written Practice 1

Choose the correct one in the parentheses, paying attention to whether the verb should be intransitive or transitive.

1. ドアが(あきました、あけました)。

   Doa ga (akimashita, akemashita).

2. まどを (あきました、あけました) 。

   Mado o (akimashita, akemashita).

3. カメラが (こわれました、こわしました) 。

   Kamera ga (kowaremashita, kowashimashita).

4. テレビを (きえました、けしました) 。

   Terebi o (kiemashita, keshimashita)

5. 電気を (ついてください、つけてください) 。

   Denki o (tsuite kudasai, tsukete kudasai).

Auxiliary Verbs That Follow the Te-Form

In Chapter 9, you saw that the verb いる **iru** (*to exist*) also functions as an auxiliary verb following another verb in the te-form to show a progressive, habitual, or resulting state. In this section, you will see additional auxiliary verbs that follow a verb in the te-form.

EXPRESSING HOW SOMETHING EXISTS WITH THE AUXILIARY VERB ある ARU

The auxiliary verb ある **aru** follows a transitive verb in the te-form and expresses how something exists. For example, the following sentence means *the TV exists after being turned on*, or *the TV is on*.

テレビがつけてあります。
Terebi ga tsukete arimasu.

The following are additional examples:

窓があけてあります。
Mado ga akete arimasu.
The window is left open.

カレンダーが壁に貼ってあります。
Karendā ga kabe ni hatte arimasu.
The calendar is posted on the wall.

花瓶がテーブルの上においてあります。
Kabin ga tēburu no ue ni oite arimasu.
The vase is placed on the table.

ジャケットがドアにかけてあります。
Jaketto ga doa ni kakete arimasu.
The jacket is hung on the door.

When the verb is an intransitive verb, ある **aru** must be replaced by いる **iru**. For example, つける **tsukeru** is a transitive verb that means *to turn on something*, but つく **tsuku** is an intransitive verb that means *something turns on*. See the contrast between the two sentences.

テレビがつけてあります。
Terebi ga tsukete arimasu.
The TV is on.

テレビがついています。
Terebi gat suite imasu.
The TV is on.

INDICATING A COMPLETED ACTION WITH THE AUXILIARY VERB しまう SHIMAU

The auxiliary verb しまう **shimau** emphasizes the fact that an action has completed and cannot be undone, indicating the speaker's regrettable feelings or happy feelings about it depending on the context. It can also just emphasize the completion of the action without indicating any feelings at all.

コーヒーをこぼしてしまいました。
Kōhī o koboshite shimaimashita.
I spilled my coffee!

パスポートをなくしてしまいました。
Pasupōto o nakushite shimaimashita.
I lost my passport.

宿題を忘れてしまいました。
Shukudai o wasurete shimaimashita.
I forgot my homework.

仕事は全部終わってしまいました。
Shigoto wa zenbu owatte shimaimashita.
I finished all of my work.

古い服は弟にあげてしまいました。
Furui fuku wa otōto ni agete shimaimashita.
I gave away my old clothes to my little brother.

行きましょう。—ちょっと待って下さい。このコーヒーを飲んでしまいます。
Ikimashō. —Chotto matte kudasai. Kono kōhī o nonde shimaimasu.
Let's get going. —Hold on. I'll finish this coffee.

INDICATING A PREPARATION ACTION WITH THE AUXILIARY VERB おく OKU

おく **oku** follows a verb in the te-form and expresses that the action is done in advance for future convenience.

忘れないように、電話番号を書いておきます。
Wasurenai yō ni, denwa-bangō o kaite okimasu.
So I won't forget, I'll write down (his) telephone number (now).

来月の電気代も払っておきます。
Raigetsu no denkidai mo haratte okimasu.
I'll pay for the electricity bill for the next month (in advance), too.

心配しないでください。ホテルは私が予約しておきます。
Shinpai shinaide kudasai. Hoteru wa watashi ga yoyaku shite okimasu.
Don't worry. I'll make the reservation for the hotel (in advance).

INDICATING A TRIAL ACTION WITH THE AUXILIARY VERB みる MIRU

みる **miru** follows a verb in the te-form and shows that the action is done just as a trial.

梅干を食べてみましたが、とてもすっぱかったです。
Umeboshi o tabete mimashita ga, totemo suppakatta desu.
I tried pickled plum, but it was very sour.

上司にこの製品のことを話してみます。
Jōshi ni kono seihin no koto o hanashite mimasu.
I'll try talking about this product to my boss.

ゴルフはしたことがありませんが、今度してみます。
Gorufu wa shita koto ga arimasen ga, kondo shite mimasu.
I've never played golf, but I'll try it next time.

Written Practice 2

Choose the appropriate item in the parentheses.

1. 宿題を忘れて（しまいました、おきました）。

   Shukudai o wasurete (shimaimashita, okimashita).

2. 明日はテストなので、よく勉強して（みます、おきます）。

   Ashita wa tesuto na node, yoku benkyō shite (mimasu, okimasu).

3. 心配しないでください。私が払って（みます、おきます）。

   Shinpai shinaide kudasai. Watashi ga haratte (mimasu, okimasu).

4. 納豆は食べたことがありませんが、今度、食べて（みます、しまいます）。

   Nattō wa tabeta koto ga arimasen ga, kondo tabete (mimasu, shimaimasu).

5. 父のカメラをこわして（みました、しまいました）。

   Chichi no kamera o kowashite (mimashita, shimaimashita).

INDICATING A CONTINUING ACTION WITH THE AUXILIARY VERBS くる KURU AND いく IKU

The auxiliary verb くる **kuru** shows that the action started a little earlier and is progressing steadily to the current.

雪が降ってきました。
Yuki ga futte kimashita.
It started to snow.

体重がふえてきました。
Taijū ga fuete kimashita.
(I) started to gain weight.

一人で子供を育ててきました。
Hitori de kodomo o sodatete kimashita.
I have brought up my child by myself (until now).

くる **kuru** is often used with なる **naru** (*to come*), as in なってくる **natte kuru**.

スミスさんは日本語がうまくなってきましたね。
Sumisu-san wa Nihon-go ga umaku natte kimashita ne.
Mr. Smith has started to improve his Japanese, didn't he?

寒くなってきました。
Samuku natte kimashita.
It is getting cold.

By contrast, the auxiliary verb いく **iku** shows that the action will start soon and will continue to progress.

日本語がうまくなっていきますよ。
Nihon-go ga umaku natte ikimasu yo.
Your Japanese will become better and better.

寒くなっていきます。
Samuku natte ikimasu.
It will get cold.

INDICATING THE BENEFICIARY OF AN ACTION WITH THE AUXILIARY VERBS あげる AGERU, くれる KURERU, AND もらう MORAU

The auxiliary verbs あげる **ageru**, くれる **kureru**, and もらう **morau** clarify who was benefited by whom from the action. The use of these auxiliary verbs parallels the use of the verbs of giving and receiving discussed in Chapter 7.

妹と遊んであげました。
Imōto to asonde agemashita.
I played with my younger sister (to be nice to her).

弟に本を読んであげました。
Otōto ni hon o yonde agemashita.
I read a book for my little brother.

私が困っている時は、いつも山田さんが助けてくれます。
Watashi ga komatte iru toki wa, itsumo Yamada-san ga tasukete kuremasu.
When I'm in trouble, Ms. Yamada always helps me.

兄が私を叱ってくれました。
Ani ga watashi o shikatte kuremashita.
My big brother scolded me (for my benefit).

私は姉に英語を教えてもらいました。
Watashi wa ane ni eigo o oshiete moraimashita.
I had my older sister teach me English.

私は友達に悩みを聞いてもらいました。
Watashi wa tomodachi ni nayami o kiite moraimashita.
I had my friend hear what I am worrying about.

In a formal context, their honorific versions 差し上げる **sashiageru**, くださる **kudasaru**, or いただく **itadaku** are used.

先生に推薦状を書いていただきました。
Sensei ni suisenjō o kaite itadakimashita.
I had my professor write a letter of recommendation for me.

推薦状を書いていただけませんか。
Suisenjō o kaite itadakemasen ka.
Could you write a letter of recommendation for me, please?

お金を貸してくださいませんか。
O-kane o kashite kudasaimasen ka.
Could you lend me some money?

社長がお金を貸してくださいました。
Shachō ga o-kane o kashite kudasaimashita.
The company president (kindly) lent me money.

ホテルを予約して差し上げました。
Hoteru o yoyaku shite sashiagemashita.
I made a hotel reservation (for him).

Although not required, あげる **ageru** may be replaced by やる **yaru** if the action is done for one's intimate subordinates.

子供にお握りを作ってやりました。
Kodomo ni onigiri o tsukutte yarimashita.
I made a rice ball for my child.

Written Practice 3

Choose the appropriate item in the parentheses.

1. 姉が私に英語を教えて(あげました、くれました)。

   Ane ga watashi ni eigo o oshiete (agemashita, kuremashita).

2. 先生が私に漢字を教えて (差し上げました、くださいました) 。

   Sensei ga watashi ni kanji o oshiete (sashiagemashita, kudasaimashita).

3. 先生に推薦状を書いて (くださいました、いただきました) 。

   Sensei ni suisenjō o kaite (kudasaimashita, itadakimashita).

4. 山田さんにお金をかして (あげました、くれました) 。

   Yamada-san ni okane o kashite (agemashita, kuremashita).

5. 私は母にいっしょに病院に行って (くれました、もらいました) 。

   Watashi wa haha ni isshoni byōin ni itte (kuremashita, moraimashita).

6. 弟に本を読んで (やりました、差し上げました) 。

   O-tōto ni hon o yonde (yarimashita, sashiagemashita).

Expressing One's Desire

In this section, you will learn how to express your and other people's desire in a variety of contexts.

THE AUXILIARY ADJECTIVE ほしい HOSHII

In Chapter 8, you learned that the adjective ほしい **hoshii** is used for expressing one's own desire for things and the suffix たい **tai** is used for expressing one's own desire for actions.

私は本がほしいです。
Watashi wa hon ga hoshii desu.
I want a book.

私は本が読みたいです。
Watashi wa hon ga yomi-tai desu.
I want to read a book.

However, when expressing one's desire for someone else to do something, the auxiliary adjective ほしい **hoshii** is used rather than the adjective ほしい **hoshii** or the suffix たい **tai**. In the following example sentences, ほしい **hoshii** follows a verb in the te-form:

私は父にもう少し厳しくなってほしいです。
Watashi wa chichi ni mō sukoshi kibishiku natte hoshii desu.
I want my father to become a bit stricter.

明日、ここに来てほしいんですが、いいですか。
Ashita, koko ni kite hoshii ndesu ga, ii desu ka.
I want you to come here tomorrow, but is it okay?

THE SUFFIX がる GARU

Some, although not all, adjectives that show a psychological state must be followed by the suffix がる **garu** if it is of the third person's psychological state. がる **garu** indicates that the person shows some signs of the feelings expressed by the adjective. It is used with adjectives such as ほしい **hoshii** (*want*), 嫌な **iya na** (*hate*),

こわい **kowai** (*scared*), and おもしろい **omoshiroi** (*fun*), but not with others such as 好きな **suki na** (*like*). がる **garu** follows an adjective in the stem form (see Chapter 4). Once がる **garu** is added to an adjective, the item the person's feeling applies to is marked by the particle を **o** rather than が **ga**.

弟はいつも宿題を嫌がります。
Otōto wa itsumo shukudai o iya-garimasu.
My younger brother always hates his homework.

妹は犬をこわがります。
Imōto wa inu o kowa-garimasu.
My younger sister is scared of dogs.

姉は車をほしがっています。
Ane wa kuruma o hoshi-gatte imasu.
My older sister wants a new car.

兄はいつも私の失敗をおもしろがります。
Ani wa itsumo watashi no shippai o omoshiro-garimasu.
My older brother always finds my failure amusing.

弟はいつも文句を言いたがります。
Otōto wa itsumo monku o ii-ta-garimasu.
My younger brother always wants to complain.

The predicate of the above sentence is composed of the verb 言う **iu**, the suffix たい **tai**, the suffix がる **garu**, and the politeness suffix ます **masu**.

Written Practice 4

Translate the following sentences into Japanese.

1. I want a new car.

   _____

2. My older brother also wants a new car.

   _____

3. I want to go to China.

   _____

4. My younger sister wants to go to Australia.

_____

5. My older brother wants to eat delicious ramen noodles.

_____

Listing Actions and Properties

In Chapter 9 you learned how to list actions and properties using the te-form, as in:

昨日は、買い物をして、レストランで食事をして、映画を見ました。
Kinō wa, kaimono o shite, resutoran de shokuji o shite, eiga o mimashita.
I went shopping, dined at the restaurant, and watched a movie yesterday.

広志さんはやさしくて、かっこよくて、頭がいいです。
Hiroshi-san wa yasashikute, kakkoyokute, atama ga ii desu.
Hiroshi is kind, good-looking, and smart.

This section presents two additional ways of listing multiple actions or properties in a sentence and shows you what subtle nuances you can convey with them.

PARTIALLY LISTING ACTIONS AND PROPERTIES WITH THE たり TARI FORM

If you want to enumerate a few actions and properties among others, emphasizing that they are only examples, use the **tari**-form for all the verbs and adjectives, and add the verb する **suru** (_to do_) in an appropriate tense, aspect, and formality at the end of the sentence. The **tari**-form can be easily created by adding り **ri** at the end of the verb or adjective in the plain past affirmative form (see Chapter 11 for the summary of plain forms of verbs and adjectives). Following are some example sentences:

昨日は、買い物をしたり、レストランで食事をしたり、映画を見たりしました。
Kinō wa, kaimono o shitari, resutoran de shokuji o shitari, eiga o mitari shimashita.
I went shopping, dined at the restaurant, watched a movie, etc., yesterday.

明日は、図書館に行ったり、数学を勉強したり、空手の道場に行ったりします。
Ashita wa, toshokan ni ittari, sūgaku o benkyō shitari, karate no dōjō ni ittari shimasu.
I will go to the library, study mathematics, go to the karate dojo, etc., tomorrow.

このレストランのステーキは小さかったり、かたかったりします。
Kono resutoran no sutēki wa chīsakattari, katakattari shimasu.
Steaks at this restaurant are sometimes small, sometimes tough, etc.

このレストランのシェフはフランス人だったり、イタリア人だったりします。
Kono resutoran no shefu wa Furansu-jin dattari, Itaria-jin dattari shimasu.
Chefs at this resutaurant are sometimes French, sometimes Italian, etc.

Written Practice 5

Convert the verbs into the **tari**-form following the example.

食べる taberu <u>食べたり tabetari</u>

読む yomu _____   買う kau _____

書く kaku _____   作る tsukuru _____

見る miru _____   する suru _____

行く iku _____   来る kuru _____

EMPHATICALLY LISTING ACTIONS AND PROPERTIES WITH THE PARTICLE し SHI

You can list actions and properties emphatically, using the particle し **shi** after each verb or adjective listed. The verbs and the adjectives are usually in the plain form.

広志さんはやさしいし、ハンサムだし、よく働くし、頭もいいです。
Hiroshi-san wa yasashii shi, hansamu da shi, yoku hataraku shi, atama mo ii desu.
Hiroshi is kind, handsome, hard-working, and also smart.

In conversations, such sentences often end in し **shi**, as in the following examples:

このクラスは本当に大変です。難しいし、宿題はたくさんあるし、先生はきびしいし。

Kono kurasu wa hontō ni taihen desu. Muzukashii shi, shukudai wa takusan aru shi, sensei wa kibishii shi.

This class is really hard. It is difficult, there is a lot of homework, and the teacher is strict.

健二君は勉強しないし、仕事もしないし、友達もいないし。大丈夫でしょうか。

Kenji-kun wa benkyō shinai shi, shigoto mo shinai shi, tomodachi mo inai shi. Daijōbu deshō ka.

Kenji doesn't study, doesn't work, and doesn't have friends. I wonder whether he is all right.

Written Practice 6

List the items using し **shi** following the example.

きれいな kirei na、やさしい yasashii、よく働く yoku hataraku

きれいだし、やさしいし、よく働くし。 Kirei da shi, yasashii shi, yoku hataraku shi.

_____

1. 頭がいい atama ga ii、ハンサムな hansamu na、まじめな majime na

_____

2. 安い yasui、おいしい oishii

_____

3. 難しい muzukashii、大変な taihen na、つまらない tsumaranai

_____

4. ハンサムじゃない hansamu ja nai、頭も悪い atama mo warui、スポーツもできない supōtsu mo dekinai (*not good in sports*)

_____

QUIZ

Circle the letter of the word or phrase that best completes each sentence.

1. 電気を_____。

   Denki o _____ .

   (a) きえました kiemashita

   (b) きえてください kiete kudasai

   (c) けしました keshimashita

   (d) きえません kiemasen

2. 電気が_____。

   Denki ga _____ .

   (a) つけてあります tsukete arimasu

   (b) けします keshimasu

   (c) けしています keshite imasu

   (d) つけます tsukemasu

3. コーヒーをこぼして_____。

   Kōhī o koboshite _____ .

   (a) おきました okimashita

   (b) しまいました shimaimashita

   (c) もらいました moraimashita

   (d) みました mimashita

4. ゴルフはしたことがありませんが、今度して_____。

   Gorufu wa shita koto ga arimasen ga, kondo shite _____ .

   (a) みます mimasu　　　　(c) しまいます shimaimasu

   (b) みました mimashita　　(d) おきました okimashita

5. 雪が降って_____。

   Yuki ga futte _____ .

   (a) みました mimashita　　(c) ありました arimashita

   (b) きました kimashita　　(d) おきました okimashita

6. 練習すると、日本語がうまくなって＿＿＿＿。

Renshū suru to, Nihon-go ga umaku natte ＿＿＿＿ .

(a) いきます ikimasu (c) あります arimasu

(b) みます mimasu (d) ほしいです hoshii desu

7. 先生に推薦状を書いて＿＿＿＿。

Sensei ni suisenjō o kaite ＿＿＿＿ .

(a) くれました kuremashita

(b) あげました agemashita

(c) いただきました itadakimashita

(d) くださいました kudasaimashita

8. 明日、ここに来て＿＿＿＿んですが、いいですか。

Ashita, koko ni kite ＿＿＿＿ ndesu ga, ii desu ka.

(a) たい tai (c) おく oku

(b) ほしい hoshii (d) がる garu

9. 昨日は食べたり、＿＿＿＿。

Kinō wa tabetari, ＿＿＿＿ .

(a) 飲みました nomimashita

(b) 飲んでいました nonde imashita

(c) 飲んだりしました nondari shimashita

(d) 飲んできました nonde kimashita

10. エミリーさんは頭がいいし、＿＿＿＿、やさしいし。

Emirī-san wa atama ga ii shi, ＿＿＿＿ , yasashii shi.

(a) きれい kirei (c) きれいに kirei ni

(b) きれいし kirei shi (d) きれいだし kirei da shi

CHAPTER 17

Expressing Attitude

In this chapter, you'll learn:

More Useful Modals
Useful Pragmatic Particles
Expressing Free Choice
Plants and Animals

More Useful Modals

In Chapter 11, you learned some modals that express the speaker's sureness or attitude toward his/her statement such as かもしれない **kamoshirenai** (*It may be the case that . . .*) and だろう **darō** (*It is probably the case that . . .*). In this section, you will learn additional useful modals that you can use for expressing your opinions and ideas.

INDICATING A STRONG OPINION WITH べきだ BEKI DA

べきだ **beki da** is placed at the end of a sentence, indicating that the statement expresses the speaker's strong subjective opinion about what should be the case. べきだ **beki da** usually follows a verb in the dictionary form (the plain present affirmative form).

> 妹はもっと本を読むべきです。
> Imōto wa motto hon o yomu beki desu.
> *My younger sister should read more.*

> 学生はまじめに勉強するべきです。
> Gakusei wa majime ni benkyō suru beki desu.
> *Students should study seriously.*

するべきだ **suru beki da** is often contracted to すべきだ **subeki da**. For example, the previous sentence can also be:

> 学生はまじめに勉強すべきです。
> Gakusei wa majime ni benkyō su beki desu.
> *Students should study seriously.*

The negative element or past tense appears not before べき **beki**, but after it.

> 東京に行くべきじゃありません。
> Tōkyō ni iku beki ja arimasen.
> *You should not go to Tokyo.*

> 若いときに、もっと勉強するべきでした。
> Wakai toki ni, motto benkyō suru beki deshita.
> *I should have studied more when I was young.*

INDICATING AN ASSUMED FACT WITH はずだ HAZU DA

はずだ **hazu da** is placed at the end of a sentence, following a verb or an adjective in the pre-nominal form. はずだ **hazu da** shows that the sentence expresses the situation that is supposed to hold or have held judging from the circumstantial facts (time, place, conditions, status, regulations, routines, actions, etc.) and other already evident facts such as scientific findings.

> 12時に飛行機に乗りましたから、2時に成田に着くはずです。
> Jūni-ji ni hikōki ni norimashita kara, ni-ji ni Narita ni tsuku hazu desu.
> *As (he) got on the plane at 12 o'clock, he is supposed to arrive at Narita at 2 P.M.*

ここに財布をおいたはずですが、ないんです。
Koko ni saifu o oita hazu desu ga, nai ndesu.
I suppose I put my wallet here, but it's not here.

今日は月曜日ですから、子供がいません。ですから、あの部屋は静かなはず
です。
Kyō wa Getsuyōbi desu kara, kodomo ga imasen. Desukara, ano heya wa
shizuka na hazu desu.
Since today is Monday, there are no kids. So, that room is supposed to be quiet.

送料は500円のはずです。
Sōryō wa gohyaku-en no hazu desu.
The shipping fee is supposed to be 500 yen.

ヨーグルトは腸にいいはずですよ。
Yōguruto wa chō ni ii hazu desu yo.
Yogurt is supposedly good for the intestines.

Written Practice 1

Fill in the blanks with either べき **beki** or はず **hazu**.

1. あなたはもっとまじめに勉強する＿＿＿です。

   Anata wa motto majime ni benkyō suru ＿＿＿ desu.

2. 2時に電車に乗りました。ですから、3時に着く＿＿＿です。

   Ni-ji ni densha ni norimashita. Desukara, 3-ji ni tsuku ＿＿＿ desu.

3. チェンさんのお母さんは日本人の＿＿＿です。

   Chen-san no okāsan wa Nihon-jin no ＿＿＿ desu.

4. 毎日そうじをする＿＿＿です。

   Mainichi sōji o suru ＿＿＿ desu.

5. この本は漢字が少ないです。ですから、簡単な＿＿＿です。

   Kono hon wa kanji ga sukunai desu. Desukara, kantan na＿＿＿desu.

INDICTATING A GUESS WITH ようだ YŌ DA

ようだ **yō da** is added at the end of a sentence, following a verb or an adjective in
the pre-nominal form. It is used to express a variety of the speaker's conjectures

such as an intuitive guess based on five senses and an educated guess based on logic and observations:

あ、すっぱい！腐っているようですよ。
A, suppai! Kusatte iru yō desu yo.
Oh, it tastes sour! It appears to be spoiled.

だれか来るようです。足音がします。
Dare ka kuru yō desu. Ashioto ga shimasu.
It appears that someone is coming. I can hear footsteps.

この町の不動産は高いようです。
Kono machi no fudōsan wa takai yō desu.
The real estate properties in this town seem to be expensive.

あの子供は頭がいいようですね。たった5歳なのに、掛け算と割り算ができますよ。
Ano kodomo wa atama ga ii yō desu ne. Tatta go-sai na noni, kakezan to warizan ga dekimasu yo.
That child seems to be smart. He is only five years old but can do multiplication and division.

道がぬれています。雨が降ったようですね。
Michi ga nurete imasu. Ame ga futta yō desu ne.
The street is wet. It seems that it has rained.

あのレストランは有名なようです。
Ano resutoran wa yūmē na yō desu.
That restaurant seems to be famous.

クリスさんはちょっと変です。何か隠しているようです。
Kurisu-san wa chotto hen desu. Nani ka kakushite iru yō desu.
Chris is acting a little strange. He appears to be hiding something.

あの男の人は日本人のようです。
Ano otoko no hito wa Nihon-jin no yō desu.
That man seems to be Japanese.

You should be cautioned that noun + のようです **no yō desu** is interpreted ambiguously. It may express a conjecture as discussed here or a simile, discussed in Chapter 14. For example, the above sentence may express a conjecture, interpreted as *that man appears to be Japanese (although I'm not sure)* or it may express a simile, interpreted as *that man is just like a Japanese (although he is not).*

INDICATING A CONJECTURE WITH らしい RASHII

らしい **rashii** is added at the end of a sentence to express the speaker's objective, logical, and non-intuitive conjecture based on what he heard, saw, or read. The verbs and adjectives that precede らしい **rashii** must be in the plain form, except that だ **da** that appears at the end of the copula and at the end of a na-type adjective must not be present.

この町の不動産は高いらしいです。
Kono machi no fudōsan wa takai rashii desu.
The real estate properties in this town seem to be expensive.

あの辞書はとても便利らしいですよ。
Ano jisho wa totemo benri rashii desu yo.
That dictionary seems to be very convenient.

今度のマネージャーは女性らしいですよ。
Kondo no manējā wa josei rashii desu yo.
The new manager seems to be a woman.

駅の横にデパートが建つらしいですよ。
Eki no yoko ni depāto ga tatsu rashii desu yo.
It seems that a department store will be built next to the train station.

Unlike ようだ **yō da** discussed in the above section, らしい **rashii** cannot be used for an intuitive instant guess based on one's five senses.

INDICATING HEARSAY WITH そうだ SŌ DA

For expressing some fact or idea as something that you heard about or read about, just add そうだ **sō da** at the end of the sentence. The verbs and the adjectives in the sentence should be in the plain form in this case. It is often used with the phrase . . .によると **ni yoruto** (*according to . . .*).

天気予報によると、明日は雪が降るそうです。
Tenki yohō ni yoru to, ashita wa yuki ga furu sō desu.
According to the weather forecast, it will snow tomorrow.

来年から、また税金が高くなるそうです。
Rainen kara, mata zeikin ga takaku naru sō desu.
I heard that the tax will go up again starting next year.

林さんは会社を辞めたそうです。
Hayashi-san wa kaisha o yameta sō desu.
I heard that Mr. Hayashi has quit the job at the company.

Written Practice 2

Rephrase the following sentences using the given modal. Make sure to conjugate the verbs and adjectives in the sentence appropriately.

(伊藤さんが会社を辞めます Itō-san ga kaisha o yamemasu,
そうです sō desu)

伊藤さんが会社をやめるそうです Itō-san ga kaisha o yameru sō desu.

1. (今度の日本語の先生はきびしくありません Kondo no Nihon-go no
   sensei wa kibishiku arimasen, らしいです rashii desu)

2. (田中さんのカメラはこわれています Tanaka-san no kamera wa kowarete
   imasu, ようです yō desu)

3. (林さんのプリンターは便利です Hayashi-san no purintā wa benri desu,
   ようです yō desu)

4. (来年から学費が高くなります Rainen kara gakuhi ga takaku narimasu,
   そうです sō desu)

Useful Pragmatic Particles

Some particles express the contextual-level speaker's view rather than the sentence-level grammatical information. They are called pragmatic particles. The particles は **wa** and も **mo** discussed in Chapter 2 and the particle ばかり **bakari** discussed in Chapter 9 are some examples of pragmatic particles. This section introduces additional pragmatic particles.

INDICATING LIMITATION AND LACK OF OTHER ITEMS WITH THE PARTICLE しか SHIKA

しか **shika** means *only* and expresses that the quantity, amount, or range of items is too few, little, or limited for the given context. Remember that the predicate must be negative if しか **shika** is used in a sentence. When しか **shika** is used for a noun, it follows the associated grammatical particle. The particles が **ga** and を **o** must be deleted when followed by しか **shika**, but other particles such as に **ni** can be directly followed by しか **shika.**

この植物はスマトラ島にしかありません。
Kono shokubutsu wa Sumatora-tō ni shika arimasen.
This plant exists only in Sumatra Island.

水しか飲みませんでした。
Mizu shika nomimasendeshita.
I only drank water.

広志さんしか来ませんでした。
Hiroshi-san shika kimasendeshita.
Only Hiroshi came.

私は300円しかありません。
Watashi wa 300-yen shika arimasen.
I only have 300 yen.

数学の宿題しかしませんでした。
Sūgaku no shukudai shika shimasendeshita.
I only did math homework.

INDICATING LIMITATION WITH THE PARTICLE だけ DAKE

だけ **dake** means *just* or *only*. It can be used for a variety of words and phrases, including nouns. When だけ **dake** occurs with a noun, the particle that is used for the noun can be placed before or after だけ **dake**, except for the particles が **ga** and を **o**, which can optionally occur only after だけ **dake**.

明子さんにだけ話しました。*or* 明子さんだけに話しました。
Akiko san ni dake hanashimashita. *or* Akiko-san dake ni hanashimashita.
I let just Akiko know (about it).

あなただけ(を)愛しています。
Anata dake (o) aishite imasu.
I only love you.

だけ **dake** and しか **shika** can be used interchangeably in some cases. For example, the above sentence and the following sentence are more or less synonymous:

あなたしか愛していません。
Anata shika aishite imasen.

However, they cannot always be interchangeably used. For example, suppose that your friend asked you to lend him 10,000 yen, but you have only 5,000 yen. In this context, it is appropriate to say:

すみません。5,000円しかありません。
Sumimasen. Gosen-yen shika arimasen,
Sorry. I only have 5,000 yen.

However, it is not appropriate to say:

すみません。5,000円だけあります。
Sumimasen. Gosen-en dake arimasu.
Sorry. I have just 5,000 yen.

This is because しか **shika**, but not だけ **dake**, highlights the lack of other items.

Written Practice 3

Complete the sentences appropriately.

1. 数学の宿題_____しました。

Sūgaku no shukudai _____ shimashita.
I just did math homework.

2. 私は５００円_____。ですから、この本は買えません。

Watashi wa gohyaku-yen _____. Desukara, kono hon wa kaemasen.
I only have 500 yen. So, I cannot buy this book.

3. 今、５００円_____。使ってください。

Ima, gohyaku-en _____ arimasu. Tsukatte kudasai.
I have just 500 yen, now. Please use it.

4. 車が一台＿＿＿＿＿＿＿＿から、5人しか行けません。

Kuruma ga ichi-dai ＿＿＿＿＿＿＿＿＿ kara, go-nin shika ikemasen.
There is only one car, so only five people can go.

5. 車がまだ一台＿＿＿＿＿＿＿＿から、私達も行けますよ。

Kuruma ga mada ichi-dai ＿＿＿＿＿＿＿＿＿ kara, watashi-tachi mo ikemasu yo.
We still have just one car, so we can also go there.

INDICATING THE LEAST EXPECTED ITEM WITH THE PARTICLE でも DEMO

でも **demo** means *even* and implies that the speaker considers the item to be one of the least expected items for the given situation. The particles が **ga** and を **o** are deleted when directly followed by でも **demo**.

弟はまずいものでも食べます。でも、妹はおいしいものでも食べません。
Otōto wa mazui mono demo tabemasu. Demo, imōto wa oishii mono demo tabemasen.
My younger brother even eats things that are not delicious. But my younger sister doesn't eat even delicious things.

こんな簡単な漢字は子供でも書けます。
Konna kantan na kanji wa kodomo demo kakemasu.
Even a child can write such an easy kanji like this.

危ない所にでも行きます。
Abunai tokoro ni demo ikimasu.
(He) even goes to dangerous places.

Written Practice 4

Choose the appropriate item in the parentheses.

1. こんな簡単なパズルは（大人でも, 子供でも）できます。

Konna kantan na pazuru wa (otona demo, kodomo demo) dekimasu.

2. こんな難しい漢字は（日本人でも, アメリカ人でも）分かりません。

Konna muzukashii kanji wa (Nihon-jin demo, Amerika-jin demo) wakarimasen.

3. この子供は (ジュースでも, お酒でも) 飲みます。

   Kono kodomo wa (jūsu demo, o-sake demo) nomimasu.

4. こんな (おいしい, まずい) ものは猫でも食べません。

   Konna (oishii, mazui) mono wa neko demo tabemasen.

Expressing Free Choice

In this section, you will learn how to express the concept of free choice, such as *anything, anyone,* and *anywhere* in Japanese. In addition, you will learn how to create concessive clauses such as *no matter how . . .* and *no matter what . . .*

EXPRESSING "ANY"

Expressions like *anyone* and *anything,* as in *Anyone can do this* and *He eats anything,* are expressed by combining a question word and でも **demo** in Japanese. For example, だれでも **dare demo** means *anyone* and 何でも **nan demo** means *anything.* The particles が **ga** and を **o** are omitted when directly followed by でも **demo.**

だれでもできます。
Dare demo dekimasu.
Anyone can do (it).

この犬は何でも食べます。
Kono inu wa nan demo tabemasu.
This dog eats anything.

どこにでも行きます。
Doko ni demo ikimasu.
(I) will go anywhere.

いつでもいいですよ。
Itsu demo ii desu yo.
Anytime is fine (with me).

木村さんはだれとでも仲良くできます。
Kimura-san wa dare to demo nakayoku dekimasu.
Ms. Kimura can get along with anyone.

EXPRESSING "NO MATTER . . ."

English phrases like *no matter who . . .*, *no matter what . . .*, and *no matter how much* *. . .* are called concessive clauses, and they are expressed by a question word, a predicate in the te-form, and the particle も **mo** in Japanese. For example:

だれが来ても、ドアをあけないでください。
Dare ga kite mo, doa o akenai de kudasai.
No matter who comes, please don't open the door.

何をやっても、失敗ばかりです。
Nani o yatte mo, shippai bakari desu.
No matter what I do, it always ends up in a failure.

何を着ても、似合いません。
Nani o kite mo, niaimasen.
No matter what I wear, it doesn't look good on me.

姉は何を食べても太りません。
Ane wa nani o tabete mo futorimasen.
My older sister doesn't gain weight no matter what she eats.

富士山はいつ見ても素晴らしいです。
Fujisan wa itsu mite mo subarashii desu.
Mt. Fuji is wonderful no matter when I look at it.

いくら勉強しても分かりません。
Ikura benkyō shite mo wakarimasen.
No matter how much (hard) I study, I don't understand it.

Written Practice 5

Choose the appropriate item in the parentheses.

1. 弟は（何でも、どこでも）食べます。

   Otōto wa (nan demo, doko demo) tabemasu.

2. こんな簡単なことは（何でも、だれでも）できます。

   Konna kantan na koto wa (nan demo, dare demo) dekimasu.

3. 陽子さんは (いつ, 何を) 着ても似合います。

Yōko-san wa (itsu, nani o) kite mo niaimasu.

4. 姉は (何を, だれが) 食べても太りません。

Ane wa (nani o, dare ga) tabete mo futorimasen.

Plants and Animals

In this section, you will learn some useful vocabulary words for plants and animals in Japanese.

PLANTS

The following are basic terms for plants in Japanese:

葉	ha	*leaf*
花	hana	*flower*
木	ki	*tree*
草	kusa	*grass*

The following are names of some plants:

松	matsu	*pine (tree)*
菊	kiku	*chrysanthemum*
竹	take	*bamboo*
チューリップ	chūrippu	*tulip*
樫	kashi	*oak (tree)*
薔薇	bara	*rose*
桜	sakura	*cherry (tree)*
柳	yanagi	*willow (tree)*

ANIMALS

The following are names of some pets:

猫	neko	*cat*
犬	inu	*dog*
兎	usagi	*rabbit*
金魚	kingyo	*goldfish*
鳥	tori	*bird*

The following are names of some animals you see in the zoo:

ライオン	raion	*lion*
虎	tora	*tiger*
猿	saru	*monkey*
象	zō	*elephant*
きりん	kirin	*giraffe*
しまうま	shimauma	*zebra*

QUIZ

Circle the letter of the word or phrase that best completes each sentence.

1. 妹はもっと本を_____べきでした。

   Imōto wa motto hon o _____ beki deshita.

   (a) 読み yomi   (c) 読んで yonde

   (b) 読む yomu   (d) 読んだ yonda

2. 2時に家を出ましたから、もうすぐ着く_____です。

   Ni-ji ni ie o demashita kara, mō sugu tsuku _____ desu.

   (a) べき beki   (c) はず hazu

   (b) つもり tsumori   (d) そうだ sō da

3. あのレストランは有名_____ようです。

   Ano resutoran wa yūmei _____ yō desu.

   (a) だ da   (c) な na

   (b) で de   (d) nothing

4. あの辞書はとても便利＿＿＿＿らしいですよ。

   Ano jisho wa totemo benri ＿＿＿＿ rashii desu yo.

   (a) の no   (c) だ da

   (b) で de   (d) nothing

5. 山田さんのお父さんは社長＿＿＿＿そうです。

   Yamada-san no otōsan wa shachō ＿＿＿＿ sō desu.

   (a) の no   (c) だ da

   (b) な na   (d) nothing

6. 今、２００円＿＿＿＿ので、このサンドイッチは買えません。

   Ima, nihyaku-en ＿＿＿＿ node, kono sandoitchi wa kaemasen.

   (a) しかない shika nai   (c) しかある shika aru

   (b) だけない dake nai   (d) だけある dake aru

7. 今、２００円＿＿＿＿ので、あのパンを買いましょう。

   Ima, nihyaku-en ＿＿＿＿ node, ano pan o kaimashō.

   (a) しかない shika nai   (c) しかある shika aru

   (b) だけない dake nai   (d) だけある dake aru

8. 兄は＿＿＿＿食べます。＿＿＿＿食べます。

   Ani wa ＿＿＿＿ tabemasu. ＿＿＿＿ tabemasu.

   (a) だれでも dare demo, まずいものでも Mazui mono demo

   (b) 何でも nan demo, おいしいものでも Oishii mono demo

   (c) 何でも nan demo, まずいものでも Mazui mono demo

   (d) だれでも dare demo, おいしいものでも Oishii mono demo

9. 姉は＿＿＿＿太りません。

   Ane wa ＿＿＿＿ futorimasen.

   (a) 何を食べても tani o tabete mo

   (b) 何も食べるも tani mo taberu mo

   (c) 何も食べても tani mo tabete mo

   (d) 何を食べるも tani o taberu mo

10. 誕生日にチューリップの＿＿＿＿をあげました。

   Tanjōbi ni chūrippu no ＿＿＿＿ o agemashita.

   (a) 葉 ha   (c) 木 ki

   (b) 花 hana   (d) 草 kusa

CHAPTER 18

Considering and Planning Your Actions

In this chapter, you'll learn:

Commands

Using the Volitional Form

Conditionals

More Terms for Occupations and Professions

Commands

In this section, you will learn two kinds of commands, plain commands and polite commands, in Japanese.

PLAIN COMMANDS WITH ろ RO

The plain command is expressed by a verb in the imperative form. You can create an imperative form by replacing the final **ru** of a ru-verb in the dictionary form with **ro**, or by replacing the final **u** of an u-verb with **e** (see Chapter 6 for a dictionary form). For example, the imperative form of たべる **taberu** (*to eat*) is たべろ **tabero**, and the imperative form of のむ **nomu** (*to drink*) is のめ **nome**. The imperative forms of する **suru** (*to do*) and くる **kuru** (*to come*) are しろ **shiro** and こい **koi**, respectively. Note that there is a minor sound change with the u-verbs that end in つ **tsu**: as you can see in the following table, **ts** becomes **t**.

Verbs in the Dictionary Form	Verbs in the Imperative Form
食べる taberu (*eat*)	食べろ tabero
見る miru (*look*)	見ろ miro
書く kaku (*write*)	書け kake
泳ぐ oyogu (*swim*)	泳げ oyoge
運ぶ hakobu (*carry*)	運べ hakobe
読む yomu (*read*)	読め yome
死ぬ shinu (*die*)	死ね shine
待つ matsu (*wait*)	待て mate
話す hanasu (*talk*)	話せ hanase
作る tsukuru (*make*)	作れ tsukure
買う kau (*buy*)	買え kae
する suru (*do*)	しろ shiro
来る kuru (*come*)	来い koi

When the imperative form is used just by itself for giving a command or an order, it sounds very blunt and rough. However, it doesn't give such a rough impression if it is used in an embedded sentence, as in:

このボタンをおせと説明書に書いてあります 。
Kono botan o ose to setsumeisho ni kaite arimasu.
It says to press this button on the instruction manual.

父が私に勉強しろと言いました。
Chichi ga watashi ni benkyō shiro to iimashita.
My father told me to study.

The negative imperative form can be created by adding な **na** after a dictionary form, as in 食べるな **taberu na** (*Don't eat!*) and 飲むな **nomu na** (*Don't drink!*).

Written Practice 1

Convert the following verbs in the dictionary form to their imperative forms.

たべる taberu (*eat*) → <u>たべろ tabero</u>

1. かく kaku (*write*) → _____
2. よむ yomu (*read*) → _____
3. みる miru (*watch*) → _____
4. ねる neru (*sleep*) → _____
5. とる toru (*take*) → _____
6. かう kau (*buy*) → _____
7. はこぶ hakobu (*carry*) → _____
8. もつ motsu (*hold*) → _____
9. する suru (*do*) → _____
10. くる kuru (*come*) → _____

POLITE COMMANDS WITH なさい NASAI

なさい **nasai** follows a verb in the stem form (see Chapter 6 for a stem form) and expresses a polite command. Unlike the plain command discussed in the previous subsection, the polite command is appropriately used by teachers to students in a classroom or by parents to children at home. It is also commonly used in instructions in exams.

早く食べなさい。
Hayaku tabe-nasai.
Eat quickly.

静かにしなさい。
Shizuka ni shi-nasai.
Be quiet.

名前を書きなさい。
Namae o kaki-nasai.
Write your name.

正しい答えを選びなさい。
Tadashii kotae o erabi-nasai.
Choose the correct answer.

10時までに帰りなさい。
10-ji made ni kaerinasai.
Come back by 10 o'clock.

Note that までに **made ni** in the last example means *by* and shows the deadline or the time by which something must be completed.

なさい **nasai** does not have a negative form. Negative polite command is usually expressed by てはいけません **te wa ikemasen** (see Chapter 10) or のをやめなさい **no o yamenasai** (*stop ...ing*), as in:

食べてはいけません。
Tabete wa ikemasen.
You must not eat.

食べるのをやめなさい。
Taberu no o yamenasai.
Stop eating.

Written Practice 2

Convert the following verbs in the dictionary form to their polite command form.

たべる taberu (*eat*) → たべなさい tabe-nasai _____

1. かく kaku (*write*) → _____
2. よむ yomu (*read*) → _____
3. みる miru (*watch*) → _____
4. ねる neru (*sleep*) → _____

5. とる toru (*take*) → _____

6. かう kau (*buy*) → _____

7. はこぶ hakobu (*carry*) → _____

8. もつ motsu (*hold*) → _____

9. する suru (*do*) → _____

10. くる kuru (*come*) → _____

Written Practice 3

Match the following Japanese sentences with English translations.

a. Please write your name.

b. Please come to my house tomorrow.

c. Wear your jacket.

d. Go!

e. Clean your room.

f. I have to do my homework.

g. Don't slack off!

h. Please don't tell anyone.

1. _____ 部屋をそうじしなさい。Heya o sōji shinasai.

2. _____ 宿題をしなくてはいけません。 Shukudai o shinakute wa ikemasen.

3. _____ 名前を書いてください。 Namae o kaite kudasai.

4. _____ だれにも言わないでください。 Dare ni mo iwanai de kudasai.

5. _____ 明日うちに来てください。 Ashita uchi ni kite kudasai.

6. _____ ジャケットを着なさい。 Jaketto o kinasai.

7. _____ 行け。 Ike!

8. _____ なまけるな。 Namakeru na!

Using the Volitional Form

In this section, you will learn a verb form called a volitional form. The volitional form can express one's volition or exhortation by itself, but its precise meaning changes depending on the context.

THE VOLITIONAL FORM よう Yō

The volitional form of a verb is created from a dictionary form (see Chapter 6 for a dictionary form), by replacing the final **ru** of a ru-verb and **u** of an u-verb with **yō** and **ō**, respectively. For example, the volitional form of 食べる **taberu** (*to eat*) is 食べよう **tabeyō**, and the volitional form of 飲む **nomu** (*to drink*) is 飲もう **nomō**. The volitional forms of する **suru** (*to do*) and 来る **kuru** (*to come*) are しよう **shiyō** and 来よう **koyō**, respectively. Note that there is a minor sound change with the u-verbs that end in つ **tsu**: as you can see in the following table, **ts** becomes **t**.

Verbs in the Dictionary Form	Verbs in the Volitional Form
食べる taberu (*eat*)	食べよう tabeyō
見る miru (*look*)	見よう miyō
書く kaku (*write*)	書こう kakō
泳ぐ oyogu (*swim*)	泳ごう oyogō
運ぶ hakobu (*carry*)	運ぼう hakobō
読む yomu (*read*)	読もう yomō
死ぬ shinu (*die*)	死のう shinō
待つ matsu (*wait*)	待とう matō
話す hanasu (*talk*)	話そう hanasō
作る tsukuru (*make*)	作ろう tsukurō
買う kau (*buy*)	買おう kaō
する suru (*do*)	しよう shiyō
来る kuru (*come*)	来よう koyō

The volitional form expresses one's volition with a strong feeling of determination or exhortation depending on the context.

私が行こう。
Watashi ga ikō.
I will go (there)!

いっしょに行こう。
Isshoni ikō.
Let's go (there) together!

The verb form with ましょう **mashō** (*Let's . . .*) discussed in Chapter 6 is actually the polite version of the volitional form.

テニスをしよう。
Tenisu o shiyō.
Let's play tennis. (Informal context)

テニスをしましょう。
Tenisu o shimashō.
Let's play tennis. (Polite/neutral context)

Written Practice 4

Convert the following verbs in the dictionary form into their volitional form.

たべる taberu (*eat*) → たべよう tabeyō _____

1. かく kaku (*write*) → _____
2. よむ yomu (*read*) → _____
3. みる miru (*watch*) → _____
4. ねる neru (*sleep*) → _____
5. とる toru (*take*) → _____
6. かう kau (*buy*) → _____
7. はこぶ hakobu (*carry*) → _____
8. もつ motsu (*hold*) → _____
9. する suru (*do*) → _____

INDICATING AN INTENTION WITH ようと思う YŌ TO OMOU

To express your intention or will to do something, use the verb in the volitional form along with a verb that expresses thinking such as 思う **omou** (*to think*) and 考える **kangaeru** (*to consider*). For example:

ハワイに行こうと思います。
Hawai ni ikō to omoimasu.
I'm thinking of going to Hawaii.

The above sentence emphasizes the speaker's willingness. On the other hand, the following sentence merely expresses what the speaker thinks will happen to him/her regardless of his/her will.

ハワイに行くと思います。
Hawai ni iku to omoimasu.
I think I will go to Hawaii.

The main verbs, for example, 思う **omou**, are often in the progressive form, as in:

ハワイに行こうと思っています。
Hawai ni ikō to omotte imasu.
I'm thinking of going to Hawaii.

奨学金をもらおうと考えています。
Shōgakukin o moraō to kangaete imasu.
I'm thinking of getting a scholarship.

将来は映画監督になろうと思っています。
Shōrai wa eiga kantoku ni narō to omotte imasu.
I'm thinking of becoming a movie director in the future.

夏休みに富士山に登ろうと思っています。
Natsu-yasumi ni Fujisan ni noborō to omotte imasu.
I'm thinking of climbing Mt. Fuji during the summer vacation.

The main verb of thinking *must* be, not just *may* be, in the progressive form when expressing the third person's intention or will:

主人は仕事をやめようと思っています。
Shujin wa shigoto o yameyō to omotte imasu.
My husband is thinking of quitting his job.

姉は台湾で日本語を教えようと思っています。
Ane wa Taiwan de Nihon-go o oshieyō to omotte imasu.
My older sister is thinking of teaching Japanese in Taiwan.

INDICATING AN ATTEMPT WITH ようとする YŌ TO SURU

To express an attempt, use the verb in the volitional form along with the particle と **to** and the verb する **suru** (*to do*). For example, the following sentence means that someone attempted or tried to drink wine by pouring wine into his glass or by bringing the glass to his mouth:

ワインを飲もうとしました。
Wain o nomō to shimashita.
I tried to drink wine.

ようとする **yō to suru** is often used when one fails to complete the action after attempting to do it. Here are additional examples of ようとする **yō to suru**:

晩ご飯を食べようとした時に、山田さんが来ました。
Bangohan o tabeyō to shita toki ni, Yamada-san ga kimashita.
When I was about to eat dinner, Ms. Yamada came over.

本当のことを言おうとしましたが、言えませんでした。
Hontō no koto o iō to shimashita ga, iemasendeshita.
I tried to tell the truth, but I couldn't.

うそをつこうとしました。
Uso o tsukō to shimashita.
I tried to lie.

起きようとしましたが、起きられませんでした。
Okiyō to shimashita ga, okiraremasendeshita.
I tried to get up, but I couldn't.

To express a continuous conscious effort rather than one-time spontaneous attempt, use ようにする **yō ni suru** discussed in Chapter 15.

できるだけ野菜を食べるようにします。
Dekiru dake yasai o taberu yō ni shimasu.
I will try to eat vegetables as much as I can.

遅れないようにしてください。
Okurenai yō ni shite kudasai.
Try not to be late, please.

Written Practice 5

Write the meaning of the following sentences.

1. 緑茶を飲むようにしています。Ryokucha o nomu yō ni shite imasu.
   (緑茶 ryokucha: *green tea*) _____

2. コーヒーを飲もうとしました。 Kohī o nomō to shimashita.

   _____

3. 中国語を勉強しようと思っています。 Chūgoku-go o benkyō shiyō to omotte imasu.

   _____

4. 明日、陽子さんにプロポーズしようと思います。　Ashita, Yōko-san ni puropōzu shiyō to omoimasu.

(プロポーズする puropōzusuru: *to propose*)

5. 野菜をできるだけたくさん食べるようにしようと思います。　Yasai o dekiru dake takusan taberu yō ni shiyō to omoimasu.

Conditionals

Some situations may hold only under some conditions. Such cases are expressed by sentences with conditional clauses. In Chapter 12 you learned the conditional clause expressed by the particle と **to**. In this section, you will learn some additional conditional clauses in Japanese.

THE たら TARA-CLAUSE

Just like the clause that ends in と **to** discussed in Chapter 12, the clause that ends in たら **tara** (*the tara-clause* for short) serves either as a time adverbial clause or a conditional clause, depending on the tense of the main clause. In either case, the situation expressed in the tara-clause must hold before the situation expressed in the main clause, just like in the case of the clause with と **to**.

The tara-form of verbs and adjectives can be created just by adding ら **ra** at the end of their plain past affirmative form. (See Chapter 11 for the summary of verbs and adjectives in the plain form). For example, the plain past affirmative form of 行く **iku** (*to go*) is 行った **itta**, and its tara-form is 行ったら **ittara**. The plain past affirmative form of 高い **takai** (*expensive*) is 高かった **takakatta** and its tara-form is 高かったら **takakattara**.

Written Practice 6

Convert the following verbs and adjectives in the dictionary form into their tara-form following the example.

たべる taberu → <u>たべたら tabetara _____</u>

1. よむ yomu → _____

2. くる kuru → _____

3. おわる owaru → _____

4. する suru → _____

5. かく kaku → _____

6. かかない kakanai → _____

7. やすい yasui → _____

8. しずかだ shizuka da → _____

9. 学生だ gakusei da → _____

When the main clause is in the past tense, the tara-clause serves as a time adverbial clause that can be used to express what happened after some event in the past, just like the clause that ends in と **to** discussed in Chapter 12. In this construction, the speaker should not have a control over the event described by the main clause.

ドアを開けたら、スミスさんが立っていました。
Doa o aketara, Sumisu-san ga tatte imashita.
When I opened the door, I saw Mr. Smith standing there.

この本を読んだら、助詞の使い方が分かりました。
Kono hon o yondara, joshi no tsukai-kata ga wakarimashita.
After reading this book, I understood how to use particles.

本を読んであげたら、弟が喜びました。
Hon o yonde agetara, otōto ga yorokobimashita.
My younger brother was very happy when I read a book to him.

桃を切ったら、中から男の子が出て来ました。
Momo o kittara, naka kara otoko no ko ga dete kimashita.
When they cut open the peach, a boy came out of it.

CONDITIONALS WITH THE たら TARA-CLAUSE

When the main clause is in the present tense, or a command, question, suggestion, request, conjecture, or volitional sentence, the tara-clause discussed above serves as a condition and expresses one of the following conditions depending on the context: a generic condition; a temporal condition; a hypothetical condition; a counterfactual condition.

Generic Condition The tara-clause in the following example sentences shows a generic condition, in which the situation described in it is almost *always* followed by some situation due to generic facts, laws, and rules in nature, mathematics, society, and family.

> 3に2をたしたら、5になります。
> San ni ni o tashitara, go ni narimasu.
> *If you add 2 to 3, you'll get 5.*

> 人を殺したら、死刑になります。
> Hito o koroshitara, shikei ni narimasu.
> *If you kill a person, you'll get the death penalty.*

> この会社の社員だったら、あのレストランで割引がもらえます。
> Kono kaisha no shain dattara, ano resutoran de waribiki ga moraemasu.
> *If you are an employee of this company, you can get a discount at that restaurant.*

> 風邪をひいたら、くしゃみがでます。
> Kaze o hiitara, kushami ga demasu.
> *If we catch a cold, we sneeze.*

Temporal Condition The tara-clause in the following example sentences shows the temporal condition, where the situation described in it is assumed to certainly take place at some time, and it is just the matter of time.

> 山田さんが来たら、これを渡してください。
> Yamada-san ga kitara, kore o watashite kudasai.
> *When Ms. Yamada comes here, please give this to her.*

> 会議がおわったら、電話しますね。
> Kaigi ga owattara, denwa shimasu ne.
> *I'll call you when the meeting is over, okay?*

Some sentences like below can express both a generic condition and a temporal condition.

春になったら、雪はとけます。
Haru ni nattara, yuki wa tokemasu.
The snow will melt when the spring comes.

Hypothetical Condition The tara-clause in the following example sentences shows the hypothetical condition, where situations described in it are just hypothetical, they may or may not take place. It is often used with the adverb もし **moshi** (*if*).

もし安かったら、買います。
Moshi yasukattara, kaimasu.
I'll buy it if it is inexpensive.

雨が降らなかったら、行きましょう。
Ame ga furanakattara, ikimashō.
Let's go there if it doesn't rain.

雨が降ったら、私は行きません。
Ame ga futtara, watashi wa ikimasen.
I won't go there if it rains.

給料が上がったら、家を買います。
Kyūryō ga agattara, ie o kaimasu.
If my salary goes up, I'll buy a house.

A sentence like the following may express either a temporal condition or a hypothetical condition depending on how likely the situation described in the conditional clause will take place.

スミスさんが来たら、私は帰ります。
Sumisu-san ga kitara, watashi wa kaerimasu.
I'll go home when Mr. Smith comes. (temporal condition)
I'll go home if Mr. Smith comes. (hypothetical condition)

Counterfactual Condition The tara-clause in the following sentences shows the counterfactual condition, where the described situation is not only hypothetical but also very unrealistic. It is usually accompanied by the adverb もし **moshi**.

もし地球に引力がなかったら、あなたは空中に浮いているでしょう。
Moshi chikyū ni inryoku ga nakattara, anata wa kūchū ni uite iru deshō.
If there were no gravity on earth, you'd be floating in the air.

もし私があなただったら、あんなことは言いません。
Moshi watashi ga anata dattara, anna koto wa iimasen.
If I were you, I wouldn't say that kind of thing.

もしもう一度生まれたら、また私と結婚しますか。
Moshi mō ichi-do umaretara, mata watashi to kekkon shimasu ka.
If you can be born again, would you want to marry me again?

毎日すしが食べられたら、私は幸せでしょう。
Mainichi sushi ga taberaretara, watashi wa shiawase deshō.
If I could eat sushi every day, I would probably be very happy.

You can see that the conditional clauses with たら **tara** offers a wide range of conditions and is compatible with a variety of main clauses including suggestions and requests. You just have to remember that the situations expressed in the tara-clause must precede the situation expressed in the main clause.

Written Practice 7

Form tara-clauses creatively, to make sensible sentences.

1. _____ら、雪がとけます。
   _____ra, yuki ga tokemasu.

2. _____ら、公園に行きませんか。
   _____ra, kōen ni ikimasen ka.

3. _____ら、電話します。
   _____ra, denwa shimasu.

4. _____ら、私はとても幸せでしょう。
   _____ra, watashi wa totemo shiawase deshō.

CONDITIONALS WITH THE なら NARA-CLAUSE

The conditional clause with なら **nara** (*the nara-clause* for short) expresses the speaker's supposition or defines the basis of the statement, meaning *if . . .* or *if you are talking about . . .* You can create a verb or an adjective in the nara-form (the form used in the nara-clause) just by adding なら **nara** at the end of the verb or the adjective in the plain form, except that だ **da** that appears at the end of a noun-copula phrase or a na-adjective in their plain present affirmative forms must drop, as in 学生なら **gakusei nara** (*if he is a student*) or 静かなら **shizuka nara** (*if it is quiet*). For example:

京都に行くなら、新幹線がいいですよ。北海道に行くなら、
飛行機がいいですよ。
Kyōto ni iku nara, Shinkansen ga ii desu yo. Hokkaidō ni iku nara, hikōki ga
ii desu yo.
If you are going to Kyoto, it is better to take the bullet train. If you are going to
Hokkaido, an airplane is better.

カメラなら、秋葉原がいいですよ。
Kamera nara, Akihabara ga ii desu yo.
For (If you are talking about) cameras, Akihabara is good.

Unlike the tara-clause that requires the two situations to be sequentially ordered,
the nara-clause does not restrict the temporal order between the two situations. For
example, the action expressed in the main clause follows or precedes the action
expressed in the nara-clause:

中国に行くなら、万里の長城を見てください。
Chūgoku ni iku nara, Banri no Chōjō o mite kudasai.
If you are going to China, please see the Great Wall.

中国に行くなら、ビザをとってください。
Chūgoku ni iku nara, biza o totte kudasai.
If you are going to China, please get a visa.

Accordingly, the nara-clause cannot express the sporadic consequence in the
past or the temporal condition for the future, which focuses on the order between
the two given events. The nara-clause is often used when the main clause expresses
suggestions, speculations, conjectures, and requests as well as the speaker's
intentions:

林さんが来ないなら、帰りませんか。
Hayashi-san ga konai nara, kaerimasen ka.
If Ms. Hayashi is not coming, why don't we go home?

日本に3年住んだことがあるなら、日本語が上手なはずですね。
Nihon ni san-nen sunda koto ga aru nara, Nihon-go ga jōzu na hazu desu ne.
If you have lived in Japan for three years, you must be good at Japanese.

新車なら、高いでしょう。
Shinsha nara, takai deshō.
If it is a brand new car, it will be expensive.

郵便局に行くなら、60円の切手を5枚買って来てください。
Yūbinkyoku ni iku nara, rokujū-en no kitte o go-mai katte kite kudasai.
If you are going to the post office, please buy five 60-yen stamps.

前の試験が難しかったなら、今度の試験も難しいかもしれません。
Mae no shiken ga muzukashikatta nara, kondo no shiken mo muzukashii kamoshiremasen.
If the previous test was hard, the next test may also be hard.

もし私が男なら、フットボールをするでしょう。
Moshi watashi ga otoko nara, futtobōru o suru deshō.
If I were a male, I would play football.

カメラを買いたいなら、秋葉原に行った方がいいですよ。
Kamera o kaitai nara, Akihabara ni itta hō ga ii desu yo.
If you want to buy a camera, it is better to go to Akihabara.

あなたが行くなら、私も行きます。
Anata ga iku nara, watashi mo ikimasu.
If you are going (there), I'll go (there), too.

Written Practice 8

The following is advice to someone who wants to make a trip to somewhere this summer. Complete it creatively.

日本に行くなら、＿＿＿＿＿＿＿＿＿＿方がいいですよ。
フランスに行くなら、＿＿＿＿＿＿＿＿＿＿方がいいですよ。
中国に行くなら、＿＿＿＿＿＿＿＿＿＿方がいいですよ。

Nihon ni iku nara, ＿＿＿＿＿＿＿＿＿＿ hō ga ii desu yo.
Furansu ni iku nara, ＿＿＿＿＿＿＿＿＿＿ hō ga ii desu yo.
Chūgoku ni iku nara, ＿＿＿＿＿＿＿＿＿＿ hō ga ii desu yo.

CONDITIONALS WITH THE ば BA-CLAUSE

The conditional clause with ば **ba** (*the ba-clause* for short) expresses a generic condition, temporal condition, hypothetical condition, and counterfactual condition, just like the tara-clause discussed earlier in this chapter. You can create a verb or an adjective in the ba-form (the form used in the ba-clause) mainly from their plain present forms although there are some irregularities. For verbs, remove **ru** at the end of the ru-verb in the plain present affirmative and add **reba** or remove **u** at the end of the u-verb in the same form and add **eba**. For example, 食べる **taberu** (*to eat*) becomes 食べれば **tabereba**, and 書く **kaku** (*to write*) becomes 書けば **kakeba**. する **suru** and くる **kuru** become すれば **sureba** and くれば **kureba**, respectively. A minor sound change occurs with a u-verb that ends in つ **tsu**: **ts** becomes **t**. For example, 待つ **matsu** (*to wait*) becomes 待てば **mateba**.

For i-type adjectives, add **kereba** after their stem. That is, remove **i** at the end of their plain present affirmative form and add **kereba**. For example, 高い **takai** (*expensive*) becomes 高ければ **takakereba**. The ba-form of いい **ii** is よければ **yokereba**.

The ba-form for na-type adjectives and the copular verb in the affirmative forms are not very simple, and they end in であれば **de areba**, as in 静かであれば **shizuka de areba** and 学生であれば **gakusei de areba**. They are often substituted by their nara-forms and optionally followed by ば **ba**, as in 静かなら(ば) **shizuka nara (ba)** and 学生なら(ば) **gakusei nara (ba)**.

For negative forms (...ない **nai**), treat them as if they are i-type adjectives, regardless of whether they are verbs or adjectives.

食べない **tabenai** (*not to eat*) → 食べなければ **tabenakereba**
高くない **takaku nai** (*not expensive*) → 高くなければ **takaku nakereba**
静かじゃない **shizuka ja nai** (*not quiet*) → 静かじゃなければ **shizuka ja nakereba**
学生じゃない **gakusei ja nai** (*not to be a student*) → 学生じゃなければ **gakusei ja nakereba**

The following are some examples:

春になれば、花が咲きます。
Haru ni nareba, hana ga sakimasu.
When it is spring, the flowers will blossom.

押せば、あきます。
Oseba, akimasu.
Once you push it, it will open.

7時になれば、父が帰ります。
Shichi-ji ni nareba, chichi ga kaerimasu.
My father will get home at 7 o'clock.

勉強すれば、Aがもらえますよ。
Benkyō sureba, Ē ga moraemasu yo.
If you study, you'll be able to get an A.

犬と話せれば、楽しいでしょう。
Inu to hanasereba, tanoshii deshō.
If I could talk with a dog, it would be enjoyable.

高ければ、買わない方がいいですよ。
Takakereba, kawanai hō ga ii desu yo.
If it is expensive, it is better not to buy it.

都合がよければ、いっしょに大阪に行きませんか。
Tsugō ga yokereba, isshoni Ōsaka ni ikimasen ka.
How about going to Osaka together if it is convenient for you?

As you can see, the main clause can be a command, a request, or a suggestion. However, if it is the case, the predicate in the ba-clause itself must express a state rather than an action. For example, unlike the above example, the following example is ungrammatical:

山田さんが来れば、いっしょに大阪に行きませんか。(Ungrammatical)
Yamada-san ga kureba, isshoni Ōsaka ni ikimasen ka. (Ungrammatical)
How about going to Osaka together if Ms. Yamada comes? (Intended meaning)

Such a restriction doesn't apply to the tara-clause or the nara-clause. The following examples are grammatical:

山田さんが来たら、いっしょに大阪に行きませんか。
Yamada-san ga kitara, isshoni Ōsaka ni ikimasen ka.
How about going to Osaka together if Ms. Yamada comes?

山田さんが来るなら、いっしょに大阪に行きませんか。
Yamada-san ga kuru nara, isshoni Ōsaka ni ikimasen ka.
How about going to Osaka together if Ms. Yamada is coming?

The ba-clause is often used to express what one should do or should have done.

あの家を買えばいいんです。
Ano ie o kaeba ii ndesu.
You should buy that house. (Literally: It would be good if you buy that house.)

私がすれば、よかったんです。
Watashi ga sureba, yokatta ndesu.
I should have done it (instead of him).

In casual conversations, such sentences often end in のに **noni** and んですよ **ndesu yo**.

あの家を買えばいいのに。
Ano ie o kaeba ii noni.
You should buy that house.

あの家を買えばよかったのに。
Ano ie o kaeba yokatta noni.
You should have bought that house.

Note that unlike a tara-clause, a ba-clause cannot relate two events that took place in the past (unless they are habitual events in the past).

Written Practice 9

Convert the following verbs and adjectives in the plain form into their ba-form.

たべる taberu → たべれば tabereba _____

1. よむ yomu → _____
2. くる kuru → _____
3. こない konai → _____
4. ある aru → _____
5. ない nai → _____
6. する suru → _____
7. いない inai → _____
8. かく kaku → _____
9. やすい yasui → _____
10. いい ii → _____
11. よくない yokunai → _____
12. べんりだ benri da → _____
13. 学生じゃない gakusei ja nai → _____

Written Practice 10

Think about your childhood. Is there anything that you feel you should have done when you were younger? For example:

ピアノを習えばよかったと思います。それから、もっと勉強すればよかったと思います。

Piano o naraeba yokatta to omoimasu. Sorekara, motto benkyō sureba yokatta to omoimasu.

_____

_____

_____

_____

More Terms for Occupations and Professions

Some terms for occupations were introduced in Chapter 2. Additional terms for occupations and professions are listed here:

警察官	keisatsukan	_police officer_
画家	gaka	_painter (art)_
会計士	kaikeishi	_accountant_
音楽家	ongakuka	_musician_
学者	gakusha	_scholar_
歌手	kashu	_singer_
通訳	tsūyaku	_interpreter_
俳優	haiyū	_actor_
女優	joyū	_actress_
作家	sakka	_writer_

QUIZ

Circle the letter of the word or phrase that best completes each sentence.

1. ここに名前を_____と書いてあります。

   Koko ni namae o _____ to kaite arimasu.

   (a) 書くに kaku ni   (c) 書け kake

   (b) 書こう kakō   (d) 書き kaki

2. 9時までに_____なさい。

   Ku-ji made ni _____ nasai.

   (a) 帰れ kaere   (c) 帰り kaeri

   (b) 帰る kaeru   (d) 帰って kaette

3. 大学院に行こう_____ 。

   Daigakuin ni ikō _____ .

   (a) 思います omoimasu

   (b) と思います to omoimasu

   (c) にしました ni shimashita

   (d) つもりです tsumori desu

4. うそをつこう_____ が、つけませんでした。

   Uso o tsukō _____ ga, tsukemasendeshita.

   (a) としました to shimashita

   (b) と思います to omoimasu

   (c) にしました ni shimashita

   (d) ようにしています yō ni shite imasu

5. できるだけ_____します。

   Dekiru dake _____ shimasu.

   (a) 遅れないと okurenai to

   (b) 遅れないに okurenai ni

   (c) 遅れないようと okurenai yō to

   (d) 遅れないように okurenai yō ni

6. 陽子さんのうちに＿＿＿＿、明子さんがいました。

Yōko-san no uchi ni ＿＿＿＿ , Akiko-san ga imashita.

(a) 行ったら ittara   (c) 行くなら iku nara

(b) 行ったなら itta nara   (d) 行って itte

7. 買い物＿＿＿＿、秋葉原がいいですよ。

Kaimono ＿＿＿＿ , Akihabara ga ii desu yo.

(a) たら tara   (c) だなら da nara

(b) なら nara   (d) ば ba

8. 山田さんが＿＿＿＿、いっしょにディズニーランドに行きませんか。

Yamada-san ga ＿＿＿＿ , isshoni Dizunīrando ni ikimasen ka.

(a) 来れば kureba   (c) 来るなら kurunara

(b) 来て kite   (d) 来たと kita to

9. 日本に＿＿＿＿、行く前に日本語を勉強してください。

Nihon ni ＿＿＿＿ , iku mae ni Nihon-go o benkyhō shite kudasai.

(a) 行けば ikeba   (c) 行くなら iku nara

(b) 行ったら ittara   (d) 行ったなら itta nara

10. 私は小説を書くのが好きで、将来は＿＿＿＿になりたいです。

Watashi wa shōsetsu o kaku no ga suki de, shōrai wa ＿＿＿＿ ni naritai desu.

(a) 作家 sakka   (c) 通訳 tsūyaku

(b) 会計士 kaikeishi   (d) 女優 joyū

CHAPTER 19

Changing the Perspective

In this chapter, you'll learn:

Passive Constructions

Causative Constructions

Causative-Passive Constructions

Loanwords

Passive Constructions

The same situation can be expressed differently depending on the speaker's perspective. In this section, you will learn two types of passive constructions in Japanese: direct passive and indirect passive.

DIRECT PASSIVE

Suppose that your father scolded your brother. You can say either *My father scolded my brother* or *My brother was scolded by my father*, depending on whether your major concern is about your father or about your brother. The first sentence is an active sentence and the second sentence is a passive sentence. Japanese also has equivalent constructions. For example:

父が弟をしかりました。
Chichi ga otōto o shikarimashita.
My father scolded my brother.

弟が父にしかられました。
Otōto ga chichi ni shikararemashita.
My brother was scolded by my father.

The second sentence is a direct passive sentence. Just like in an English passive sentence, the action receiver is the subject in a direct passive sentence in Japanese. The action performer is marked by the particle に **ni**, and the verb is a passive verb.

PASSIVE VERBS

You can convert a verb into a passive verb by adding **rareru** or **areru** to its dictionary form without the final **ru** or **u**. If a verb is a ru-verb, remove **ru** and add **rareru**. For example, 食べる **taberu** becomes 食べられる **taberareru**. If a verb is a u-verb, remove **u** and add **areru**. For example, 書く **kaku** becomes 書かれる **kakareru**. As you can see in the following table, a minor sound change occurs with u-verbs whose dictionary forms end in the hiragana う **u** or つ **tsu**, just like when we create the plain present negative forms (Chapter 7). The resulting passive verbs are ru-verbs, so you can conjugate them accordingly, as in 食べられる **taberareru**, 食べられない **taberarenai**, 食べられます **taberaremasu**, and so on. The passive forms of する **suru** and くる **kuru** are される **sareru** and こられる **korareru**, respectively. These are summarized in the following table.

Verbs in the Dictionary Form	Passive Counterparts
食べる taberu (*eat*)	食べられる taberareru
見る miru (*look*)	見られる mirareru
書く kaku (*write*)	書かれる kakareru
泳ぐ oyogu (*swim*)	泳がれる oyogareru
運ぶ hakobu (*carry*)	運ばれる hakobareru

読む yomu (*read*)	読まれる yomareru
死ぬ shinu (*die*)	死なれる shinareru
待つ matsu (*wait*)	待たれる matareru
話す hanasu (*talk*)	話される hanasareru
作る tsukuru (*make*)	作られる tsukurareru
買う kau (*buy*)	買われる kawareru
する suru (*do*)	される sareru
来る kuru (*come*)	来られる korareru

The passive verbs for intransitive verbs such as 泳ぐ **oyogu** and 死ぬ **shinu** do not make sense in direct passive, but do make sense in indirect passive, which is discussed in the following section.

Written Practice 1

Convert the following verbs into their passive forms following the example.

たべる taberu (*eat*) → たべられる taberareru _____

1. ぬすむ nusumu (*steal*) → _____
2. たたく tataku (*hit*) → _____
3. つかう tsukau (*use*) → _____
4. とる toru (*take*) → _____
5. しかる shikaru (*scold*) → _____
6. ほめる homeru (*praise*) → _____

THE PARTICLE に NI IN PASSIVE SENTENCES

In direct passive sentences, the action performer is marked by the particle に **ni**.

ネックレスがどろぼうに盗まれました。
Nekkuresu ga dorobō ni nusumaremashita.
The necklace was stolen by a thief.

弟が父にたたかれました。
Otōto ga chichi ni tatakaremashita.
My younger brother was hit by my father.

Written Practice 2

Convert the following sentences into direct passive sentences.

1. どろぼうがネックレスを盗みました。

   Dorobō ga nekkuresu o nusumimashita.

   _____

2. 父が弟をしかりました。

   Chichi ga otōto o shikarimashita.

   _____

3. たくさんの人が日本語を話しています。

   Takusan no hito ga Nihon-go o hanashite imasu. (たくさんの人 takusan no hito: _many people_)

   _____

4. 知らない人が私の電話を使いました。

   Shiranai hito ga watashi no denwa o tsukaimashita. (知らない人 shiranai hito: _a stranger_)

   _____

INDIRECT PASSIVE

Interestingly, passive verbs can also be used without converting the direct object to the subject noun. The direct object can either remain as the direct object or can be absent to start with. Thus, even an intransitive verb such as "to die" or "to cry" can be in the passive form. Such passive constructions are called "indirect passive" as opposed to the "direct passive" discussed in the previous section, where a direct object is converted to the subject noun. In indirect passive sentences, the action performer is marked by the particle に **ni** rather than が **ga**. Interestingly, the person denoted by the subject in an indirect passive sentence is usually the one disturbed, annoyed, or saddened by the action. For this reason, indirect passive is also called adversative passive.

またマイクさんにうちに来られました。
Mata Maiku-san ni uchi ni koraremashita.
Mike came to my house again (although I don't enjoy his visiting me.)

兄は電車の中で女の人に足を踏まれました。
Ani wa densha no naka de onna no hito ni ashi o fumaremashita.
A woman stepped on my brother's foot on the train (and he was unhappy about it).

兄は昨日雨にふられました。
Ani wa kinō ame ni furaremashita.
It rained on my brother yesterday.

あの人は子供に死なれたんです。
Ano hito wa kodomo ni shinareta ndesu.
That person's child died (which is an awful thing that happened to her).

どろぼうに逃げられました。
Dorobō ni nigeraremashita.
The thief ran away (which was very unfortunate for me).

私が100点を取ったと言ったら、みんなにびっくりされました。
Watashi ga 100-ten o totta to ittara, minna ni bikkuri saremashita.
When I said that I got 100, everyone was surprised (and I was offended).

弟に先に卒業されました。
Otōto ni sakini sotsugyō saremashita.
My younger brother graduated before me (and I was embarrassed).

Written Practice 3

State the following unfortunate situations in Japanese using indirect passive.

1. Mr. Tanaka was caught in the rain.

   _____

2. Yoko's cat died, and she is very upset about it.

   _____

3. Mike's dog ran away, which made him unhappy.

   _____

Causative Constructions

Using a causative verb, you can express a situation where someone makes or lets someone else do something.

CAUSATIVE VERBS

You can create a causative verb from a regular verb by adding **saseru** or **aseru** to its dictionary form without the final **ru** or **u**. If a verb is a ru-verb, remove **ru** and add **saseru**. For example, 食べる **taberu** becomes 食べさせる **tabesaseru**. If a verb is a u-verb, remove **u** and add **aseru**. For example, 書く **kaku** becomes 書かせる **kakaseru**. As you can see in the following table a minor sound change occurs with u-verbs whose dictionary forms end in the hiragana う **u** or つ **tsu**, as in the passive verbs discussed earlier in this chapter. The resulting causative verbs are ru-verbs, so you can conjugate them accordingly, as in 食べさせる **tabesaseru**, 食べさせない **tabesasenai**, 食べさせます **tabesasemasu**, and so on. The causative forms of する **suru** and くる **kuru** are させる **saseru** and こさせる **kosaseru**, respectively. These are summarized in the following table.

Verbs in the Dictionary Form	Causative Form
食べる taberu (*eat*)	食べさせる tabesaseru
見る miru (*look*)	見させる misaseru
書く kaku (*write*)	書かせる kakaseru
泳ぐ oyogu (*swim*)	泳がせる oyogaseru
運ぶ hakobu (*carry*)	運ばせる hakobaseru
読む yomu (*read*)	読ませる yomaseru
死ぬ shinu (*die*)	死なせる shinaseru
待つ matsu (*wait*)	待たせる mataseru
話す hanasu (*talk*)	話させる hanasaseru
作る tsukuru (*make*)	作らせる tsukuraseru
買う kau (*buy*)	買わせる kawaseru
する suru (*do*)	させる saseru
来る kuru (*come*)	来させる kosaseru

Written Practice 4

Convert the following verbs into their causative forms following the example.

たべる taberu (*eat*)　　たべさせる tabesaseru _____

1. ならう narau (*learn*) _____
2. いく iku (*go*) _____
3. あらう arau (*wash*) _____
4. たつ tatsu (*stand up*) _____

5. くる kuru (*come*)   _____

6. する suru (*do*)   _____

THE PARTICLE に NI IN CAUSATIVE SENTENCES

In causative sentences, the causer (the person who causes someone else's action) becomes the subject, and the action performer is marked by the particle に **ni** if the verb is originally a transitive verb. (See Chapter 16 for transitive verbs and intransitive verbs.) The following are additional examples of simple action sentences and their causative counterparts:

妹が皿を洗いました。
Imōto ga sara o araimashita.
My sister washed dishes.

母が妹に皿を洗わせました。
Haha ga imōto ni sara o arawasemashita.
My mother made my younger sister wash dishes.

弟が剣道を習いました。
Otōto ga kendō o naraimashita.
My younger brother took kendo lessons.

父が弟に剣道を習わせました。
Chichi ga otōto ni kendō o narawasemashita.
My father made my younger brother take kendo lessons.

If the verb is originally an intransitive verb, the action performer is marked by を **o** rather than by に **ni**.

兄は弟を泣かせました。
Ani wa otōto o nakasemashita.
My big brother made my younger brother cry.

母を休ませました。
Haha o yasumasemashita.
(We) made our mother rest.

父は弟をオーストラリアに行かせました。
Chichi wa otōto o Ōsutoraria ni ikasemashita.
My father made my younger brother go to Australia.

However, note that some intransitive verbs allow the action performer to be marked either by に **ni** or by を **o** depending on the context.

MAKE-CAUSATIVE AND LET-CAUSATIVE

Depending on the context, the interpretation of the causative sentences is either *make someone do something* (make-causative) or *let someone do something* (let-causative). It all depends on whether the action performer is willing to perform the action or not. For example, the first sentence is a make-causative whereas the second sentence is a let-causative.

弟は野菜が嫌いですが、母は弟に毎日野菜を食べさせます。
Otōto wa yasai ga kirai desu ga, haha wa otōto ni mainichi yasai o tabesasemasu.
My younger brother hates vegetables, but my mother makes him eat them every day.

弟はチョコレートが大好きです。母は少しなら弟にチョコレートを食べさせます。
Otōto wa chokorēto ga daisuki desu. Haha wa sukoshi nara otōto ni chokorēto o tabesasemasu.
My younger brother loves chocolate very much. My mother lets him eat it if it is a little bit.

Let-causative sentences are usually accompanied by auxiliary verbs such as あげる **ageru**, くれる **kureru**, and もらう **morau**, discussed in Chapter 16. For example, the following sentences are all let-causatives:

母は私に料理をさせてくれました。
Haha wa watashi ni ryōri o sasete kuremashita.
My mother let me cook.

子供に専攻を決めさせてあげます。
Kodomo ni senkō o kimesasete agemasu.
I'll let my child decide his major.

兄の車を使わせてもらいました。
Ani no kuruma o tsukawasete moraimashita.
I was allowed to use my big brother's car.

Written Practice 5

Translate the following sentences into Japanese. You may want to use the phrases in the parentheses.

1. My mother made me take piano lessons. (ピアノを習う piano o narau *to take piano lessons*)

   _____

2. My mother let me watch TV. (テレビを見る terebi o miru *to watch TV*)

   _____

3. The teacher made me stand up. (立つ tatsu *to stand up*)

   _____

Causative-Passive Constructions

A passive version of a causative verb expresses the situation where one is made to do something. For example, compare the following three sentences: the first one is a simple action sentence with the action performer as the subject; the second one is a causative sentence with the action causer as the subject; the third one is a causative-passive sentence where the person who was made to do something is the subject:

兄が部屋を掃除しました。
Ani ga heya o sōji shimashita.
My older brother cleaned the room.

母が兄に部屋を掃除させました。
Haha ga ani ni heya o sōji sasemashita.
My mother made my brother clean the room.

兄が母に部屋を掃除させられました。
Ani ga haha ni heya o sōji saseraremashita.
My brother was made to clean the room by my mother.

The following are additional examples of causative-passive sentences:

学生は先生に漢字を練習させられました。
Gakusei wa sensei ni kanji o renshū saseraremashita.
The students were made to practice kanji by their teacher.

僕はガールフレンドに荷物を持たせられました。
Boku wa gārufurendo ni nimotsu o motaseraremashita.
I was made to carry the baggage by my girlfriend.

病院で3時間待たせられました。
Byōin de san-jikan mataseraremashita.
I was made to wait for 3 hours at the hospital.

私は父に書道を習わせられました。
Watashi wa chichi ni shodō o narawaseraremashita.
I was made to take calligraphy lessons by my father.

The ending of the causative-passive verb **aserareru** often contracts to **asareru** in colloquial Japanese for u-verbs whose dictionary forms do not end in す **su**. For example, instead of 待たせられる **mataserareru**, they may say 待たされる **matasareru**.

Written Practice 6

Convert the following verbs into the causative-passive forms following the example.

たべる taberu (*eat*) → たべさせられる tabesaserareru _____

1. まつ matsu (*wait*) → _____
2. はこぶ hakobu (*carry*) → _____
3. うたう utau (*sing*) → _____
4. てつだう tetsudau (*assist*) → _____
5. はたらく hataraku (*work*) → _____
6. よむ yomu (*read*) → _____
7. する suru (*do*) → _____
8. くる kuru (*come*) → _____

Loanwords

There are many English words used in Japanese, and their number is constantly increasing. They are usually written in katakana. The following are some examples:

コーヒー	kōhī	*coffee*
オレンジジュース	orenji-jūsu	*orange juice*
ラジオ	rajio	*radio*
ベッド	beddo	*bed*
ネクタイ	nekutai	*necktie*

Some items are shortened into about four syllables:

エアコン	eakon	*air conditioning*
コンビニ	konbini	*convenience store*
パソコン	pasokon	*personal computer*
リモコン	rimokon	*remote control*

Some items have different meanings from modern (American) English.

マンション	manshon	*condominium*
スマート	sumāto	*skinny, slim*

QUIZ

Refer to the text in this chapter if necessary. A good score is eight correct. Answers are in the back of the book. Circle the letter of the word or phrase that best completes each sentence.

1. 兄が弟 _____ ほめました。

   Ani ga otōto _____ homemashita.

   (a) を o   (c) で de

   (b) が ga   (d) に ni

2. 弟が兄＿＿＿＿ほめられました。

Otōto ga ani ＿＿＿＿＿ homeraremashita.

(a) を   (c) で

(b) が   (d) に

3. マイクさんは知らない人に＿＿＿＿＿。

Maiku-san wa shiranai hito ni ＿＿＿＿＿ .

(a) パソコンを使いました pasokon o tsukaimashita

(b) パソコンを使われました pasokon o tsukawaremashita

(c) パソコンが使いました pasokon ga tsukaimashita

(d) パソコンが使われました pasokon ga tsukawaremashita

4. マイクは猫＿＿＿＿＿。

Maiku wa neko ＿＿＿＿＿ .

(a) に死にました ni shinimashita

(b) に死なれました ni shinaremashita

(c) を死なれました o shinaremashita

(d) が死なれました ga shinaremashita

5. 5歳のとき、母は私＿＿＿＿。

Go-sai no toki, haha wa watashi ＿＿＿＿＿ .

(a) にピアノを習いました ni piano o naraimashita

(b) にピアノを習わせました ni piano o narawasemashita

(c) にピアノを習わせられました ni piano o narawaseraremashita

(d) をピアノが習わせました o piano ga narawasemashita

6. 5歳のとき、私は母＿＿＿＿＿。

Go-sai no toki, watashi wa haha ＿＿＿＿＿ .

(a) をピアノを習いました o piano o naraimashita

(b) にピアノを習わせました ni piano o narawasemashita

(c) にピアノを習わせられました ni piano o narawaseraremashita

(d) をピアノが習わせました o piano ga narawasemashita

7. 弟は野菜が嫌いですが、母は弟に毎日野菜を ＿＿＿＿ ます。

   Otōto wa yasai ga kirai desu ga, haha wa otōto ni mainichi yasai o ＿＿＿＿ masu.

   (a) 食べ tabe

   (b) 食べさせ tabesase

   (c) 食べさせてあげ tabesasete age

   (d) 食べさせてもらい tabesasete morai

8. 弟はチョコレートが好きです。母は少しなら弟にチョコレートを ＿＿＿＿ ます。

   Otōto wa chokorēto ga suki desu. Haha wa sukoshi nara otōto ni chokorēto o ＿＿＿＿ masu.

   (a) 食べ tabe   (c) 食べさせてあげ tabesasete age

   (b) 食べられ taberare   (d) 食べさせてもらい tabesasete morai

9. 先生は学生 ＿＿＿＿ 。

   Sensei wa gakusei ＿＿＿＿ .

   (a) に勉強しました ni benkyō shimashita

   (b) を勉強されました o benkyō saremashita

   (c) に勉強させました ni benkyō sasemashita

   (d) に勉強させられました ni benkyō saseraremashita

10. ＿＿＿＿ でコーヒーを買いました。

    ＿＿＿＿ de kōhī o kaimashita.

    (a) パソコン pasokon   (c) リモコン rimokon

    (b) エアコン eakon   (d) コンビニ konbini

CHAPTER 20

Using Honorifics

In this chapter, you'll learn:

Japanese Honorifics
Honorific and Humble Verb Forms
Honorific/Polite Noun Forms
Honorific/Polite Adjective Forms
Honorific/Polite Question Words

Japanese Honorifics

Japanese has three speech styles: informal, polite, and formal. In the informal speech style, sentences mostly end in the plain form, for example, 食べた **tabeta** (*ate*) and きれいだ **kirei da** (*pretty*). In the polite speech style, they end in the polite form, which are typically characterized by ます **masu** and です **desu**. (See Chapter 6 for plain and polite forms.) These two speech styles are selected based on who

is the addressee, the person whom the speaker is talking to. In the formal speech style, sentences end in the polite form but also include verbs and other items in the honorific (respectful) forms, humble forms, or very polite forms. The honorific form is used to elevate the stature of the referent, the person who is being talked about, when the speaker is talking about his social superiors such as his boss, teacher, client, or customer. The referent can be the addressee at the same time. The humble form is used to lower the speaker's stature, when the speaker is talking about himself or his in-group such as his family and teammates in front of his out-group or those from whom the speaker feels distant. The very polite form is used to emphasize the formality of the situation, as you see in public announcements and speeches. The term *honorific* is also used to refer to the formal speech style in general.

Honorific and Humble Verb Forms

The Japanese honorifics are most evidently manifested in verb forms. They are reflected in special verb forms, grammatical items, and conventionally used words and phrases.

SPECIAL FORMS FOR SOME FREQUENTLY USED VERBS

Some frequently used verbs have their own special honorific and humble forms. For example, as discussed in Chapter 5, the honorific form for the verb いる **iru** (*to exist*) is いらっしゃる **irassharu**. As discussed in Chapter 7, the honorific form for the verb くれる **kureru** (*to give*) is 下さる **kudasaru**, the humble form for the verb あげる **ageru** (*to give*) is 差し上げる **sashiageru**, and the humble form for the verb もらう **morau** (*to receive*) is 頂く**itadaku**. The following table lists additional examples. The footnotes offer further explanation.

Plain form	Honorific form	Humble form
いる iru (*exist*)	いらっしゃる irassharu[1]	おる oru
行く iku (*go*)	いらっしゃる irassharu[1]	参る mairu[2] 伺う ukagau[2]
来る kuru (*come*)	いらっしゃる irassharu[1]	参る mairu
する suru (*do*)	なさる nasaru[1]	致す itasu

食べる taberu (*eat*) 飲む nomu (*drink*)	召し上がる meshiagaru	頂く itadaku
見る miru (*look*)	ご覧になる go-ran ni naru	拝見する haiken suru[3]
言う iu (*say*)	おっしゃる o-ssharu[1]	申す mōsu
知っている shitte iru (*know*)	ご存知だ go-zonji da	存じている zonjite iru
ある (*exist*)	not applicable	ござる gozaru[1, 4]
...だ da (copular verb)	...でいらっしゃる de irassharu[1]	...でござる de gozaru[1, 4]

Oral Practice

 TRACK 59

Practice asking a question and answering it by reading the following sentences out loud. Pay attention to the level of formality in each conversational interaction.

陽子さんはいらっしゃいますか。
Yōko-san wa irasshaimasu ka.
Is Yoko in?

いいえ、おりません。
Īe, orimasen.
No, she is not in.

召し上がってください。
Meshiagatte kudasai.
Please eat (it).

はい、頂きます。
Hai, itadakimasu.
Yes, I'll have it.

---

1. These verbs are u-verbs, but り **ri** that appears right before the polite suffix (ます **masu**, ません **masen**, etc.) changes to い **i**.
2. If the speaker is going to the place of the addressee, use 伺う **ukagau** rather than 参る **mairu**.
3. Use 拝見する **haiken suru** only if the item to be seen belongs to the addressee.
4. ござる **gozaru** and ... でござる **de gozaru** function either as humble forms or very polite forms.

この写真をご覧になりましたか。
Kono shashin o go-ran ni narimashita ka.
Did you see this photo?

はい。
Hai.
Yes.

ホワイトと申します。宜しくお願いいたします。
Howaito to mōshimasu. Yoroshiku o-negai itashimasu.
My name is White. I am pleased to meet you.

ああ、こちらこそ宜しく。
Ā, kochira koso yoroshiku.
Oh, pleased to meet you, too.

ゴルフをなさいますか。
Gorufu o nasaimasu ka.
Do you play golf?

はい。毎週しています。
Hai. Maishū shite imasu.
Yes. I do it every week.

明日7時にうちに来てください。
Ashita shichi-ji ni uchi ni kite kudasai.
Please come to my house at 7 o'clock.

はい。7時に伺います。
Hai. Shichi-ji ni ukagaimasu.
Certainly. I will come to your place at 7 o'clock.

スミスさんでいらっしゃいますか。
Sumisu-san de irasshaimasu ka.
Are you Mr. Smith?

はい、そうですが。
Hai, sō desu ga.
Yes, that's right, but . . .

営業時間は何時から何時までですか。
Eigyō-jikan wa nan-ji kara nan-ji made desu ka.
What are your business hours? (From what time to what time are you open?)

午前10時から午後5時まででございます。
Gozen jū-ji kara gogo go-ji made de gozaimasu.
From 10 A.M. to 5 P.M.

すみません。近くに郵便局はありますか。
Sumimasen. Chikaku ni yūbinkyoku wa arimasu ka.
Excuse me. Is there a post office nearby?

はい、この建物の隣にございます。
Hai, kono tatemono no tonari ni gozaimasu.
Yes, it is next to this building.

HONORIFIC AND HUMBLE VERB FORMS WITH お...になる O ... NI NARU AND お...する O ... SURU

There is a general way of creating a honorific form and a humble form of verbs. For the honorific form, use the construction お **o** + verb stem + に **ni** + なる **naru**. For example:

先生がお書きになりました。
Sensei ga o-kaki ni narimashita.
The teacher wrote (it).

For the humble form, use the construction お **o** + verb stem + する **suru**. For example:

私がお届けしました。
Watashi ga o-todoke shimashita.
I delivered (it).

You may use いたす **itasu** instead of する **suru** (*to do*) to make the humble form even more humble. For example, the last example sentence can also be said as:

私がお届けいたしました。
Watashi ga o-todoke itashimashita.

These constructions do not apply to the verbs that have their special honorific/humble forms, for example, 行く **iku** (*to go*) and 食べる **taberu** (*to eat*), discussed in the above section in this chapter.

Oral Practice

 TRACK 60

Practice speaking politely by reading the following sentences out loud.

これは先生がお書きになった本ですか。
Kore wa sensei ga o-kaki ni natta hon desu ka.
Is this the book you wrote, Professor?

はい、そうです。
Hai, sō desu.
Yes, it is.

この本をお借りしてもよろしいですか。
Kono hon o o-kari shite mo yoroshii desu ka.
Is it okay to borrow this book?

ええ、どうぞ。
Ē, dōzo.
Yes, go ahead.

ありがとうございます。明日お返しいたします。
Arigatō gozaimasu. Ashita o-kaeshi itashimasu.
Thank you. I'll return it to you tomorrow.

いつでもいいですよ。
Itsu demo ii desu yo.
Anytime is fine.

どうぞここでお休みになってください。
Dōzo koko de o-yasumi ni natte kudasai.
Please take a rest here.

ああ、ありがとうございます。
Ā, arigatō gozaimasu.
Oh, thank you.

Written Practice 1

Following the examples, form a sentence using the given items. Carefully think about whether you should use the honorific form or the humble form.

先生 sensei, 書きました kakimashita (*wrote*)

先生がお書きになりました。 (Sensei ga o-kaki ni narimashita.)

私 watashi, 届けました todokemashita (*delivered*)

私がお届けいたしました。 (Watashi ga o-todoke itashimashita.)

1. 社長 shachō, 決めました kimemashita (*decided*)

   _____

2. 私 watashi, 作りました tsukurimashita (*made*)

   _____

3. 先生 sensei, 考えました kangaemashita (*thought about it*)

   _____

4. 私 watashi, 見せました misemashita (*showed*)

   _____

5. 私 watashi, 知らせました shirasemashita (*notified*)

   _____

HONORIFIC VERB FORMS WITH られる RARERU

Another way of creating an honorific verb form is to use the same verb form as the passive form (Chapter 19). For example:

あの本は読まれましたか。
Ano hon wa yomaremashita ka.
Did you read that book?

辞書を買われましたか。
Jisho o kawaremashita ka.
Did you buy a dictionary?

However, the degree of politeness expressed by this form is lower than that expressed by the honorific form with お...になる **o ... ni naru** discussed in the above subsection.

Written Practice 2

Rephrase the following questions so they sound polite.

辞書を買いましたか。 Jisho o kaimashita ka.

辞書を買われましたか。 Jisho o kawaremashita ka.

_____

1. 田中さんと話しましたか。 Tanaka-san to hanashimashita ka.

_____

2. よく車を使いますか。 Yoku kuruma o tsukaimasu ka.

_____

3. 手紙を書きましたか。 Tegami o kakimashita ka.

_____

4. 今朝の新聞を読みましたか。 Kesa no shinbun o yomimashita ka.

_____

POLITELY SEEKING PERMISSION WITH させてください SASETE KUDASAI

The let-causative discussed in Chapter 19 is often used for seeking permission to do something very politely. For example, the following sentences all have a causative verb, and they can be used for asking for permission to go home.

うちに帰らせてください。
Uchi ni kaerasete kudasai.
Please let me go home.

うちに帰らせていただきたいんですが。
Uchi ni kaerasete itadaki-tai ndesu ga.
I'd like to be allowed to go home.

うちに帰らせていただけませんか。
Uchi ni kaerasete itadakemasen ka.
Can I be allowed to go home?

Depending on the nature of the action as well as the context of the conversation, the *let*-causative can be used for offering help very politely rather than seeking permission. For example:

私に荷物を持たせてくださいませんか。
Watashi ni nimotsu o motasete kudasaimasen ka.
Could you let me carry the luggage?

Written Practice 3

Create sentences that politely ask for permission to do the following.

うちに帰る uchi ni kaeru

うちに帰らせていただけませんか。 Uchi ni kaerasete itadakemasen ka.

1. 東京に行く Tokyō ni iku

    _____

2. 手紙を読む tegami o yomu

    _____

3. 車を使う kuruma o tsukau

    _____

POLITELY REQUESTING AN ACTION WITH お...ください O ... KUDASAI

For requesting someone to do something very politely, you can use the construction お **o** + verb stem + ください **kudasai**. (See Chapter 6 for the stem form.) For example, instead of just saying 書いてください **Kaite kudasai** (*Please write it*), you can say お書きください **O-kaki kudasai**. The following are some examples:

どうぞお入りください。
Dōzo o-hairi kudasai.
Please come in.

チケットをお取りください。
Chiketto o o-tori kudasai.
Please take the ticket.

もうしばらくお待ちください。
Mō shibaraku o-machi kudasai.
Please wait a little bit more.

お名前とご住所をお教えくださいませんか。
O-namae to go-jūsho o o-oshie kudasaimasen ka.
Could you let me know your name and your address?

Honorific/Polite Noun Forms

In this section, you will learn honorific/polite forms of many Japanese nouns.

USING お O AND ご GO BEFORE A NOUN

The polite prefixes お **o** and ご **go** can be placed before a noun to show respect to the person who is talked to or talked about or the things that belong to him/her. Make sure not to use a polite prefix for yourself or for your insiders. The basic rule is to use お **o** before a native Japanese word and ご **go** before a Sino-Japanese word (a word with Chinese origin), but there are numerous exceptions.

お名前	o-namae	*name*
ご自身	go-jishin	*self*
ご住所	go-jūsho	*address*
ご病気	go-byōki	*illness*
お電話番号	o-denwa-bangō	*telephone number*
お勉強	o-benkyō	*study*
お車	o-kuruma	*car*
ご結婚	go-kekkon	*marriage*

お食事	o-shokuji	*meal*
ご出産	go-shussan	*childbirth*
ご家族	go-kazoku	*family*
ご注文	go-chūmon	*order*

There are some nouns that are always preceded by a polite prefix regardless of who is talking to whom or to whom the item belongs to. For example, the following words almost always appear with a polite prefix:

お金	o-kane	*money*
お茶	o-cha	*tea*
お湯	o-yu	*hot water*
ご飯	go-han	*(cooked) rice*

MORE TERMS FOR FAMILY MEMBERS

As discussed in Chapter 3, family terms such as *mother* and *father* have a few different forms depending on the use. Plain forms such as 父 **chichi** (*father*) and 母 **haha** (*mother*) are used to refer to the speaker's family members in front of outsiders. Honorific forms such as お父さん **otōsan** (*father*) and お母さん **okāsan** (*mother*) can be used politely referring to someone else's family members. The following table lists additional examples of family terms in the honorific form and in the plain form.

Meaning	Honorific Form	Plain Form
grandfather	おじいさん ojīsan	祖父 sofu
grandmother	おばあさん obāsan	祖母 sobo
uncle	おじさん ojisan	おじ oji
aunt	おばさん obasan	おば oba
husband	ご主人 go-shujin	主人 shujin
wife	奥さん okusan	家内 kanai, 妻 tsuma
child	お子さん okosan	子供 kodomo
son	息子さん musukosan	息子 musuko
daughter	お嬢さん ojōsan	娘 musume
grandchild	お孫さん omagosan	孫 mago
parents	ご両親 go-ryōshin	両親 ryōshin
siblings	ご兄弟 go-kyōdai	兄弟 kyōdai
relatives	ご親戚 go-shinseki	親戚 shinseki

For the terms of occupation such as 先生 **sensei** (*teacher*) and 教師 **kyōshi** (*teacher*), see Chapter 2.

Honorific/Polite Adjective Forms

To create an honorific form for an adjective, add お **o** to i-type adjectives, and add お **o** or ご **go** to na-type adjectives depending on the word.

お元気ですか。
O-genki desu ka.
How are you?

お忙しいですか。
O-isogashii desu ka.
Are you busy?

お肌がおきれいですね。
O-hada ga o-kirei desu ne.
(Your) skin is pretty.

お若いですね。
O-wakai desu ne.
(You) are young.

おひまなときに、お電話下さい。
O-hima na toki ni, o-denwa kudasai.
Please call me when you are free.

ご親切にありがとうございました。
Go-shinsetsu ni arigatō gozaimashita.
Thank you for (your) kindness.

ご立派です。
Go-rippa desu.
(You) are great.

おやさしい方ですね。
O-yasashii kata desu ne.
(He) is a kind person.

ピアノがお上手ですね。
Piano ga o-jōzu desu ne.
(You) are good at piano.

Honorific/Polite Question Words

There are some question words that have their polite version. For example, as discussed in Chapter 3, the polite counterparts of だれ **dare** (*who*) and どこ **doko** (*where*) are どなた **donata** and どちら **dochira**, respectively. Similarly, the polite counterpart of どう **dō** (*how*) is いかが **ikaga** (*how*).

あの方はどなたですか。
Ano kata wa donata desu ka.
Who is that person?

どちらからですか。
Dochira kara desu ka.
Where are you from?

ご旅行はいかがでしたか。
Go-ryokō wa ikaga deshita ka.
How was your trip?

QUIZ

Circle the letter of the word or phrase that best completes each sentence.

1. 先生はいつ東京に_____んですか。

   Senei wa itsu Tokyō ni _____ ndesu ka.

   (a) 行く iku   (c) いらっしゃる irassharu

   (b) 参る mairu   (d) 伺う ukagau

2. A: _____ ください。B: はい。では、_____ ます。

   A: _____ kudasai. B: Hai. Dewa, _____ masu.

   (a) 頂いて itadaite, 召し上がり meshiagari

   (b) 頂いて itadaite, 頂き itadaki

   (c) 召し上がって meshiagatte, 召し上がり meshiagari

   (d) 召し上がって meshiagatte, 頂き itadaki

3. 私がお運び_____致します。先生はここでお休み_____なってください。

   Watashi ga o-hakobi _____ itashimasu. Sensei wa koko de
   o-yasumi _____ natte kudasai.

   (a) に ni, に ni   (c) nothing, に ni

   (b) に ni, nothing   (d) nothing, nothing

4. 社長、新聞はもう_____ましたか。

   Shachō, shinbun wa mō _____ mashita ka.

   (a) 読めれ yomere   (c) 読まれ yomare

   (b) 読められ yomerare   (d) 読まられ yomarare

5. ちょっと頭が痛いので、_____くださいませんか。

   Chotto atama ga itai node, _____ kudasai masen ka.

   (a) 休ませて yasumasete   (c) 休んで yasunde

   (b) 休まれて yasumarete   (d) 休めて yasumete

6. もうしばらくお待ち_____ください。

   Mō shibaraku o-machi _____ kudasai.

   (a) に ni   (c) なって natte

   (b) にして ni shite   (d) nothing

7. ＿＿＿＿＿名前と、＿＿＿＿＿住所と、＿＿＿＿＿電話番号をお願いします。

    ＿＿＿＿＿ -namae to, ＿＿＿＿＿ -jūsho to, ＿＿＿＿＿ -denwa-bangō o o-negai shimasu.

    (a) お o, お o, お o   (c) お o, お o, ご go

    (b) ご go, ご go, ご go   (d) お o, ご go, お o

8. A: ＿＿＿＿＿ひまなときに＿＿＿＿＿電話下さい。

    B: ＿＿＿＿＿親切にありがとうございます。

    A: ＿＿＿＿＿ -hima na toki ni, ＿＿＿＿＿ -denwa kudasai.

    B: ＿＿＿＿＿ -shinsetsu ni arigatō gozaimasu.

    (a) お o, お o, お o   (c) お o, お o, ご go

    (b) ご go, ご go, ご go   (d) お o, ご go, お o

9. A: ご旅行は＿＿＿＿＿でしたか。B: とてもよかったです。

    A: Go-ryokō wa ＿＿＿＿＿ deshita ka. B: Totemo yokatta desu.

    (a) どなた donata   (c) いくら ikura

    (b) いかが ikaga   (d) どちら dochira

10. 私の＿＿＿＿＿と、マイクさんの＿＿＿＿＿は友達です。

    Watashi no ＿＿＿＿＿ to, Maiku-san no ＿＿＿＿＿ wa tomodachi desu.

    (a) 祖母 sobo, 祖母 sobo

    (b) おばあさん obāsan, おばあさん obāsan

    (c) 祖母 sobo, おばあさん obāsan

    (d) おばあさん obāsan, 祖母 sobo

Circle the letter of the word or phrase that best completes each sentence.

1. A: 窓が＿＿＿＿＿ましたよ。B: 弟が＿＿＿＿＿たんですよ。

   A: Mado ga ＿＿＿＿＿ mashita yo. B: Otōto ga ＿＿＿＿＿ ta ndesu yo.
   - (a) あき aki, あい ai
   - (b) あき aki, あけ ake
   - (c) あけ ake, あい ai
   - (d) あけ ake, あけ ake

2. 納豆は食べたことがありませんが、今度食べて＿＿＿＿＿。

   Nattō wa tabeta koto ga arimasen ga, kondo tabete ＿＿＿＿＿ .
   - (a) おきました okimashita
   - (b) あります arimasu
   - (c) みました mimashita
   - (d) みます mimasu

3. 最近英語が話せるようになって＿＿＿＿＿。

   Saikin eigo ga hanaseru yō ni natte ＿＿＿＿＿ .
   - (a) いきました ikimashita
   - (b) いきます ikimasu
   - (c) きました kimashita
   - (d) きます kimasu

4. 私は妹に本を読んで＿＿＿＿＿ました。

   Watashi wa imōto ni hon o yonde ＿＿＿＿＿ mashita.
   - (a) くれ kure
   - (b) あげ age
   - (c) 差し上げ sashiage
   - (d) ください kudasai

5. 姉は車を＿＿＿＿＿。

   Ane wa kuruma o ＿＿＿＿＿ .
   - (a) ほしいです hoshii desu
   - (b) 買いたいです kaitai desu
   - (c) ほしがっています hoshigatte imasu
   - (d) ほしくありません hoshiku arimasen

6. 学生は勉強する＿＿＿＿＿です。

   Gakusei wa benkyō suru ＿＿＿＿＿ desu.
   - (a) べき beki
   - (b) のべき no beki
   - (c) のはず no hazu
   - (d) のよう no yō

7. マイクさんのお母さんは日本人＿＿＿ です。

Maiku-san no okāsan wa Nihon-jin ＿＿＿ desu.

  (a) だらしい da rashii   (c) のらしい no rashii

  (b) だよう da yō   (d) のよう no yō

8. 田中さん＿＿＿よると、あのレストランは有名＿＿＿そうです。

Tanaka-san ＿＿＿ yoru to, ano resutoran wa yūmei ＿＿＿ sō desu.

  (a) に ni, だ da   (c) に ni, な na

  (b) と to, だ da   (d) で de, だ da

9. こんな簡単なテストはだれ＿＿＿ 。

Konna kantan na tesuto wa dare ＿＿＿ .

  (a) もできます mo dekimasu.

  (b) でもできます demo dekimasu.

  (c) でもできません demo dekimasen

  (e) もできません mo dekimasen

10. いくら勉強しても、３０点＿＿＿ 。

Ikura benkyō shite mo, sanjut-ten ＿＿＿ .

  (a) だけとれます dake toremasu

  (b) しかとれます shika toremasu

  (c) だけとれません dake toremasen

  (d) しかとれません shika toremasen

11. 部屋を掃除＿＿＿なさい。

Heya o sōji ＿＿＿ nasai.

  (a) する suru   (c) しろ shiro

  (b) し shi   (d) して shite

12. ＿＿＿ましたが、足が痛くて立てませんでした。びっくりしました。

＿＿＿ mashita ga, ashi ga itakute tatemasendeshita. Bikkuri shimashita.

  (a) 立とうとし tatō to shi

  (b) 立つように思い tatsuyō ni omoi

  (c) 立つようにし tatsu yō ni shi

  (d) 立ってみ tatte mi

13. できるだけタバコを _____ しました。

Dekiru dake tabako o _____ shimashita.

(a) すうに suu ni

(b) すわないように suwanai yō ni

(c) すって sutte

(d) すわないに suwanai ni

14. 都合が _____ 、明日うちに来ませんか。

Tsugō ga _____ , ashita uchi ni kimasen ka.

(a) いければ ikereba   (c) いいば iiba

(b) よければ yokereba   (d) よいば yoiba

15. フランスに5年_____、もうフランス語が上手なはずです。

Furansu ni go-nen _____ , mō Furansu-go ga jōzu na hazu desu.

(a) 住んだなら sunda nara   (c) 住んだのに sunda noni

(b) 住むなら sumu nara   (d) 住むのに sumu noni

16. 学生が先生_____ました。

Gakusei ga sensei _____ mashita.

(a) にしかり ni shikari   (c) にしかられ ni shikarare

(b) がしかり ga shikari   (d) をしかられ o shikarare

17. 100点をとったら、友達_____ました。

Hyaku-ten o tottara, tomodachi _____ mashita.

(a) をびっくりし o bikkuri shi

(b) にびっくりし ni bikkuri shi

(c) にびっくりされ ni bikkuri sare

(d) にびっくりさせられ ni bikkuri saserare

18. 母は私_____マンガを_____くれます。

Haha wa watashi _____ manga o _____ kuremasu.

(a) に ni, 読まれて yomarete   (c) を o, 読まれて yomarete

(b) に ni, 読ませて yomasete   (d) を o, 読ませて yomasete

19. 私は姉のドレスを＿＿＿＿ました。

Watashi wa ane no doresu o ＿＿＿＿ mashita.

(a) 使われてもらい tsukawarete morai

(b) 使われてあげ tsukawarete age

(c) 使わせてもらい tsukawasete morai

(d) 使わせてくれ tsukawasete kure

20. 僕は病院で2時間＿＿＿＿。

Boku wa byōin de ni-jikan ＿＿＿＿ .

(a) 待たせました matasemashita

(b) 待たれました mataremashita

(c) 待たせられました mataseraremashita

(d) 待たれてもらいました matarete moraimashita

21. 先生。どうぞ＿＿＿＿ください。

Senei. Dōzo ＿＿＿＿ kudasai.

(a) 見て mite

(b) 拝見して haiken shite

(c) ご覧にして go-ran ni shite

(d) ご覧になって go-ran ni natte

22. どうぞお入り＿＿＿＿ください。

Dōzo o-hairi ＿＿＿＿ kudasai.

(a) して shite

(b) にして ni shite

(c) なって natte

(d) になって ni natte

23. この本をお借り＿＿＿＿もよろしいですか。

Kono hon o o-kari ＿＿＿＿ mo yoroshii desu ka.

(a) して shite

(b) にして ni shite

(c) なって natte

(d) になって ni natte

24. 先生、今日は車を＿＿＿＿ますか。

Sensei, kyō wa kuruma o ＿＿＿＿ masu ka.

(a) 使い tsukai

(b) 使われ tsukaware

(c) お使いにいたし o-tsukai ni itashi

(d) お使いなり o-tsukai nari

25. 社長、私をニューヨークに＿＿＿＿ください。

Shachō, watashi o Nyūyōku ni ＿＿＿＿ kudasai.

(a) 行って itte

(b) 行かれて ikarete

(c) 行かせて ikasete

(d) お行き o-iki

Circle the letter of the word or phrase that best completes each sentence.

1. 私の＿＿＿＿は医者です。

   Watashi no ＿＿＿＿ wa isha desu.

   (a) 姉 ane

   (b) お姉さん onēsan

   (c) お父さん okōsan

   (d) お兄さん onīsan

2. この建物は＿＿＿＿です。

   Kono tatemono wa ＿＿＿＿ desu.

   (a) 教師 kyōshi

   (b) 図書館 toshokan

   (c) 数学 sūgaku

   (d) 弁護士 bengoshi

3. 本は机の＿＿＿＿です。

   Hon wa tsukue no ＿＿＿＿ desu.

   (a) 間 aida

   (b) 上 ue

   (c) 東 higashi

   (d) 北 kita

4. 病院は＿＿＿＿です。

   Byōin wa ＿＿＿＿ desu.

   (a) 駅のとなり eki no tonari

   (b) 西の駅 nishi no eki

   (c) 駅と東 eki to higashi

   (d) 西と北 nishi to kita

5. ＿＿＿＿。マイクです。よろしく。

   ＿＿＿＿ . Maiku desu. Yoroshiku

   (a) どうぞ Dōzo

   (b) こちらこそ Kochira koso

   (c) はじめまして Hjimemashite

   (d) すみません Sumimasen

6. あれは犬じゃ＿＿＿＿。

   Are wa inu ja ＿＿＿＿ .

   (a) です desu

   (b) あります arimasu

   (c) ありません arimasen

   (d) ございます gozaimasu

381

7. ＿＿＿＿＿本は私のです。

＿＿＿＿＿ hon wa watashi no desu.

(a) これ Kore   (c) あれ Are

(b) その Sono   (d) それ Sore

8. ＿＿＿＿＿は何ですか。

＿＿＿＿＿ wa nan desu ka.

(a) あの Ano   (c) この Kono

(b) あれ Are   (d) その Sono

9. あの＿＿＿＿＿はどなたですか。

Ano ＿＿＿＿＿ wa donata desu ka.

(a) 犬 inu   (c) 学生 gakusei

(b) 方 kata   (d) 車 kuruma

10. あの人は＿＿＿＿＿です。

Ano hito wa ＿＿＿＿＿ desu.

(a) 学生の日本語 gakusei no Nihon-go

(b) 数学の学生 sūgaku no gakusei

(c) 日本語のアメリカ人 Nihon-go no Amerika-jin

(d) 学生のアメリカ gakusei no Amerika

11. 姉は弁護士です。兄＿＿＿＿＿弁護士です。

Ane wa bengoshi desu. Ani ＿＿＿＿＿ bengoshi desu.

(a) は wa   (c) に ni

(b) も mo   (d) と to

12. ジョンさんは＿＿＿＿＿人です。

Jon-san wa ＿＿＿＿＿ hito desu.

(a) まじめ majime   (c) まじめの majime no

(b) まじめな majime na   (c) まじめだ majime da

13. すみません。駅は＿＿＿＿＿ですか。

Sumimasen. Eki wa ＿＿＿＿＿ desu ka.

(a) どこに doko ni   (c) どこ doko

(b) だれ dare   (d) どなた donata

14. _____ に来てください。

_____ ni kite kudasai.

(a) ここ koko   (c) そこ soko

(b) どこ doko   (d) どちら dochira

15. 日本語のクラスは _____ ですか。

Nihongo no kurasu wa _____ desu ka.

(a) どう dō   (c) どんな donna

(b) だれ dare   (d) 何 nan

16. このラーメンはあまり _____ 。

Kono rāmen wa amari _____ .

(a) おいしいです oishii desu

(b) おいしくありません oishiku arimasen

(c) まずいです mazui desu

(d) 安いです yasui desu

17. このホテルは便利です。それに、_____ です。

Kono hoteru wa benri desu. Soreni, _____ desu.

(a) せまい semai   (c) きたない kitanai

(b) 安い yasui   (d) うるさい urusai

18. あのホテルは便利です。でも、_____ です。

Ano hoteru wa benri desu. Demo, _____ desu.

(a) 高い takai   (c) 新しい atarashii

(b) 静か shizuka   (d) きれい kirei

19. うちには桜の木が _____ 。

Uchi ni wa sakura no ki ga _____ .

(a) あります arimasu   (c) いらっしゃいます irasshaimasu

(b) います imasu   (d) です desu

20. うちには猫が2匹 _____ 。

Uchi ni wa neko ga ni-hiki _____ .

(a) あります arimasu   (c) いらっしゃいます irasshaimasu

(b) います imasu   (d) です desu

21. 山田さんのお母さんはカフェテリアに_____。

    Yamada-san no okāsan wa kafeteria ni _____ .

    (a) あります arimasu   (c) いらっしゃいます irasshaimasu

    (b) います imasu   (d) です desu

22. 水曜日は仕事が_____。

    Suiyōbi wa shigoto ga _____ .

    (a) ありません arimasen   (c) いらっしゃいません irasshaimasen

    (b) いません imasen   (d) じゃありません ja arimasen

23. 切手が_____あります。

    Kitte ga _____ arimasu.

    (a) 3枚 san-mai   (c) 3人 san-nin

    (b) 2本 ni-hon   (d) 2つ futa-tsu

24. 専攻は_____ですか。

    Senkō wa _____ desu ka.

    (a) 何本 nan-bon   (c) おいくつ o-ikutsu

    (b) 何歳 nan-sai   (d) 何 nan

25. テレビ_____ラジオを買いました。

    Terebi _____ rajio o kaimashita.

    (a) を o   (c) が ga

    (b) と to   (d) も mo

26. 昨日は_____。

    Kinō wa _____ .

    (a) 寒かったです samukatta desu

    (b) 寒いかったです samuikatta desu

    (c) 寒いでした samui deshita

    (d) 寒かったでした samukatta deshita

27. 本_____兄_____読みました。

    Hon _____ ani _____ yomimashita

    (a) が ga, が ga   (c) を o, が ga

    (b) が ga, を o   (d) を o, を o

28. 仕事には車_____行きます。

    Shigoto ni wa kuruma _____ ikimasu.

    (a) に ni   (c) で de
    (b) と to   (d) が ga

29. 図書館の中_____食べてはいけません。

    Toshokan no naka _____ tabete wa ikemasen.

    (a) に ni   (c) で de
    (b) と to   (d) が ga

30. 私_____カラオケに行きませんか。

    Watashi _____ karaoke ni ikimasen ka.

    (a) に ni   (c) で de
    (b) と to   (d) が ga

31. すしは手_____食べてもいいですか。

    Sushi wa te _____ tabete mo ii desu ka.

    (a) に ni   (c) で de
    (b) と to   (d) が ga

32. １００円の切手と、６０円の切手を_____買いました。

    Hyaku-en no kitte to, rokujū-en no kitte o _____ kaimashita.

    (a) ２枚目 ni-mai-me   (c) ２枚ずつ ni-mai-zutsu
    (b) ２本目 ni-hon-me   (d) ２本ずつ ni-hon-zutsu

33. 私は母にネックレスを_____ 。

    Watashi wa haha ni nekkuresu o _____ .

    (a) あげます agemasu   (c) くれます kuremasu
    (b) 下さいます kudasaimasu   (d) 差し上げます sashiagemasu

34. 私は社長にお酒を_____ 。

    Watashi wa shachō ni o-sake o _____ .

    (a) あげました agemashita
    (b) 下さいました kudasaimashita
    (c) くれました kuremashita
    (d) 差し上げました sashiagemashita

35. 先生は私に辞書を _____ 。

Sensei wa watashi ni jisho o _____ .

(a) あげました agemashita

(b) 下さいました kudasaimashita

(c) くれました kuremashita

(d) 差し上げました sashiagemashita

36. A: 春休みは _____ 行きましたか。B: いいえ、_____ 行きませんでした。

A: Haru-yasumi wa _____ ikimashita ka. B: Īe, _____ ikimasendeshita.

(a) どこか dokoka, どこに doko ni

(b) どこにか doko ni ka, どこにも doko ni mo

(c) どこかに dokoka ni, どこもに doko mo ni

(d) どこかに dokoka ni, どこにも doko ni mo

37. シュノーケリングを _____ ありますか。

Shunōkeringu o _____ arimasu ka.

(a) するが suru ga

(b) したが shita ga

(c) したことが shita koto ga

(d) するのが suru no ga

38. 私は猫 _____ 好きです。

Watashi wa neko _____ suki desu.

(a) が ga   (c) に ni

(b) を o   (d) の no

39. 日本に _____ たいです。

Nihon ni _____ tai desu.

(a) 行く iku   (c) 行って itte

(b) 行き iki   (d) 行った itta

40. 昨日はゲームを _____ 、寝ました。

Kinō wa gēmu o _____ , nemashita.

(a) します shimasu   (c) して shite

(b) する suru   (d) した shita

41. エミリーさんは＿＿＿＿、　＿＿＿＿、頭がいいです。

Emirī-san wa ＿＿＿＿ , ＿＿＿＿ , atama ga ii desu.

(a) きれいて kireite, やさしいて yasashiite

(b) きれいて kireite, やさしくて yasashikute

(c) きれいで kirei de, やさしいて yasashiite

(d) きれいで kirei de, やさしくて yasashikute

42. ここでタバコを＿＿＿＿ください。

Koko de tabako o ＿＿＿＿ kudasai.

(a) すわなくて suwanakute

(b) すい sui

(c) すわない suwanai

(d) すわないで suwanai de

43. あの交差点＿＿＿＿左＿＿＿＿曲がってください。

Ano kōsaten ＿＿＿＿ hidari ＿＿＿＿ magatte kudasai.

(a) を o, で de　　　　　(c) に ni, で de

(b) を o, に ni,　　　　(d) に ni, を o,

44. A: 山田さんはいますか。B: いいえ、山田さんは東京に＿＿＿＿。

A: Yamada-san wa imasu ka. B: Īe, Yamada-san wa Tōkyō ni ＿＿＿＿ .

(a) 行きます ikimasu

(b) 行っています itte imasu

(c) 行っていました itte imashita,

(d) 行きませんでした ikimasendeshita

45. A: うちに＿＿＿＿いいですか。B: いいえ、＿＿＿＿いけません。

A: Uchi ni ＿＿＿＿ ii desu ka. B: Īe, ＿＿＿＿ ikemasen.

(a) 帰っては kaette wa, 帰っては kaette wa

(b) 帰っても kaette mo, 帰っても kaette mo

(c) 帰っては kaette wa, 帰っても kaette mo

(d) 帰っても kaette mo, 帰っては kaette wa

46. A: 薬を_____いけませんか。B: いいえ、_____いいです。

    A: Kusuri o _____ ikemasen ka. B: Īe, _____ ii desu.

    (a) 飲まなくては nomanakute wa, 飲まなくても nomanakute mo
    (b) 飲まなくては nomanakute wa, 飲まなくては nomanakute wa
    (c) 飲まなくても nomanakute mo, 飲まなくても nomanakute mo
    (d) 飲まなくても nomanakute mo, 飲まなくては nomanakute wa

47. _____いいですが、きれい_____いけません。

    _____ ii desu ga, kirei _____ ikemasen.

    (a) 高くても takakute mo, でも de mo
    (b) 高くても takakute mo, じゃなくては ja nakute wa
    (c) 高くては takakute wa, じゃなくては ja nakute wa
    (d) 高くては takakute wa, では de wa

48. 高校生ですからお酒が_____ 。

    Kōkōsei desu kara o-sake ga _____ .

    (a) 飲めません nomemasen
    (b) 飲みませんでした nomimasendeshita
    (c) 飲みません nomimasen
    (d) 飲んではいけません nonde wa ikemasen

49. 足音が_____ 。

    Ashioto ga _____ .

    (a) 聞きます kikimasu
    (c) 聞きません kikimasen
    (b) 聞こえます kikoemasu
    (d) 聞いてください kiite kudasai

50. まだ泳ぐ_____できません。

    Mada oyogu _____ dekimasen.

    (a) が ga
    (c) ことが koto ga
    (b) を o
    (d) ことを koto o

51. あの山は富士山_____思います。

    Ano yama wa Fujisan _____ omoimasu.

    (a) だ da
    (c) だと da to
    (b) と to
    (d) nothing

52. 社長さんは何時に帰られる ＿＿＿＿＿ 分かりますか。

    Shachō-san wa nan-ji ni kaerareru ＿＿＿＿＿ wakarimasu ka.

    (a) かどうか ka dōka   (c) と to

    (b) か ka   (d) nothing

53. 水曜日はテストがある ＿＿＿＿＿ 分かりません。

    Suiyōbi wa tesuto ga aru ＿＿＿＿＿ wakarimasen.

    (a) かどうか ka dōka   (c) と to

    (b) を o   (d) nothing

54. 咳がでます。風邪 ＿＿＿＿＿ かもしれません。

    Seki ga demasu. Kaze ＿＿＿＿＿ kamoshiremasen.

    (a) だ da   (c) の no

    (b) な na   (d) nothing

55. あの人はマイクさんの友達 ＿＿＿＿＿ でしょう。

    Ano hito wa Maiku-san no tomodachi ＿＿＿＿＿ deshō.

    (a) だ da   (c) の no

    (b) な na   (d) nothing

56. 静か ＿＿＿＿＿ ときに勉強します。

    Shizuka ＿＿＿＿＿ toki ni benkyō shimasu.

    (a) だ da   (c) の no

    (b) な na   (d) nothing

57. 寝る ＿＿＿＿＿ 、パジャマを着ます。

    Neru ＿＿＿＿＿ , pajama o kimasu.

    (a) 間 に aida ni   (c) ながら nagara

    (b) 後に ato ni   (d) 前に mae ni

58. 大学生 ＿＿＿＿＿ ときに、カラオケボックスによく行きました。

    Daigakusei ＿＿＿＿＿ toki ni, karaoke-bokkusu ni yoku ikimashita.

    (a) だ da   (c) な na

    (b) の no   (d) nothing

59. 話して＿＿＿＿と、やさしい人でした。

Hanashite ＿＿＿＿ to, yasashii hito deshita.

(a) みる miru   (c) みて mite

(b) みた mita   (d) nothing

60. こわさない＿＿＿＿に運んでください。

Kowasanai ＿＿＿＿ ni hakonde kudasai.

(a) そう sō   (c) よう yō

(b) ながら nagara   (d) nothing

61. 兄は父＿＿＿＿背が高いです。

Ani wa chichi ＿＿＿＿ se ga takai desu.

(a) より yori   (c) ほど hodo

(b) 同じ onaji   (d) で de

62. 父は兄＿＿＿＿背が高くありません。

Chichi wa ani ＿＿＿＿ se ga takaku arimasen.

(a) より yori   (c) ほど hodo

(b) 同じ onaji   (d) で de

63. ピザと、スパゲッティーと、＿＿＿＿の方が好きですか。

Piza to, supagettī to, ＿＿＿＿ no hō ga suki desu ka.

(a) どちら dochira   (c) 何 nani

(b) どれ dore   (d) だれ dare

64. 動物の中では、＿＿＿＿が一番好きですか。

Dōbutsu no naka de wa, ＿＿＿＿ ga ichi-ban suki desu ka.

(a) 何 nani   (c) どれ dore

(b) どこ doko   (d) だれ dare

65. ＿＿＿＿と、＿＿＿＿とでは、どちらが難しいですか。

＿＿＿＿ to, ＿＿＿＿ to de wa, dochira ga muzukashii desu ka.

(a) 習う narau, 教える oshieru

(b) 習うが narau ga, 教えるが oshieru ga

(c) 習うの narau no, 教えるの oshieru no

(d) 習って naratte, 教えて oshiete

66. このバッグは_____やすいです。

Kono baggu wa _____ yasui desu.

(a) 使う tsukau
(c) 使い tsukai
(b) 使って tsukatte
(d) 使わない tsukawanai

67. ちょっと食べ_____しまいました。

Chotto tabe _____ shimaimashita.

(a) すぎる sugiru
(c) すぎて sugite
(b) すぎ sugi
(d) すぎない suginai

68. あのドレスは_____そうですね。

Ano doresu wa _____ -sō desu ne.

(a) 高 taka
(c) 高くに takaku ni
(b) 高く takaku
(d) 高くて takakute

69. 先生はやさしくて、天使_____です。

Sensei wa yasashikute, tenshi _____ desu.

(a) よう yō
(c) らしい rashii
(b) のよう no yō
(d) そう sō

70. _____を知っていますか。

_____ o shitte imasu ka.

(a) 明子さんいう人 Akiko-san iu hito
(b) 明子さんという人 Akiko-san to iu hito
(d) 人という明子さん hito to iu Akiko-san
(d) 明子さんをいう人 Akiko-san o iu hito

71. すみませんが、もう少し_____ください。

Sumimasen ga, mō sukoshi _____ kudasai.

(a) しずかにして shizuka ni shite
(b) しずか shizuka
(c) しずかな shizuka na
(d) しずかに shizuka ni

72. 5歳のときに＿＿＿＿＿なりました。

Go-sai no toki ni ＿＿＿＿＿ narimashita.

(a) 話す hanasu

(b) 話せるように hanaseru yō ni

(c) 話すに hanasu ni

(d) 話せないに hanasenai ni

73. 日本に留学する＿＿＿＿＿。

Nihon ni ryūgaku suru ＿＿＿＿＿ .

(a) ことにしました koto ni shimashita

(b) ようにしました yō ni shimashita

(c) ようなりました yō narimashita

(d) になりました ni narimashita

74. 今年＿＿＿＿アメリカに来て10年になります。

Kotoshi ＿＿＿＿＿ Amerika ni kite jū-nen ni narimasu.

(a) に ni   (c) を o

(b) で de   (d) が ga

75. 兄はセーターを＿＿＿＿＿、ジーンズを＿＿＿＿＿います。

Ani wa sētā o ＿＿＿＿＿ , jīnzu o ＿＿＿＿＿ imasu.

(a) きて kite, はいて haite

(b) はいて haite, して shite

(c) かぶって kabutte, かけて kakete

(d) かぶって kabutte, して shite

76. カメラが＿＿＿＿＿しまいました。

Kamera ga ＿＿＿＿＿ shimaimashita.

(a) こわれ koware   (c) こわして kowashite

(b) こわれて kowarete   (d) こわれる kowareru

77. このスカートをちょっとはいて＿＿＿＿＿

Kono sukāto o chotto haite ＿＿＿＿＿ .

(a) すぎます sugimasu   (c) にくいです nikui desu

(b) やすいです yasui desu   (d) みます mimasu

78. 日本語の映画が最近分かるようになって＿＿＿＿。

Nihongo no eiga ga saikin wakaru yō ni natte ＿＿＿＿ .

(a) いきました ikimashita   (c) きました kimashita

(b) いきます ikimasu   (d) きます kimasu

79. 先生は私に日本の歌を教えて＿＿＿＿ました。

Sensei wa watashi ni Nihon no uta o oshiete ＿＿＿＿ mashita.

(a) くれ kure   (c) 差し上げ sashiage

(b) あげ age   (d) ください kudasai

80. 弟は先生を＿＿＿＿。

Otōto wa sensei o ＿＿＿＿ .

(a) こわいです kowai desu

(b) こわいがっています kowai gatte imasu

(c) こわがっています kowagatte imasu

(d) こわくています kowakute imasu

81. 高いものは＿＿＿＿。

Takai mono wa ＿＿＿＿ .

(a) 買うべきじゃありません kau beki ja arimasen

(b) 買わないべきです kawanai beki desu

(c) 買いべきです kai beki desu

(d) 買ってべきです katte beki desu

82. 今度のマネージャーは若い人＿＿＿＿です。

Kondo no manējā wa wakai hito ＿＿＿＿ desu.

(a) のらしい no rashii   (c) のよう no yō

(b) だらしい da rashii   (d) だよう da yō

83. エミリーさんは車を2台＿＿＿＿そうです。

Emirī-san wa kuruma o ni-dai ＿＿＿＿ sō desu.

(a) 買って katte   (c) 買ってしまって katte shimatte

(b) 買った katta   (d) 買いすぎた kai-sugita

84. こんな簡単なことはだれ＿＿＿＿。

Konna kantan na koto wa dare ＿＿＿＿ .

(a) もできます mo dekimasu

(b) でもできます demo dekimasu.

(c) でもできません demo dekimasen

(e) もできません mo dekimasen

85. 昨日はパン＿＿＿＿。

Kinō wa pan ＿＿＿＿ .

(a) をしか食べませんでした o shika tabemasendeshita

(b) しかを食べませんでした shika o tabemasendeshita

(c) しか食べませんでした shika tabemasendeshita

(d) しか食べました shika tabemashita

86. 9時までに＿＿＿＿なさい。

Ku-ji made ni ＿＿＿＿ nasai.

(a) 帰る kaeru   (c) 帰ろ kaero

(b) 帰り kaeri   (d) 帰って kaette

87. 昨日は雨に＿＿＿＿。

Kinō wa ame ni ＿＿＿＿ .

(a) 降りました furimashita

(b) 降れました furemashita

(c) 降られました furaremashita

(d) 降ろうとしました furō to shimashita

88. ＿＿＿＿としたときに、山田さんが来ました。

＿＿＿＿ to shita toki ni, Yamada-san ga kimashita.

(a) 出かける dekakeru

(b) 出かけよう dekakeyō

(c) 出かけて dekakete

(d) 出かけろ dekakero

89. できるだけテレビを＿＿＿＿＿しました。

    Dekiru dake terebi o ＿＿＿＿＿ shimashita.

    (a) 見るに miru ni   (c) 見ないように minai yō ni

    (b) 見ないに minai ni   (d) 見ように miyō ni

90. 小さいときにピアノを習って＿＿＿＿＿よかった。

    Chīsai toki ni piano o ＿＿＿＿＿ yokatta.

    (a) おくば oku ba   (c) しまうば shimau ba

    (b) おけば okeba   (d) みてば mite ba

91. 渋谷に＿＿＿＿＿、秋葉原にも行ってください。

    Shibuya ni ＿＿＿＿＿ , Akihabara ni mo itte kudasai.

    (a) 行ってなら itte nara   (c) 行くと iku to

    (b) 行くなら iku nara   (d) 行ったと itta to

92. 忙しいときにお客さん＿＿＿＿＿。

    Isogashii toki ni o-kyaku-san ＿＿＿＿＿ .

    (a) に来ました ni kimashita

    (b) に来られました ni koraremashita

    (c) を来られました o koraremashita

    (d) を来ました o kimashita

93. 母は私＿＿＿＿＿好きなことを＿＿＿＿＿くれます。

    Haha wa watashi ＿＿＿＿＿ sukina koto o ＿＿＿＿＿ kuremasu.

    (a) に ni, されてsarete   (c) を o, されて sarete

    (b) に ni, させてsasete   (d) を o, させて sasete

94. そのネックレスはかわいいですね。ちょっと＿＿＿＿＿。

    Sono nekkuresu wa kawaii desu ne. Chotto ＿＿＿＿＿ .

    (a) 見られてください mirarete kudasai

    (b) 見せてお願いします misete o-negai shimasu

    (c) 見せてもらえますか misete moraemasu ka

    (d) 見せるもらえますか miseru moraemasu ka

95. 僕は病院で2時間_____。

    Boku wa byōin de ni-jikan _____ .

    (a) 待たせました matasemashita

    (b) 待たれました mataremashita

    (c) 待たせられました mataseraremashita

    (d) 待たれてもらいました matarete moraimashita

96. ちょっと_____いたします。

    Chotto _____ itashimasu.

    (a) 見て mite　　　　　　　　(c) 拝見して haiken shite

    (b) 拝見 haiken　　　　　　　(d) ご覧 go-ran

97. どうぞお楽しみ_____ください。

    Dōzo o-tanoshimi _____ kudasai.

    (a) して shite　　　　　　　　(c) なって natte

    (b) にして ni shite　　　　　　(d) nothing

98. ちょっとお伺い_____もよろしいですか。

    Chotto o-ukagai _____ mo yoroshii desu ka.

    (a) して shite　　　　　　　　(c) なって natte

    (b) にして ni shite　　　　　　(d) になって ni natte

99. スミスさんは肉は_____らしいです。

    Sumisu-san wa niku wa _____ rashii desu.

    (a) 食べない tabenai　　　　　(c) 食べて tabete

    (b) 食べないで tabenai de　　　(d) 食べ tabe

100. 日本語はちょっと難しいですが、勉強し_____ます。

    Nihon-go wa chotto muzukashii desu ga, benkyō shi _____ masu.

    (a) あり ari　　　　　　　　　(c) しまい shimai

    (b) つづけ tsuduke　　　　　　(d) おき oki

APPENDIX A

Sentence Predicates in Japanese

		Plain		Polite	
		Present	Past	Present	Past
Verb	Affirmative	食べる taberu	食べた tabeta	食べます tabemasu	食べました tabemashita
	Negative	食べない tabenai	食べなかった tabenakatta	食べません tabemasen	食べませんでした tabemasendeshita
(Noun +) Copula	Affirmative	学生だ gakusei da	学生だった gakusei datta	学生です gakusei desu	学生でした gakusei deshita
	Negative	学生じゃない gakusei ja nai	学生じゃなかった gakusei ja nakatta	学生じゃありません gakusei ja arimasen	学生じゃありませんでした gakusei ja arimasendeshita
Na-type Adjective	Affirmative	便利だ benri da	便利だった benri datta	便利です benri desu	便利でした benri deshita
	Negative	便利じゃない benri ja nai	便利じゃなかった benri ja nakatta	便利じゃありません benri ja arimasen	便利じゃありませんでした benri ja arimasendeshita
I-type Adjective	Affirmative	高い takai	高かった takakatta	高いです takai desu	高かったです takakatta desu
	Negative	高くない takaku nai	高くなかった takaku nakatta	高くありません takaku arimasen	高くありませんでした takaku arimasendeshita

じゃ **ja** in the negative forms of the copular verb and na-type adjectives in the above table can be では **de wa**. ありません **arimasen** and ありませんでした **arimasendeshita** in the negative forms in the table can be ないです **naidesu** and なかったです **nakattadesu**, respectively.

APPENDIX B

Verb Forms

(ru): ru-verb
(u): u-verb
(irr.): irregular verbs

Dictionary Form	Stem Form	Plain Present Negative	Plain Past Affirmative	Te-Form	Potential Form
たべる taberu (ru)	たべ tabe	たべない tabenai	たべた tabeta	たべて tabete	たべられる taberareru
みる miru (ru)	み mi	みない minai	みた mita	みて mite	みられる mirareru
とる toru (u)	とり tori	とらない toranai	とった totta	とって totte	とれる toreru
かく kaku (u)	かき kaki	かかない kakanai	かいた kaita	かいて kaite	かける kakeru
およぐ oyogu (u)	およぎ oyogi	およがない oyoganai	およいだ oyoida	およいで oyoide	およげる oyogeru
はなす hanasu (u)	はなし hanashi	はなさない hanasanai	はなした hanashita	はなして hanashite	はなせる hanaseru
かう kau (u)	かい kai	かわない kawanai	かった katta	かって katte	かえる kaeru
まつ matsu (u)	まち machi	またない matanai	まった matta	まって matte	まてる materu
のむ nomu (u)	のみ nomi	のまない nomanai	のんだ nonda	のんで nonde	のめる nomeru
しぬ shinu (u)	しに shini	しなない shinanai	しんだ shinda	しんで shinde	しねる shineru
とぶ tobu (u)	とび tobi	とばない tobanai	とんだ tonda	とんで tonde	とべる toberu
する suru (irr.)	し shi	しない shinai	した shita	して shite	できる dekiru
くる kuru (irr.)	き ki	こない konai	きた kita	きて kite	こられる korareru

Volitional Form	Plain Command	Passive Form	Causative Form	Ba-Conditional Form
たべよう tabeyō	たべろ tabero	たべられる taberareru	たべさせる tabesaseru	たべれば tabereba
みよう miyō	みろ miro	みられる mirareru	みさせる misaseru	みれば mireba
とろう torō	とれ tore	とられる torareru	とらせる toraseru	とれば toreba
かこう kakō	かけ kake	かかれる kakareru	かかせる kakaseru	かけば kakeba
およごう oyogō	およげ oyoge	およがれる oyogareru	およがせる oyogaseru	およげば oyogeba
はなそう hanasō	はなせ hanase	はなされる hanasareru	はなさせる hanasaseru	はなせば hanaseba
かおう kaō	かえ kae	かわれる kawareru	かわせる kawaseru	かえば kaeba
まとう matō	まて mate	またれる matareru	またせる mataseru	まてば mateba
のもう nomō	のめ nome	のまれる nomareru	のませる nomaseru	のめば nomeba
しのう shinō	しね shine	しなれる shinareru	しなせる shinaseru	しねば shineba
とぼう tobō	とべ tobe	とばれる tobareru	とばせる tobaseru	とべば tobeba
しよう shiyō	しろ shiro	される sareru	させる saseru	すれば sureba
こよう koyō	こい koi	こられる korareru	こさせる kosaseru	くれば kureba

JAPANESE-ENGLISH GLOSSARY

(irr): irregular verb
(ru): ru-verb
(u): u-verb
(v): verbs
s.th.: something

ageru (ru) to give (v)
akachan baby
akeru (ru) to open s.th. (v)
aku (u) to open (v)
amai sweet
ame rain
aru (u) to exist (v)
aruku (u) to walk (v)
asa morning
ashi foot, leg
asobu (u) to play (v)
atama head
atarashii new
atatakai warm
atsui hot
bengoshi lawyer
benkyō studying
benri na convenient
bijutsukan art museum

bōshi hat
bukka prices (cost of living)
bunka culture
buta pig
buta-niku pork
byōin hospital
byōki illness
chikatetsu subway
chīsai small
chizu map
chūmon order
chūshajō parking lot
chūshoku lunch
daidokoro kitchen
daigaku university
daisuki na like very much
deguchi exit
dekakeru (ru) to go out (v)
densha train
denwa telephone
denwa-bangō telephone number
dōbutsuen zoo
dōryō colleague
e drawing, painting
eiga movie

eigo English
fune boat
furui old
futoru (u) to gain weight (v)
gaikoku foreign country
gakkō school
gakusei student
gakusha scholar
gekijō theater
genkin cash
ginkō bank
gohan rice (cooked), meal
gyūniku beef
gyūnyū milk
hairu (u) to enter (v)
haisha dentist
haiyū actor
hakobu (u) to carry (v)
haku (u) to put on (v)
hakubutsukan museum
hana flower, nose
hanasu (u) to speak (v)
harau (u) to pay (v)
hashi chopsticks, bridge
hataraku (u) to work (v)
hayai early, fast
hen na weird
heya room
hi day
hikōki airplane
hiroi wide, spacious
hiru-gohan lunch
hisho secretary
hito person
hiza knee
hon book
hontō no true, real
hon'ya bookstore
hoshii want
ie house
ii good

iku (u) to go (v)
inaka countryside
inu dog
irassharu to exist (v)
iru (ru) to exist (v)
iru (u) to need (v)
isha physician
itadaku (u) to receive (v)
iu (u) to say (v)
ji letter, character
jibun self
jiko accident
jishin earthquake
jisho dictionary
jitensha bicycle
jōshi superior, boss
joyū actress
jōzu na skillful
jūsho address
kaban bag
kaeru (ru) to change (v)
kaeru (u) to return (v)
kaesu (u) to return s.th. (v)
kagi key
kaisha company
kaishain company employee
kaku (u) to write (v)
kami hair, paper
kangoshi nurse
kantan na easy
kao face
karendā calendar
kariru (ru) to borrow (v)
kasa umbrella
kasu (u) to lend (v)
kata shoulder
kau (u) to buy (v)
kawa river
kazoku family
keisatsu police
kekkon marriage

kenkō health
keshigomu eraser
kesu (u) to turn off s.th. (v)
ki tree
kieru (ru) to turn off (v)
kikoeru (ru) to hear (v)
kiku (u) to listen (v)
kingyo goldfish
kirai na hate
kirei na beautiful
kiru (ru) to wear, to put on (v)
kiru (u) to cut (v)
kissaten coffee shop
kitte stamp
kobosu (u) to spill (v)
kōen park
kōkō high school
kokuseki nationality
kome rice (uncooked)
konban tonight
kōsaten intersection
kotae answer
kōzui flood
kubi neck
kuchi mouth
kudamono fruit
kudasaru (u) to give (v)
kūkō airport
kuni country
kurai dark
kureru (ru) to give (v)
kuro black
kuru (irr) to come (v)
kuruma car
kusa grass
kushi comb
kusuri medicine
kutsu shoe
kutsushita sock
kyōkai church
kyōkasho textbook

kyōshi teacher
kyūkyūsha ambulance
mado window
magaru to turn (v)
majime na serious
magaru (u) to turn (v)
matsu (u) to wait (v)
mazui bad-tasting
me eye
megane eyeglasses
michi road
mieru (ru) to see (v)
mijikai short
mimi ear
miru (ru) to look (v)
mise store
mizu water
mizuumi lake
mono thing
morau (u) to receive (v)
mune chest
mura village
muzukashii difficult
nagai long
namae name
nedan price
neko cat
neru (ru) to sleep (v)
netsu fever
nezumi mouse
Nihon Japan
Nihon-go Japanese language
Nihon-jin Japanese person
niku meat
nimotsu luggage
nishi west
nomu (u) to drink (v)
noru (u) to get (into/on a means of transportation) (v)
oboeru (ru) to memorize (v)
o-cha tea

odoru (u) to dance (v)
oishii delicious
o-kane money
ōkii big
oku (u) to put (v)
omoshiroi interesting
onaka abdomen
ongaku music
ongakuka musician
onna, onna no hito woman
oshieru (ru) to teach (v)
osoi late, slow
oto sound
otoko, otoko no hito man (male person)
owaru (u) to end (v)
oyasuminasai good night
oyogu (u) to swim (v)
renshū practice
rikon divorce
ringo apple
risu squirrel
ryō dormitory
ryōjikan consulate
ryokan Japanese-style inn
ryokō trip
ryōri cooking
ryōshūsho receipt
ryūgaku study abroad
saifu wallet
sakana fish
saku (u) to bloom (v)
samui cold (weather)
sashiageru (ru) to give (v)
satō sugar
sayōnara goodbye
se height, stature
sekai world
sensei teacher
shachō company president
shashin photograph

shimaru (u) to close (v)
shimeru (ru) to close s.th. (v)
shinbun newspaper
shinseki relatives
shinsetsu na kind
shinu (u) to die (v)
shiru (u) to come to know (v)
shitsumon question
shizen nature
shizuka na quiet
shodō calligraphy
shokugyō occupation
shokuji meal
shōrai future
shōsetsu novel
shumi hobby
shuppatsu departure
kashu singer
sōji cleaning
sora sky
sōsu sauce
soto outside
sūgaku mathematics
sugiru (ru) to pass (v)
suiei swimming
suki na like
suppai sour
suru (irr) to do (v)
suwaru (u) to sit (v)
suzushii cool (weather)
tabako o suu to smoke (v)
taberu (ru) to eat (v)
taihen na terribly difficult, terrible
taishikan embassy
taiyō sun
takai expensive
tamago egg
tanjōbi birthday
tanoshii fun
tasukeru(ru) to help, rescue (v)

tatsu (u) to stand (v)
te hand, arm
tegami letter
tenshi angel
terebi TV
tetsudau (u) to help, assist (v)
tobu (u) to fly (v)
tōi far
tokei watch
tokoro place
tomodachi friend
tori bird
tōri street
toriniku chicken
toru (u) to take (v)
toshokan library
tsukau (u) to use (v)
tsukeru (ru) to turn on s.th. (v)
tsuku (u) to arrive (v)
tsuku (u) to turn on (v)
tsukuru (u) to make (v)
tsuri fishing
uchi home
udetatefuse pushup
uma horse

umi ocean, sea
undō exercise (physical)
unten driving
uru (u) to sell (v)
urusai noisy
utau (u) to sing (v)
wakai young
warui bad
wataru (u) to cross (v)
yakyū baseball
yama mountain
yameru (ru) to quit (v)
yanagi willow (tree)
yasai vegetable
yaseru (ru) to lose weight (v)
yasui cheap
yasumi vacation
yōfuku clothes
yomu (u) to read (v)
yoyaku reservation
yubi finger
yūbinkyoku post office
yuki snow
zasshi magazine
zubon pants, trousers

ENGLISH–JAPANESE GLOSSARY

(irr): irregular verbs
(ru): ru-verb
(u): u-verb
(v): verbs
s.th.: something

abdomen **onaka**
accident **jiko**
actor **haiyū**
actress **joyū**
address **jūsho**
airplane **hikōki**
airport **kūkō**
ambulance **kyūkyūsha**
angel **tenshi**
answer **kotae**
apple **ringo**
arrive (v) **tsuku** (u)
art museum **bijutsukan**
baby **akachan**
bad **warui**
bad-tasting **mazui**
bag **kaban**
bank **ginkō**
baseball **yakyū**

beautiful **kirei na**
beef **gyūniku**
bicycle **jitensha**
big **ōkii**
bird **tori**
birthday **tanjōbi**
black **kuro**
bloom (v) **saku** (u)
boat **fune**
book **hon**
bookstore **hon'ya**
borrow (v) **kariru** (ru)
bridge **hashi**
buy (v) **kau** (u)
calendar **karendā**
calligraphy **shodō**
car **kuruma**
carry (v) **hakobu** (u)
cash **genkin**
cat **neko**
change (v) **kaeru** (ru)
cheap **yasui**
chest **mune**
chicken **toriniku**
chopsticks **hashi**

church **kyōkai**
cleaning **sōji**
close (v) **shimaru** (u)
close s.th. (v) **shimeru** (ru)
clothes **yōfuku**
coffee shop **kissaten**
cold (weather) **samui**
colleague **dōryō**
comb **kushi**
come (v) **kuru** (irr)
come to know (v) **shiru** (u)
company **kaisha**
company employee **kaishain**
company president **shachō**
consulate **ryōjikan**
convenient **benri na**
cooking **ryōri**
cool (weather) **suzushii**
country **kuni**
countryside **inaka**
cross (v) **wataru** (u)
culture **bunka**
cut (v) **kiru** (u)
dance (v) **odoru** (u)
dark **kurai**
day **hi**
delicious **oishii**
dentist **haisha**
departure **shuppatsu**
dictionary **jisho**
die (v) **shinu** (u)
difficult **muzukashii**
divorce **rikon**
do (v) **suru** (irr)
dog **inu**
dormitory **ryō**
drawing, painting **e**
drink (v) **nomu** (u)
driving **unten**
ear **mimi**
early, fast **hayai**

earthquake **jishin**
easy **kantan na**
eat (v) **taberu** (ru)
egg **tamago**
embassy **taishikan**
end (v) **owaru** (u)
English **eigo**
enter (v) **hairu** (u)
eraser **keshigomu**
exercise (physical) **undō**
exist (v) **iru** (ru), **aru** (u),
    irassharu (u)
exit **deguchi**
expensive **takai**
eye **me**
eyeglasses **megane**
face **kao**
family **kazoku**
far **tōi**
fever **netsu**
finger **yubi**
fish **sakana**
fishing **tsuri**
flood **kōzui**
flower **hana**
fly (v) **tobu** (u)
foot, leg **ashi**
foreign country **gaikoku**
friend **tomodachi**
fruit **kudamono**
fun **tanoshii**
future **shōrai**
gain weight (v) **futoru** (u)
get (into/on a means of transporta-
    tion) (v) **noru** (u)
give (v) **ageru** (ru), **kureru** (ru),
    sashiageru (ru), **kudasaru** (u)
go (v) **iku** (u)
go out (v) **dekakeru** (ru)
goldfish **kingyo**
good night **oyasuminasai**

good **ii**
goodbye **sayōnara**
grass **kusa**
hair **kami**
hand, arm **te**
hat **bōshi**
hate **kirai na**
head **atama**
health **kenkō**
hear (v) **kikoeru** (ru)
height, stature **se**
help, assist (v) **tetsudau** (u)
help, rescue (v) **tasukeru**(ru)
high school **kōkō**
hobby **shumi**
home **uchi**
horse **uma**
hospital **byōin**
hot **atsui**
house **ie**
illness **byōki**
interesting **omoshiroi**
intersection **kōsaten**
Japan **Nihon**
Japanese language **Nihon-go**
Japanese person **Nihon-jin**
Japanese-style inn **ryokan**
key **kagi**
kind **shinsetsu na**
kitchen **daidokoro**
knee **hiza**
lake **mizuumi**
late, slow **osoi**
lawyer **bengoshi**
lend (v) **kasu** (u)
letter **tegami**
letter, character **ji**
library **toshokan**
like **suki na**
like very much **daisuki na**
listen (v) **kiku** (u)

long **nagai**
look (v) **miru** (ru)
lose weight (v) **yaseru** (ru)
luggage **nimotsu**
lunch **chūshoku**
lunch **hiru-gohan**
magazine **zasshi**
make (v) **tsukuru** (u)
man (male person) **otoko, otoko no hito**
map **chizu**
marriage **kekkon**
mathematics **sūgaku**
meal **shokuji**
meat **niku**
medicine **kusuri**
memorize (v) **oboeru** (ru)
milk **gyūnyū**
money **o-kane**
morning **asa**
mountain **yama**
mouse **nezumi**
mouth **kuchi**
movie **eiga**
museum **hakubutsukan**
music **ongaku**
musician **ongakuka**
name **namae**
nationality **kokuseki**
nature **shizen**
neck **kubi**
need (v) **iru** (u)
new **atarashii**
newspaper **shinbun**
noisy **urusai**
nose **hana**
novel **shōsetsu**
nurse **kangoshi**
occupation **shokugyō**
ocean, sea **umi**
old **furui**

open (v) **aku** (u)
open s.th. (v) **akeru** (ru)
order **chūmon**
outside **soto**
pants, trousers **zubon**
paper **kami**
park **kōen**
parking lot **chūshajō**
pass (v) **sugiru** (ru)
pay (v) **harau** (u)
person **hito**
photograph **shashin**
physician **isha**
pig **buta**
place **tokoro**
play (v) **asobu** (u)
police **keisatsu**
pork **buta-niku**
post office **yūbinkyoku**
practice **renshū**
price **nedan**
prices (cost of living) **bukka**
pushup **udetatefuse**
put (v) **oku** (u)
question **shitsumon**
quiet **shizuka na**
quit (v) **yameru** (ru)
rain **ame**
read (v) **yomu** (u)
receipt **ryōshūsho**
receive (v) **morau** (u), **itadaku** (u)
relatives **shinseki**
reservation **yoyaku**
return (v) **kaeru** (u)
return s.th. (v) **kaesu** (u)
rice (cooked), meal **gohan**
rice (uncooked) **kome**
river **kawa**
road **michi**
room **heya**
sauce **sōsu**

say (v) **iu** (u)
scholar **gakusha**
school **gakkō**
secretary **hisho**
see (v) **mieru** (ru)
self **jibun**
sell (v) **uru** (u)
serious **majime na**
shoe **kutsu**
short **mijikai**
shoulder **kata**
sing (v) **utau** (u)
singer **kashu**
sit (v) **suwaru** (u)
skillful **jōzu na**
sky **sora**
sleep (v) **neru** (ru)
small **chīsai**
smoke (v) **tabako o suu**
snow **yuki**
sock **kutsushita**
sound **oto**
sour **suppai**
speak (v) **hanasu** (u)
spill (v) **kobosu** (u)
squirrel **risu**
stamp **kitte**
stand (v) **tatsu** (u)
store **mise**
street **tōri**
student **gakusei**
study abroad **ryūgaku**
studying **benkyō**
subway **chikatetsu**
sugar **satō**
sun **taiyō**
superior, boss **jōshi**
sweet **amai**
swim (v) **oyogu** (u)
swimming **suiei**
take (v) **toru** (u)

tea **o-cha**
teach (v) **oshieru** (ru)
teacher **kyōshi, sensei**
telephone number **denwa-bangō**
telephone **denwa**
terribly difficult, terrible **taihen na**
textbook **kyōkasho**
theater **gekijō**
thing **mono**
tonight **konban**
train **densha**
tree **ki**
trip **ryokō**
true, real **hontō no**
turn (v) **magaru** (u)
turn off (v) **kieru** (ru)
turn off s.th. (v) **kesu** (u)
turn on (v) **tsuku** (u)
turn on s.th. (v) **tsukeru** (ru)
TV **terebi**
umbrella **kasa**
university **daigaku**
use (v) **tsukau** (u)

vacation **yasumi**
vegetable **yasai**
village **mura**
wait (v) **matsu** (u)
walk (v) **aruku** (u)
wallet **saifu**
want (v) **hoshii**
warm **atatakai**
watch **tokei**
water **mizu**
wear, put on (v) **kiru** (ru), **haku** (u),
    kaburu (u)
weird **hen na**
west **nishi**
wide, spacious **hiroi**
willow (tree) **yanagi**
window **mado**
woman **onna, onna no hito**
work (v) **hataraku** (u)
world **sekai**
write (v) **kaku** (u)
young **wakai**
zoo **dōbutsuen**

ANSWER KEY

CHAPTER 1

Written Practice 1

1. からて   2. うなぎ   3. おかあさん   4. がっこう
5. とうきょう

Written Practice 2

1. テニス   2. カメラ   3. サッカー   4. コーヒー   5. ボストン
6. ニューヨーク

Written Practice 3

1. c   2. a   3. b   4. e   5. d

Quiz

1. b   2. d   3. d   4. b   5. d   6. d   7. d   8. a
9. b   10. a

CHAPTER 2

Written Practice 1

1. b   2. d   3. e   4. c   5. a

Written Practice 2

1. スミスさんは学生です。 Sumisu-san wa gakusei desu.
2. 私は日本人です。 Watashi wa Nihon-jin desu.
3. チェンさんは中国人です。 Chen-san wa Chūgoku-jin desu.

Written Practice 3

not applicable

Written Practice 4

1. ブラウンさんはアメリカ人です。 Burarun-san wa Amerika-jin desu.
2. ホワイトさんはアメリカ人じゃありません。 Howaito-san wa Amerika-jin ja arimasen. 3. スミスさんは学生です。 Sumisu-san wa gakusei desu.
4. 山田さんは学生じゃありません。 Yamada-san wa gakusei ja arimasen.

Written Practice 5

1. も mo 2. は wa 3. は wa 4. は wa 5. も mo

Written Practice 6

1. この kono 2. その sono 3. あの ano

Written Practice 7

1. この kono 2. あれ are 3. その sono 4. あの ano
5. あの ano 6. あの ano

Written Practice 8

1. a 2. e 3. d 4. c 5. b

Quiz

1. c 2. c 3. a 4. a 5. b 6. c 7. c 8. a
9. c 10. d

CHAPTER 3

Written Practice 1

1. あの女の人はだれですか。 Ano onna no hito wa dare desu ka.
2. あの学生はだれですか。Ano gakusei wa dare desu ka.
3. あの先生はどなたですか。 Ano sensei wa donata desu ka.
4. あの方はどなたですか。 Ano kata wa donata desu ka.

Written Practice 2

1. それは何ですか。Sore wa nan desu ka. 2. あの建物は何ですか。 Ano tatemono wa nan desu ka. 3. 専攻は何ですか。 Senkō wa nan desu ka.
4. 趣味は何ですか。 Shumi wa nan desu ka. 5. あの人はだれですか。
Ano hito wa dare desu ka.

Written Practice 3

1. 本はどこですか。 Hon wa doko desu ka. 2. 本はテーブルの上です。
Hon wa tēburu no ue desu. 3. 田中さんはどちらですか。 Tanaka-san wa dochira desu ka. 4. ヤンさんはどちらからですか。 Yan-san wa dochira kara desu ka.

Quiz

1. b   2. a   3. a   4. d   5. a   6. d   7. a   8. c
9. c   10. a

CHAPTER 4

Written Practice 1

1. 難しい muzukashii   2. きれい kirei   3. きびしい kibishii
4. きれいじゃ kirei ja   5. 難しくmuzukashiku

Written Practice 2

1. 難しいです muzukashii desu   2. おもしろくありません omoshiroku
arimasen   3. 忙しいです isogashii desu   4. 安いです yasui desu

Written Practice 3

(Example Answers) 1. 私の母はやさしいです。でも、ちょっと厳しいです。
Watashi no haha wa yasashii desu. Demo, chotto kibishii desu.   2. 私の父は
厳しいです。それに、ちょっと意地悪です。 Watashi no chichi wa kibishii desu.
Soreni, chotto ijiwaru desu.   3. 私の部屋は広いです。それに、明るいです。
Watashi no heya wa hiroi desu. Soreni, akarui desu.   4. 日本語は難しいです。
でも、おもしろいです。Nihon-go wa muzukashii desu. Demo, omoshiroi desu.

Written Practice 4

1. マイクさんの本 Maiku-san no hon   2. マイクさんの日本語の本 Maiku-
san no Nihon-go no hon   3. マイクさんの日本人の友達 Maiku-san no
Nihon-jin no tomodachi   4. 日本語の学生 Nihon-go no gakusei
5. マイクさんの友達の日本語の本 Maiku-san no tomodachi no Nihon-go
no hon

Quiz

1. c   2. b   3. a   4. c   5. c   6. a   7. b   8. a
9. b   10. c

CHAPTER 5

Written Practice 1

1. 駅のとなりには銀行があります。Eki no tonari ni wa ginkō ga arimasu.
2. うちにはねこと犬がいます。Uchi ni wa neko to inu ga imasu.
3. 机の上には鉛筆と辞書と消しゴムがあります。Ttsukue no ue ni wa enpitsu

to jisho to keshigomu ga arimasu.　　　 4. 日本語のクラスにはアメリカ人 と中国人と韓国人がいます。Nihon-go no kurasu ni wa Amerika-jin to Chūgoku-jin to Kankoku-jin ga imasu.

Written Practice 2
1. 山田さんは兄弟がいますか 。 Yamada-san wa kyōdai ga imasu ka.
2. 今日はクラスがありますか。Kyō wa kurasu ga arimasu ka.
3. 今、時間がありますか。Ima, jikan ga ariamsu ka.
4. 私はお金がありません。Watashi wa o-kane ga arimasen.

Written Practice 3
1. 郵便局はどこにありますか。 Yūbinkyoku wa doko ni arimasu ka.
2. 陽子さんはどこにいますか。 Yōko-san wa doko ni imasu ka.
3. 陽子さんのお母さんはどちらにいらっしゃいますか。 Yōko-san no okāsan wa dochira ni irasshaimasu ka.　　　 4. 母 はどこにいますか。Haha wa doko ni imasu ka.　　　 5. 日本語の辞書 はどこにありますか。 Nihon-go no jisho wa doko ni arimasu ka.

Written Practice 4
1. が ga, none　　 2. が ga, と to, が ga, none　　 3. が ga, と to, が ga, と to, が ga, none　　 4. が ga, と to, が ga, none　　 5. が ga, と to, が ga, none

Quiz
1. a　 2. b　 3. c　 4. d　 5. a　 6. a　 7. b　 8. c
9. b　 10. c

Part One Test
1. c　 2. b　 3. c　 4. a　 5. c　 6. c　 7. d　 8. b
9. b　 10. c　 11. a　 12. c　 13. c　 14. a　 15. b
16. b　 17. a　 18. b　 19. a　 20. b　 21. c　 22. a
23. b　 24. c　 25. b

CHAPTER 6

Written Practice 1
1. 父は毎日会社に行きます。 Chichi wa mainichi kaisha ni ikimasu.
2. 今日はうちに帰りません。 Kyō wa uchi ni kaerimasen.
3. 週末は京都へ行きます。 Shūmatsu wa Kyōto e ikimasu.
4. 田中さんはあまりうちに来ません。 Tanaka-san wa amari uchi ni kimasen.
5. 母はときどき病院に行きます。 Haha wa tokidoki byōin ni ikimasu.

Written Practice 2
1. と to, に ni 2. で de, に ni 3. と to, へ e 4. と to, に ni
5. で de, に ni

Written Practice 3
1. さんびゃくごじゅうに sanbyaku-gojū-ni 2. せんにひゃく sen-nihyaku
3. にせんきゅうひゃくきゅうじゅう nisen-kyūhyaku-kyūjū
4. さんまんごせん sanman-gosen 5. はちまんきゅうせんさんじゅうなな
hachiman-kyūsen-sanjū-nana

Quiz
1. a 2. d 3. b 4. b 5. b 6. c 7. c 8. b
9. c 10. b

CHAPTER 7

Written Practice 1
たたく tataku もらう morau かかる kakaru はこぶ hakobu
おとす otosu たのむ tanomu かつ katsu しぬ shinu こぐ kogu

Written Practice 2
1. もたない motanai, もちます mochimasu 2. かさない kasanai, かします
kashimasu 3. とらない toranai, とります torimasu 4. のまない
nomanai, のみます nomimasu 5. かわない kawanai, かいます kaimasu

Written Practice 3
1. かえらない kaeranai, かえります kaerimasu 2. かえない kaenai,
かえます kaemasu 3. みない minai, みます mimasu 4. しない shinai,
します shimasu 5. こない konai, きます kimasu 6. はいらない
hairanai, はいります hairimasu

Written Practice 4
今日は友達が来ます。晩ご飯を姉が作ります。兄がワインを買います。 Kyō wa
tomodachi ga kimasu. Bangohan o ane ga tsukurimasu. Ani ga wain o kaimasu.

Written Practice 5
1. 日本語を勉強します。 Nihon-go o benkyō shimasu. 2. 毎日図書館で新
聞を読みます。 Mainichi toshokan de shinbun o yomimasu. 3. はしですし
を食べます。 Hashi de sushi o tabemasu. 4. 明日学生がここに来ます。
Ashita gakusei ga koko ni kimasu.

Written Practice 6
1. くれます kuremasu   2. あげます agemasu   3. くれます kuremasu
4. 差し上げます sashiagemasu   5. 下さいます kudasaimasu
6. やりました yarimashita

Written Practice 7
1. もらいました moraimashita   2. あげました agemashita
3. 頂きました itadakimashita   4. くれました kuremashita

Written Practice 8
1. c   2. a   3. e   4. d   5. b

Quiz
1. a   2. d   3. a   4. b   5. d   6. b   7. c   8. a
9. a   10. d

CHAPTER 8

Written Practice 1
I didn't go to class yesterday. I stayed home. I watched an interesting movie on TV. Then, I read a book.

Written Practice 2
1. 本を読みました。 Hon o yomimashita.   2. このかばんは高かったです。 Kono kaban wa takakatta desu.   3. レストランは静かでした。 Resutoran wa shizuka deshita.   4. 部屋はきれいじゃありませんでした。 Heya wa kirei ja arimasendeshita.   5. クラスには行きませんでした。 Kurasu ni wa ikimasendeshita.

Written Practice 3
1. 何か食べましたか。 Nanika tabemashita ka.   2. 何かしましたか。 Nanika shimashita ka.   3. どこかに行きましたか。 Dokoka ni ikimashita ka.   4. だれか来ましたか。 Dareka kimashitaka.

Written Practice 4
1. いいえ、何も食べませんでした。 Īe, nani mo tabemasendeshita.
2. いいえ、何もしませんでした。 Īe, nani mo shimasendeshita.
3. いいえ、どこにも行きませんでした。 Īe, doko ni mo ikimasendeshita.
4. いいえ、だれも来ませんでした。 Īe, dare mo kimasendeshita.
5. いいえ、だれとも話しませんでした。 Īe, dare to mo hanashimasendeshita.

Written Practice 5
1. 黒澤の映画を見たことがありますか。 Kurosawa no eiga o mita koto ga arimasu ka.   2. アラスカに行ったことがありますか。 Arasuka ni itta koto

ga arimasu ka.   3. 着物を着たことがありますか。 Kimono o kita koto ga arimasu ka.   4. 留学したことがありますか。 Ryūgaku shita koto ga arimasu ka.

Written Practice 6
The answers vary.

Quiz
1. d   2. b   3. c   4. a   5. d   6. d   7. c   8. c
9. b   10. a

CHAPTER 9

Written Practice 1
1. 新聞を読んで、テレビを見ました。 Shinbun o yonde, terebi o mimashita.
2. 地下鉄に乗って、友達のうちに行きます。 Chikatetsu ni notte, tomodachi no uchi ni ikimasu.   3. 優しくて、きれいで、頭がいいです。 Yasashikute, kirei de, atama ga ii desu.   4. かぜをひいて、クラスを休みました。 Kaze o hiite, kurasu o yasumimashita.   5. 難しくて、わかりませんでした。 Muzukashikute, wakarimasendeshita.

Written Practice 2
1. を o   2. の no   3. に ni   4. まで made   5. に ni

Written Practice 3
Go straight on this street. Then, turn right at the third intersection. Then, you'll see a bookstore on your right. Pass that bookstore. Then, cross the bridge. Then, you'll see a hospital on your left. My house is next to that hospital.

Written Practice 4
1. My older brother plays tennis every morning.   2. Where is the cat? —It is sleeping on the sofa now.   3. Is Ms. Yamada in? —No. Ms. Yamada is in Tokyo now.   4. My older brother is 35 years old. He works at a bank.
5. What are you doing now? — I'm reading a newspaper now.   6. Ms. Yamada hasn't come yet.

Quiz
1. c   2. a   3. b   4. c   5. a   6. c   7. d   8. d
9. d   10. a

CHAPTER 10

Written Practice 1
1. テニスをしてはいけません。 Tenisu o shite wa ikemasen.　　2. うちに帰ってもいいです。 Uchi ni kaette mo ii desu.　　3. これはテストです。ですから、辞書を使ってはいけません。 Kore wa tesuto desu. Desukara, jisho o tsukatte wa ikemasen.　　4. ここに座ってもいいですか。 Koko ni suwatte mo ii desu ka.　5. この本を借りてもいいですか。 Kono hon o karite mo ii desu ka.

Written Practice 2
1. テレビを見てはいけません。 Terebi o mite wa ikemasen.　　2. 漢字を覚えなくてはいけません。 Kanji o oboenakute wa ikemasen.　　3. ビールを飲んではいけません。 Bīru o nonde wa ikemasen.　　4. 私は9時から5時まで働かなくてはいけません。 Watashi wa ku-ji kara go-ji made hatarakanakute wa ikemasen.　　5. 山田さんのうちに行かなくてはいけませんか。 Yamada-san no uchi ni ikanakute wa ikemasen ka.

Written Practice 3
Answers vary.

Written Practice 4
1. はしで食べられます。 Hashi de taberaremasu.　　2. 自転車に乗れます。 Jitensha ni noremasu.　　3. テニスができます。 Tenisu ga dekimasu.　4. 漢字が書けます。 Kanji ga kakemasu.　　5. 日本語が話せます。 Nihon-go ga hanasemasu.

Written Practice 5
1. ジョアナさんは折り紙でバラを作ることができます。 Joana-san wa origami de bara o tsukuru koto ga dekimasu.　　2. スコットさんは日本のうたをうたうことができます。 Sukotto-san wa Nihon no uta o utau koto ga dekimasu.　3. トムさんは大きいトラックを運転することができます。 Tomu-san wa ōkii torakku o unten-suru koto ga dekimasu.　　4. マリアさんは一人で着物を着ることができます。 Maria-san wa hitori de kimono o kiru koto ga dekimasu.

Quiz
1. b　　2. b　　3. d　　4. a　　5. c　　6. b　　7. a　　8. c　9. d　　10. c

Part Two Test
1. d　　2. c　　3. c　　4. b　　5. a　　6. b　　7. b　　8. b　9. d　　10. a　　11. a　　12. d　　13. b　　14. a　　15. b　　16. c　17. d　　18. d　　19. b　　20. b　　21. d　　22. a　　23. b　24. a　　25. b

CHAPTER 11

Written Practice 1

1. 田中さんは社長になると思います。　Tanaka-san wa shachō ni naru to omoimasu.　　2. マイクさんはやさしいと思います。　Maiku-san wa yasashii to omoimasu.　　3. 日本の映画はおもしろいと思います。　Nihon no eiga wa omoshiroi to omoimasu.　　4. 漢字は難しくないと思います。　Kanji wa muzukashiku nai to omoimasu.　　5. トムさんは毎日イタリア語を勉強していると思います。　Tomu-san wa mainichi Itaria-go o benkyō shite iru to omoimasu.

Written Practice 2

1. どのレストランがいいか分かりますか。　Dono resutoran ga ii ka wakarimasu ka.　　2. 郵便局はどこにあるか教えてください。　Yūbinkyoku wa doko ni aru ka oshiete kudasai.　　3. あの人の名前は何か教えてください。　Ano hito no namae wa nani ka oshiete kudasai.　　4. どの映画がおもしろいか知っていますか。　Dono eiga ga omoshiroi ka shitte imasu ka.　　5. プレゼントは何がいいか考えてください。　Purezento wa nani ga ii ka kangaete kudasai.

Written Practice 3

1. 日本の大学に行くつもりです。　Nihon no daigaku ni iku tsumori desu.
2. あの人は韓国人かもしれません。　Ano hito wa Kankoku-jin kamoshiremasen.　　3. 明日は晴れるでしょう。　Ashita wa hareru deshō.
4. 今、数学を勉強しているんです。　Ima sūgaku o benkyō shite iru ndesu.
5. この辞書は便利なんです。　Kono jisho wa benri na ndesu.

Written Practice 4

1. どうして日本語を勉強しているんですか。　Dōshite Nihon-go o benkyō shite iru ndesu ka.　　2. どうして漢字が嫌いなんですか。　Dōshite kanji ga kirai na ndesu ka.　　3. どうして納豆が好きなんですか。　Dōshite nattō ga suki na ndesu ka.　　4. どうしてパーティーに行かなかったんですか。　Dōshite pātī ni ikanakatta ndesu ka.　　5. どうして看護師になりたいんですか。　Dōshite kangoshi ni nari-tai ndesu ka.

Quiz

1. c　　2. c　　3. b　　4. b　　5. d　　6. a　　7. d　　8. c
9. b　　10. a

CHAPTER 12

Written Practice 1

1. 大きい ōkii (no change)　　2. 大きく ōkiku　　3. 高く takaku
4. 静か shizuka　　5. 静かに shizuka ni　　6. まじめな majime na (no change)　　7. まじめじゃ majime ja

Written Practice 2

1. 行く iku　　2. 食べている tabete iru　　3. 前 mae　　4. 食べた tabeta

Written Practice 3

1. 静かな shizuka na　　2. 食事の shokuji no　　3. 読む yomu
4. 起きた okita　　5. している shite iru

Written Practice 4

1. 聞きながら kiki-nagara　　2. 来ないうちに konai uchi ni
3. 明るいうちに akarui uchi ni　　4. 飲みながら nomi nagara

Written Practice 5

1. よく勉強する yoku benkyō suru　　2. よく勉強しない yoku benkyō shinai
3. たくさん食べる takusan taberu　　4. 雪がふります yuki ga furimasu

Written Practice 6

1. ので node　　2. のに noni　　3. のに noni　　4. ので node
5. が ga　　6. から kara　　7. から kara　　8. 申しますが mōshimasu ga

Written Practice 7

1. 映画を見に行きましょう。 Eiga o mini ikimashō.　　2. 切手を買いに郵便局に行きます。 Kitte o kai ni yūbinkyoku ni ikimasu.　　3. 祖母に会いに日本に行きます。 Sobo ni ai ni Nihon ni ikimasu.　　4. 昼ご飯を食べにうちに帰りました。 Hirugohan o tabe ni uchi ni kaerimashita.

Written Practice 8

1. 見える mieru　　2. 読める yomeru　　3. 分かる wakaru　　4. こわさない kowasanai　　5. こぼさない kobosanai

Quiz

1. c　　2. d　　3. a　　4. b　　5. d　　6. b　　7. c　　8. d
9. c　　10. b

CHAPTER 13

Written Practice 1

Answers vary.

Written Practice 2

1. お父さんと、お母さんとでは、どちらの方が厳しいですか。 Otōsan to, okāsan to de wa, dochira no hō ga kibishii desu ka.　　2. コーヒーと、紅茶とでは、どちらの方をよく飲みますか。 Kōhī to, kōcha to de wa, dochira no hō o yoku nomimasu ka.　　3. 寝るのと、食べるのとでは、どちらの方が好きですか。 Neru no to, taberu no to de wa, dochira no hō ga sukidesu ka.
4. 日本語を話すのと、日本語を聞くのとでは、どちらの方が難しいですか。 Nihon-go o hanasu no to, Nihon-go o kiku no to de wa, dochira no hō ga muzukashii desu ka.

Written Practice 3

1. 何 nani　　2. どこ doko　　3. どちら dochira　　4. だれ dare
5. だれ dare　　6. どれ dore

Quiz

1. a　　2. c　　3. b　　4. a　　5. b　　6. c　　7. b　　8. d
9. a　　10. d

CHAPTER 14

Written Practice 1

1. にくいです nikui desu　　2. はじめ ました hajimemashita　　3. 高 taka
4. つくしました tsukushimashita　　5. つづけます tsuzukemasu

Written Practice 2

1. おいし oishi　　2. まじめ Majime　　3. やさし yasashi
4. こわれてい kowarete i　　5. よさ yosa　　6. なさ nasa

Written Practice 3

1. 女 onna　　2. 女 onna　　3. 子供 kodomo　　4. みたい mitai

Written Practice 4

1. 昨日食べたすきやきはおいしかったです。 Kinō tabeta sukiyaki wa oishikatta desu.　　2. 昨日ここに来た人はフランス人でした。 Kinō koko ni kita hito wa Furansu-jin deshita.　　3. あそこでピザを食べている男の人は私の友達です。 Asoko de piza o tabete iru otoko no hito wa watashi no tomodachi desu.　　4. 五嶋みどりというバイオリニストを知っていますか。 Gotō Midori to iu baiorinisuto o shitte imasu ka.

Quiz

1. b　　2. a　　3. b　　4. a　　5. b　　6. d　　7. b　　8. a
9. a　　10. b

CHAPTER 15

Written Practice 1
1. 大きく ōkiku   2. 静かに shizuka ni   3. きれいに kirei ni
4. 少なく sukunaku   5. 安く yasuku

Written Practice 2
1. こと koto   2. よう yō   3. こと koto   4. よう yō   5. よう yō
6. よう yō

Written Practice 3
1. I go to school by subway.   2. There will be a cultural festival at the university tomorrow.   3. I did my homework at Yoko's house.   4. (I) became able to walk when I was one year old.   5. I eat with chopsticks.
6. I went to Japan by myself.   7. My job ends next week.

Written Practice 4
姉はジーンズをはいています。それから、セーターを着ています。それから、ネックレスをしています。　Ane wa jīnzu o haite imasu. Sorekara, sētā o kite imasu. Sorekara, nekkuresu o shite imasu.

Quiz
1. a   2. d   3. b   4. a   5. a   6. b   7. b   8. d
9. b   10. a

Part Three Test
1. b   2. b   3. a   4. d   5. a   6. d   7. b   8. c
9. a   10. c   11. a   12. c   13. a   14. c   15. c
16. d   17. c   18. a   19. b   20. a   21. a   22. b
23. b   24. b   25. d

CHAPTER 16

Written Practice 1
1. あきました akimashita   2. あけました akemashita   3. こわれました kowaremashita   4. けしました keshimashita   5. つけてください tsukete kudasai

Written Practice 2
1. しまいました shimaimashita   2. おきます okimasu   3. おきます okimasu   4. みます mimasu   5. しまいました shimaimashita

Written Practice 3

1. くれました kuremashita   2. くださいました kudasaimashita
3. いただきました itadakimashita   4. あげました agemashita
5. もらいました moraimashita   6. やりました yarimashita

Written Practice 4

1. 私は新しい車がほしいです。 Watashi wa atarashii kuruma ga hoshii desu.
2. 兄も新しい車をほしがっています。 Ani mo atarashii kuruma o hoshigatte
imasu.   3. 私は中国に行きたいです。 Watashi wa Chūgoku ni iki-tai desu.
4. 妹はオーストラリアに行きたがっています。 Imōto wa Ōsutoraria ni iki-ta-
gatte imasu.   5. 兄はおいしいラーメンを食べたがっています。 Ani wa
oishii ramen o tabe-ta-gatte imasu.

Written Practice 5

読んだり yondari   書いたり kaitari   見たり mitari   行ったり ittari 買ったり
kattari   作ったり tsukuttari   したり shitari   来たり kitari

Written Practice 6

1. 頭がいいし、ハンサムだし, まじめだし。 Atama ga ii shi, hansamu da shi,
majime da shi.   2. 安いし、おいしいし。Yasui shi, oishii shi.   3. 難しいし、
大変だし、つまらないし。 Muzukashii shi, taihen da shi, tsumaranai shi.
4. ハンサムじゃないし、頭も悪いし、スポーツもできないし。 Hansamu ja
nai shi, atama mo warui shi, supōtsu mo dekinai shi.

Quiz

1. c   2. a   3. b   4. a   5. b   6. a   7. c   8. b
9. c   10. d

CHAPTER 17

Written Practice 1

1. べき beki   2. はず hazu   3. はず hazu   4. べき beki
5. はず hazu

Written Practice 2

1. 今度の日本語の先生はきびしくないらしいです。 Kondo no Nihon-go no
sensei wa kibishiku nai rashii desu.   2. 田中さんのカメラはこわれているよ
うです。 Tanaka-san no kamera wa kowarete iru yō desu.   3. 林さんのプリ
ンターは便利なようです。 Hayashi-san no purintā wa benri na yō desu.
4. 来年から学費が高くなるそうです。 Rainen kara gakuhi ga takaku naru sō
desu.

Written Practice 3
1. だけ dake   2. しかありません shika arimasen   3. だけあります dake arimasu   4. しかありません shika arimasen   5. だけあります dake arimasu

Written Practice 4
1. 子供でも kodomo demo   2. 日本人でも Nihon-jin demo
3. お酒でも o-sake demo   4. まずい mazui

Written Practice 5
1. 何でも nan demo   2. だれでも dare demo   3. 何を nani o
4. 何を nani o

Quiz
1. b   2. c   3. c   4. d   5. c   6. a   7. d   8. c
9. a   10. b

CHAPTER 18

Written Practice 1
1. かけ kake   2. よめ yome   3. みろ miro   4. ねろ nero
5. とれ tore   6. かえ kae   7. はこべ hakobe   8. もて mote
9. しろ shiro   10. こい koi

Written Practice 2
1. かきなさい kaki-nasai   2. よみなさい yomi-nasai   3. みなさい mi-nasai   4. ねなさい ne-nasai   5. とりなさい tori-nasai
6. かいなさい kai-nasai   7. はこびなさい hakobi-nasai   8. もちなさい mochi-nasai   9. しなさい shi-nasai   10. きなさい ki-nasai

Written Practice 3
1. e   2. f   3. a   4. h   5. b   6. c   7. d   8. g

Written Practice 4
1. かこう kakō   2. よもう yomō   3. みよう miyō   4. ねよう neyō
5. とろう torō   6. かおう kaō   7. はこぼう hakobō   8. もとう motō
9. しよう shiyō

Written Practice 5
1. I try to drink green tea (as much as I can).   2. I tried to drink coffee.
3. I am thinking of studying Chinese.   4. I am thinking of proposing to Yoko tomorrow.   5. I am thinking of trying to eat vegetables as much as I can.

Written Practice 6
1. よんだら yondara   2. きたら kitara   3. おわったら owattara
4. したら shitara   5. かいたら kaitara   6. かかなかったら
kakanakattara   7. やすかったら yasukattara   8. しずかだったら shizuka
dattara   9. 学生だったら gakusei dattara

Written Practice 7
Answers vary.

Written Practice 8
Answers vary.

Written Practice 9
1. よめば yomeba   2. くれば kureba   3. こなければ konakereba
4. あれば areba   5. なければ nakereba   6. すれば sureba
7. いなければ inakereba   8. かけば kakeba   9. やすければ yasukereba
10. よければ yokereba   11. よくなければ yokunakereba
12. べんりであれば benri de areba (or べんりなら[ば] benri nara [ba])
13. 学生じゃなければ gakusei ja nakereba

Written Practice 10
Answers vary.

Quiz
1. c   2. c   3. b   4. a   5. d   6. a   7. b   8. c
9. c   10. a

CHAPTER 19

Written Practice 1
1. ぬすまれる nusumareru   2. たたかれる tatakareru   3. つかわれる
tsukawareru   4. とられる torareru   5. しかられる shikarareru
6. ほめられる homerareru

Written Practice 2
1. ネックレスがどろぼうに盗まれました。 Nnekkuresu ga dorobō ni
nusumaremashita.   2. 弟が父にしかられました。 Otōto ga chichi ni
shikararemashita.   3. 日本語がたくさんの人に話されています。 Nihon-go
ga takusan no hito ni hanasarete imasu.   4. 私の電話が知らない人に使われ
ました。 Watashi no denwa ga shiranai hito ni tsukawaremashita.

Written Practice 3
1. 田中さんは雨にふられました。 Tanaka-san wa ame ni furaremashita.
2. 陽子さんは猫に死なれました。 Yōko-san wa neko ni shinaremashita.
3. マイクさんは犬に逃げられました。 Maiku-san wa inu ni nigeraremashita.

Written Practice 4
1. ならわせる narawaseru　　2. いかせる ikaseru　　3. あらわせる arawaseru　　4. たたせる tataseru　　5. こさせる kosaseru
6. させる saseru

Written Practice 5
1. 母は私にピアノを習わせました。 Haha wa watashi ni piano o narawasemashita.　　2. 母は私にテレビを見させました。 Haha wa watashi ni terebi o misasemashita.　　3. 先生は私を立たせました。 Sensei wa watashi o tatasemashita.

Written Practice 6
1. またせられる mataserareru　　2. はこばせられる hakobaserareru
3. うたわせられる utawaserareru　　4. てつだわせられる tetsudawaserareru
5. はたらかせられる hatarakaserareru　　6. よませられる yomaserareru
7. させられる saserareru　　8. こさせられる kosaserareru

Quiz
1. a　　2. d　　3. b　　4. b　　5. b　　6. c　　7. b　　8. c
9. c　　10. d

CHAPTER 20

Written Practice 1
1. 社長がお決めになりました。 Shachō ga o-kime ni narimashita.　　2. 私がお作りいたしました。 Watashi ga o-tsukuri itashimashita.　　3. 先生がお考えになりました。 Sensei ga o-kangae ni narimashita.　　4. 私がお見せいたしました。 Watashi ga o-mise itashimashita.　　5. 私がお知らせいたしました。 Watashi ga o-shirase itashimashita.

Written Practice 2
1. 田中さんと話されましたか。 Tanaka-san to hanasaremashita ka.　　2. よく車を使われますか。 Yoku kuruma o tsukawaremasu ka.　　3. 手紙を書かれましたか。 Tegami o kakaremashita ka　　4. 今朝の新聞を読まれましたか。 Kesa no shinbun o yomaremashita ka.

Written Practice 3
1. 東京に行かせていただけませんか。 Tokyō ni ikasete itadakemasen ka.
2. 手紙を読ませていただけませんか。 Tegami o yomasete itadakemasen ka.
3. 車を使わせていただけませんか。 Kuruma o tsukawasete itadakemasen ka.

Quiz
1. c   2. d   3. c   4. c   5. a   6. d   7. d   8. c
9. b   10. c

Part Four Test
1. b   2. d   3. c   4. b   5. c   6. a   7. d   8. a
9. b   10. d   11. b   12. a   13. b   14. b   15. a
16. c   17. c   18. b   19. c   20. c   21. d   22. d
23. a   24. b   25. c

Final Exam
1. a   2. b   3. b   4. a   5. c   6. c   7. b   8. b
9. b   10. b   11. b   12. b   13. c   14. a   15. a
16. b   17. b   18. a   19. a   20. b   21. c   22. a
23. a   24. d   25. b   26. a   27. c   28. c   29. c
30. b   31. c   32. c   33. a   34. d   35. b   36. d
37. c   38. a   39. b   40. c   41. d   42. d   43. b
44. b   45. d   46. a   47. b   48. a   49. b   50. c
51. c   52. b   53. a   54. d   55. d   56. b   57. d
58. b   59. a   60. c   61. a   62. c   63. a   64. a
65. c   66. c   67. c   68. a   69. b   70. b   71. a
72. b   73. a   74. b   75. a   76. b   77. d   78. c
79. d   80. c   81. a   82. c   83. b   84. b   85. c
86. b   87. c   88. b   89. c   90. b   91. b   92. b
93. b   94. c   95. c   96. b   97. d   98. a   99. a
100. b

INDEX

Index

439